C0-AKU-034

MORE THAN WORDS

MORE THAN WORDS

Transforming Script, Agency, and Collective Life in Bali

RICHARD FOX

CORNELL UNIVERSITY PRESS
ITHACA AND LONDON

Copyright © 2018 by Cornell University

All rights reserved. Except for brief quotations in a review, this book, or
parts thereof, must not be reproduced in any form without permission in
writing from the publisher. For information, address Cornell University
Press, Sage House, 512 East State Street, Ithaca, New York 14850. Visit
our website at cornellpress.cornell.edu.

First published 2018 by Cornell University Press

Printed in the United States of America

Library of Congress Cataloging-in-Publication Data

Names: Fox, Richard, 1972– author.
Title: More than words : transforming script, agency, and collective life
    in Bali / Richard Fox.
Description: Ithaca : Cornell University Press, 2018. | Includes
    bibliographical references and index.
Identifiers: LCCN 2017053343 (print) | LCCN 2017056751 (ebook) |
    ISBN 9781501725371 (epub/mobi) | ISBN 9781501725364 (pdf) |
    ISBN 9781501725340 | ISBN 9781501725340 (cloth ; alk. paper) |
    ISBN 9781501725357 (pbk. ; alk. paper)
Subjects: LCSH: Balinese language—Writing. | Balinese language—
    Alphabet. | Manuscripts, Balinese. | Bali Island (Indonesia)—
    Civilization.
Classification: LCC PL5162 (ebook) | LCC PL5162 F69 2018 (print) |
    DDC 499/.223811—dc23
LC record available at https://lccn.loc.gov/2017053343

All photographs are by the author unless otherwise noted.

For Zachary and Aaron

Contents

ILLUSTRATIONS

Photographs

Figures

Preface and Acknowledgments

What is a text? By now the question probably seems passé, calling to mind an earlier moment when anthropological theorizing was preoccupied with poststructuralism and the "writing culture" debates. Academic fashion has long since moved on, to cultivate a more self-assured interest in things such as affect, ethics, and ontology. And yet, despite these more recent developments, the idea of "the text" has perdured, doing most of its work covertly—underwriting all manner of enquiry, but often without the scrutiny of a self-consciously theoretical stance. Scholarship on religion in Southeast Asia is a case in point, where "texts" of various kinds—canonical, colonial, literary, commercial—continue to figure in our work as prominently as ever. But what does it mean to study a text? Or to cite a manuscript as an evidentiary source? What are the practices involved? On what grounds do they proceed? And precisely what can we hope to accomplish in the process?

Consider the following example. Late one afternoon a Balinese priest told me about a palm-leaf manuscript, or *lontar*, that enumerated the offerings required for a rite he had just performed. Having carefully filmed the proceedings, I wanted to have a look at the manuscript and review its résumé of offerings. But the priest did not have a copy at hand. So later that evening I sent an email to a colleague, and she replied within hours, forwarding an attachment that we both quite naturally called "a copy of the manuscript." The attachment itself was a Microsoft Word file containing the romanized transliteration of a *lontar* from an aristocratic house at the eastern end of the island that had been borrowed for copying some four years before. This file was part of a collection of several thousand similar files held in a well-known digital archive of Balinese and Old Javanese manuscripts. Of course, these "manuscripts" are not actually manuscripts. They are computerized transliterations of manuscripts, painstakingly typed, checked, and cataloged by a team of experts. Occasional technical glitches notwithstanding, the regular typeface of the digital files makes them easier to read than the palm leaves they are meant to represent—which may be damaged or inscribed in an idiosyncratic hand. What is more, the electronic format enables an array of critical procedures that would be difficult, if not impossible, before digitization—from quick word searches and instant comparisons across expansive textual corpora, to more sophisticated morphological, syntactical, and statistical forms of analysis. It is in this respect that the digital archive has facilitated and extended traditional lines of philological enquiry, while at the same time enabling a new style of research. Displacing notecards, typewriters, and hard-copy dictionaries, the indispensable tools of the trade are now digital cameras, laptops, and an Internet connection.

Clearly none of this will come as news to readers familiar with current philological practice. Yet it is worth noting a certain ambivalence in the response to these developments. On the one hand, there is an understandable *enthusiasm* for the ever more powerful lexicographical tools, archival resources, and visual imaging afforded by the new technology. But, on the other, there is also a palpable sense of *loss* that may be detected in the growing number of studies focused on issues of "textual materiality"—that is, the sheer physicality of the inscribed object, which is absent from its digitally "preserved" copy. The ambivalence itself is hardly unique; new media often inspire an equivocal response. What makes this case most interesting is the underlying assumption that links technological enhancement with material diminution—namely, the unexamined notion of a textual "degree zero," to which new features are seen to be added, and others subtracted, through the process of digital storage and analysis. Put another way, our mixed feelings about the digital archive are premised on a largely unreflective commitment to the idea of writing *in itself*—the supposedly brute fact of letters on a page. This book takes that assumption as its point of departure, using the ethnography from Bali to reflect on how a tacit understanding of script and writing has helped to shape anthropological thinking about broader questions regarding the nature of human agency and collective life.

A couple of cautionary notes are in order before carrying on ahead. The first pertains to the idea of religion. The history and theoretical difficulties associated with this term are the subject of an extensive critical literature, which this book mostly takes for granted. But, with specific reference to Bali, it is particularly important to distinguish between state-bureaucratic representations of "Hindu religion" (I. *Agama Hindu*) and the innumerable rites and related activities that permeate day-to-day life on the island. The former is characterized by a moralizing monotheism that aspires to the universal status of a world religion. By contrast, the latter rites and activities are often inextricably tied to a particular locale, incorporating aims and ideals that anthropologists and other regional specialists have more commonly associated with the less rigorously institutionalized activities of healing, sorcery, and self-fortification. The historical interplay between these variously overlapping articulations of "Balinese religion" is one of the book's central concerns.

There is second a question of ethnographic anonymity. The research for this book was conducted in and around "Batan Nangka," a pseudonym for the southerly Balinese ward in which I have done some two years' fieldwork over the past decade. In a previous monograph I explained my reasons for disguising the identity of my interlocutors and their community—a decision to which a number of colleagues have objected. Anonymity, they have said, will prevent others from doing follow-up studies and forecloses on the possibility of a public response from those with whom I have been working. I recognize the problem and accept the criticism. But the simple fact is that many in Batan Nangka have expressly—and at times insistently—requested anonymity. It is not my place to deny it.

Research for this book was supported by the Collaborative Research Centre 933, Materiale Textkulturen: Materialität und Präsenz des Geschriebenen in non-typographischen Gesellschaften (Subproject C07) at Ruprecht-Karls-Universität Heidelberg. The CRC 933 is funded by the German Research

Foundation (DFG). I owe a substantial debt of gratitude both to the CRC and to the university's Institut für Ethnologie for providing an exceptionally collegial environment for research and teaching. I would also like to acknowledge the generous support of a Fulbright Senior Scholar Award, which enabled a prior period of fieldwork, between September 2010 and July 2011. However, none of this would have been possible without the ongoing support of the Indonesian Ministry of Research and Technology. In particular, I would like to thank Madé Suastra of Universitas Udayana for sponsoring and helping to coordinate my research.

Several people have offered assistance and support along the way. First among these are the people of Batan Nangka and the wider administrative village of "Pateluan," who hosted my family during periods of fieldwork. No acknowledgment could possibly do justice to their kindness, patience, and generosity. I am also grateful to my Balinese colleagues, Wayan Griya, Nyoman Darma Putra, Nyoman Wijaya, and Ketut Kodi. In Germany I additionally received important institutional support from my *Habilmutter*, Annette Hornbacher, as well as from Markus Hilgert, Ludger Lieb, Monika Fest, Nele Schneidereit, and Friederike Elias. I remain in their debt.

The writing of this book more generally took place against the backdrop of ongoing conversations with friends, colleagues, mentors, and others. Among those who generously shared their time and experience, I am especially thankful to Mark Hobart, Hildred Geertz, Annette Hornbacher, Nengah Susila, Tom Hunter, Ketut Kodi, Margaret Wiener, and the late Ketut Sueca. These have been my teachers—both formally and otherwise—and I have endeavored in my work to emulate their erudition and critical sensitivity. More recently, I have also benefited from a series of exchanges with new friends and colleagues, including Dan Birchok, Jake Carbine, Tom Patton, and Sri Ratna Saktimulya. Their enthusiasm—and criticism—has been an inspiration.

As importantly, there are also conversations that did *not* happen—and for which I feel a deep sense of loss. When we left Chicago, a regular feature of our family life was abruptly cut short. We had spent many fine evenings sharing food and conversation with our dear friends Sascha Ebeling and Nisha Kommattam. While Skype and periodic reunions are a most welcome diversion, Sascha and Nisha's absence is sorely felt by the whole family. My hope is that we might soon find ourselves once again laughing and talking over good food and drink.

Returning to Bali, archival research was facilitated by the learned advice and assistance that I received from Hedi Hinzler and Déwa Gedé Catra. Hedi graciously answered what must have seemed an endless barrage of questions. But she also sent numerous files by email and even photographed manuscripts when the latter were not already part of the electronic database of the Proyék Tik (see chapter 1). I am also indebted to Hedi for introducing me to Déwa Gedé, who, in addition to helping me locate and photograph pertinent *lontar*, also sat for hours at a time patiently instructing me on the idiom of the ritual manuals discussed in chapter 4. Without their help, an important part of this research would not have taken place.

In the course of writing, I also received helpful commentary from numerous friends, family members, and colleagues. Several gave very generously of their time and read the manuscript in its entirety. These include Judith Fox, Hildred Geertz, Mark Hobart, Annette Hornbacher, Verena Meyer, Michel Picard, and the two anonymous reviewers for Cornell University Press. Others read one or more chapters. For the latter I am grateful to Dan Birchok, Megan Brankley Abbas, Wendy Doniger, Jonathan Doherty, Faruk ht, Johannes Fabian, David Halperin, Anne Hansen, Birgitta Hauser-Schäublin, John Holt, Tom Hunter, Kelvin Knight, Christopher Lutz, Tom Patton, Kostas Retsikas, Natalia Theodoridou, Kate Wakeling, Margaret Wiener, Rebecca Wollenberg, and Peter Worsley. Their criticism and suggestions have undoubtedly helped to make this a better book. I should probably have paid closer attention to their advice.

Additionally, I had the privilege of presenting drafts for several chapters at various institutions. These included the Centre for Southeast Asian Studies at the University of London's School of Oriental and African Studies; the Centre national de la recherche scientifique in Paris; the Department of Anthropology at the University of Victoria in Canada; the Fakultas Sastra at Universitas Udayana in Denpasar, Bali; the Pusat Kebudayaan Koesnadi Hardjasoemantri at Universitas Gadjah Mada in Yogyakarta, Java; Soka University in Southern California; the Institut für Ethnologie, Georg-August-Universität Göttingen; and the Institut für Ethnologie, Ruprecht-Karls-Universität Heidelberg. I also benefited from input from several colleagues at the symposium "The Power and Efficacy of Balinese Letters," which was hosted by the Heidelberg Institut für Ethnologie and sponsored by the CRC 933.

I am grateful to the *Jurnal Kajian Bali* and Brill for their permission to reprint materials already published. Parts of chapter 2 first appeared as "*Ngelidin Sétra, Nepukin Sema?* Thoughts on Language and Writing in Contemporary Bali," *Jurnal Kajian Bali* 2, no. 2 (2012): 21–48. An earlier version of chapter 3 was previously published in the volume I coedited with Annette Hornbacher, entitled *The Materiality and Efficacy of Balinese Letters: Situating Scriptural Practice* (Leiden: Brill, 2016). Warm thanks also go to the *Bali Post* for generously allowing me to reprint images from the newspaper. I am also grateful to Cynthia Col for producing such a sharp index, and in such short order. And I would be remiss not to mention Jim Lance, Michelle Witkowski, and Cornell University Press for all their work in seeing this project through to publication—thank you very much!

It is customary to thank one's family for their support, and to apologize for the time that might otherwise have been spent together. Like so many of the preceding expressions of gratitude, this would be grossly inadequate. But here we go . . . To Jude, my wife: We did this together. You know that. Others should, too. To my mother, Ruth: I apologize for my grumpiness and impatience, which I have too often blamed on this book. To my late father, Dick: I miss you. Terribly. Much of this book was written aloud, as if I were speaking to you. To my sister, Megan: We need to spend more time together. To Siobhan and Alex, our girls: Please come home more often—we miss you! Finally, to Zachary and Aaron, our boys: It may seem a strange or even unwanted gift, but this book was written for you. The rest of what I want to say is, well . . . more than words.

A Note on Orthography
and Related Conventions

Day-to-day life in Bali is marked by the interplay of multiple languages and scripts, much as it is in many other parts of the world. Accordingly, questions of translation, transcription, and transliteration are a central concern for this book. The conversations making up my primary research were mostly conducted in Balinese and Indonesian. But they also included words and expressions borrowed from other languages—most notably Kawi, Sanskrit, and English. Key terms and phrases have been provided in their original languages where pertinent, usually with a specification of linguistic register—for example, Balinese (B), Indonesian (I), Kawi (K), or Sanskrit (S). There is often a degree of overlap between these registers, and so my designations have aimed to privilege the way these terms were used and understood by the people with whom I was speaking. (Theoretical questions pertaining to language and translation are addressed in chapter 7.) For example, the term *aksara* is commonly recognized as both Balinese and Indonesian. But when used in Balinese conversation—in a recognizably Balinese manner—I have marked it with a *B* and specified its associations as I understood them.

Where the register was uncertain, or had multiple associations, I have tried to provide an appropriate indication. So words like *cocok* and *guna* have been marked "B./I." because they are widely recognized as both Balinese and Indonesian. But, while *guru* is also marked as both Balinese and Indonesian, it is not marked as Sanskrit or Kawi, despite its readily recognizable etymology.

I have generally adhered to contemporary scholarly conventions for the transcription and transliteration of Balinese, Kawi, and Sanskrit, and I have used the modern spelling for Indonesian in the official *ejaan yang disempurnakan* introduced in 1972 (see Kridalaksana 1978). For reasons addressed elsewhere (Fox and Hornbacher 2016, viii), I have not followed the system for romanization proposed by Acri and Griffiths (2014). For Balinese the conventions are those of Wayan Warna et al. (1990). But I have not followed their Indonesianized spelling of the prefix vowel that appears as *e* in terms such as *pedanda* and *penasar*. In my own text, these terms appear as *padanda* and *panasar*, following a model that more accurately reflects Balinese orthography (cf. Van der Tuuk 1897–1912). Additional exceptions are noted and explained where they occur. In citing others, I have retained their original spellings and transliterations.

Unless indicated otherwise, all translations are my own.

More Than Words

Chapter 1

Manuscripts, Madness

Most who study religion in Southeast Asia will have come across uses of writing, and of scripture, that exceed their expectations. Eating sutras. Meditating on the alphabet. Making offerings to manuscripts. Wearing bulletproof tattoos. The regional scholarship points time and again to the idea that writing is *more than words* and that the expert handling of script may confer power and protection. From modern-day Burmese sorcery to Old Javanese curse inscriptions, these "other" uses of writing are crucial for our understanding of Southeast Asian iterations of Buddhism, Brahmanism, and Islam. Yet, with some notable exceptions, scholars have tended to devalue such nonliterary uses of writing as secondary to a more conventional model of "the text" understood as a medium for the transmission of religious ideas and ideals. What would happen if we inverted this assumption and approached ostensibly literary objects as if they were amulets, or even living beings? Would it really be such a stretch? Is there not already a certain "word magic" at work in the commonsense notion of *meaning* as an ethereal substance passing between minds?

Drawing on ethnographic and archival fieldwork conducted on the Indonesian island of Bali, this book aims to unsettle received understandings of textuality and writing as they pertain to the religious traditions of Southeast Asia. Through a study of Balinese script as employed in rites of healing, sorcery, and self-defense, it explores the aims and desires embodied in the production and use of palm-leaf manuscripts, amulets, and other inscribed objects. In so doing, the book sets out to accomplish three things. The first is to make a positive contribution to the scholarship on religious uses of script and writing in Indonesia and the wider Malay region. This is, in turn, directed to problematizing our more general understanding of textual practice and its assumptions regarding history and precedent. And the broader purpose driving this critique is to open up new avenues for thinking differently about our relationship to writing as a practice and as a medium for actualizing ideals of human flourishing and collective life.

In reflecting on script and writing, the ethnography from Bali offers much food for thought. We find, for example, that Balinese often attribute both life and independent volition to manuscripts and copperplate inscriptions, presenting them with elaborate offerings on specified occasions. Commonly addressed with personal honorifics, these script-bearing objects may become partners with humans and other sentient beings in relations of exchange and mutual obligation. The question is how such practices of "the living letter" may be related to other ideas about the island's traditional script. There is first the state bureaucratic articulation of reform Hinduism, for which Balinese letters figure primarily as a symbol of cultural heritage. But there is also the more broadly philological assumption that script serves as a neutral medium for the expression and transmission of textual meaning—an idea that has long guided scholarship in the historical study of religions. Balinese practices of apotropaic writing—on palm leaves, amulets, and bodies—challenge both of these notions and yet coexist alongside them. One of my primary aims in this book is to theorize the coexistence of these seemingly contradictory sensibilities, with an eye to its wider significance for the history and contemporary practice of religion in Southeast Asia and elsewhere. So, while my argument is presented with detailed attention to the materials from Bali, my examples have been chosen for their pertinence to problems of broader import.

Photo 1.1. A palm-leaf manuscript from the personal collection of Déwa Gedé Catra in Karangasem. As with many palm-leaf "books" (B. *cakepan*) of this kind, the manuscript brings together four separately named parts, each addressing a different topic—likely copied together for a particular purpose or occasion.

A Lecture on Letters and Lamps

On December 20, 1980, I Gusti Ngurah Bagus delivered his inaugural address to the Faculty of Letters at Udayana University, Bali's flagship institution of higher learning.[1] Only the eighth full professor at Udayana, Bagus was also the university's first professor of anthropology. One might have expected to hear a lecture on issues of current anthropological interest, such as agricultural development or the social effects of urbanization. Another possible topic would have been the temple festivals and performing arts for which Bali was famous as a leading tourist destination. But Professor Bagus chose instead to discuss the letters of the Balinese alphabet, known collectively as *aksara Bali*.[2] He described first the standard eighteen letters used for writing colloquial Balinese (B. *wréastra*; see figure 1.1), and then the special characters (B. *swalalita*) employed in more literary forms of composition. This, however, was but a prologue to a more detailed explication of the esoteric configurations of Balinese script commonly known as *modré*, which are utilized in the performance of ceremonial rites, healing, and sorcery. Why might he have thought such an arcane subject suitable for his inaugural address?

It appears Bagus himself was aware of the need for an explanation, offering by way of introduction a numbered list of reasons for his choice of topic. Having cited a series of institutional, intellectual, and personal grounds, he went on to suggest that the *aksara* themselves bore a special relationship to Balinese religion and culture—a relationship, he argued, that was in need of closer scholarly attention. He explained there had been numerous attempts—by the Dutch, and later by Balinese themselves—to simplify the island's traditional script and later replace it with roman transliteration. But these were bound to fail. For *aksara Bali* were not simply arbitrary signs for representing the sounds of the Balinese language. And for this reason, he insisted, they could not "be erased or rubbed out as easily as Balinese oil lamps were replaced with electric lights" (Bagus 1980, 23).[3]

The contrast between lamps and letters appeared to work at several levels. For Balinese and non-Balinese alike, the island's traditional script might have been seen as part of a cultural heritage they were loath to abandon.

ᬳ	ᬦ	ᬘ	ᬭ	ᬓ	ᬤ
(h)a	na	ca	ra	ka	da

ᬢ	ᬲ	ᬯ	ᬮ	ᬫ	ᬕ
ta	sa	wa	la	ma	ga

ᬩ	ᬗ	ᬧ	ᬚ	ᬬ	ᬜ
ba	nga	pa	ja	ya	nya

Figure 1.1. The standard eighteen *aksara wréastra* used for writing colloquial Balinese.

ꦤ	ꦤꦶ	ꦤꦺ	ꦤꦺ	ꦤꦸ	ꦤꦺꦴ	ꦤ꧀
na	ni	né	ne	nu	no	n

Figure 1.2. By adding specific marks to the basic /na/ syllable, it can be transformed into /ni/, /né/, /ne/ ("nĕ"), /nu/, or /no/ or reduced to /n/.

Unlike a lamp, the *aksara* were in this respect more than a mere instrument. But for Balinese—and particularly for those in the Faculty of Letters—the language of "erasure" (I. *penghapusan*) would also likely have been recognized as an allusion to the dangers associated with mishandling *aksara*, and especially overwriting or scratching them out. In working with palm-leaf manuscripts, Balinese scribes have often made a special effort to avoid doing so—employing a distinctive set of orthographic marks to indicate where one ought to read past an erroneously written character. This was at least in part because Balinese letters were seen to embody a power of their own, which must be handled with care. As Rachelle Rubinstein has noted (2000, 194), to scratch out written *aksara* is an act of "killing letters," and so potentially an affront to this power. And, indeed, Bagus acknowledged the potency of *aksara* at several points in his address. Beyond more general links to religion (I. *agama*) and "the supersensory world" (I. *dunia gaib*),[4] he referred to their efficacy in rites of self-fortification and empowerment—and so the preference for secrecy among many of those adept in their use.

Cultural Tension

The specific uses of *aksara* aside, what is in many ways most remarkable about Bagus's inaugural address is how the collision of subject matter and occasion required a linkage of at least two differing, and potentially conflicting, frames of reference. Bagus may have emphasized occult powers and esoteric forms of knowledge in his substantive discussion of *aksara*. But his more general framing of the address called on a rather different conception of "Balinese culture"—one grounded in the state bureaucratic sensibilities befitting a senior civil servant. This may be seen most conspicuously in his opening remarks, where he situated the lecture with reference to the recent celebration of National Language Month, and its appeal for good grammar, proper spelling, and standardized pronunciation. Along similar lines, albeit more subtly, the terminology he employed in specifying the particularity of Balinese script was that of the developmentalist state.[5] Bagus spoke, for instance, of the pride with which Balinese society looked on the *aksara* as a medium for accessing the religious and cultural teachings of their ancestors (B. *leluhur*; Bagus 1980, 22; cf. 3, 15). His use of terms such as *religion* (I. *agama*), *culture* (I. *kebudayaan*), and *society* (I. *masyarakat*) may seem at first unremarkable. But these terms have a unique genealogy in Indonesia, where their use has been closely tied to programs for national development and religious reform—which, by the early 1980s, were well underway throughout the archipelago.[6]

Balinese script was, and very much remains, caught between these conflicting ideals. On the one hand, Bagus's address exemplified a modernizing and ultimately reductive conception of cultural difference, for which *aksara* would figure primarily as a symbol of Balinese tradition, and perhaps secondarily as a medium for representing Balinese language. It is on these grounds that one now finds Balinese script, language, and literature taught in schools and promoted through programs for the preservation of cultural heritage. On the other hand, however, Bagus's account of the tradition's self-understanding attributed to these letters a potency that exceeded both their "cultural" significance and their utility as a means of communication. These latter sensibilities are still very much alive in Bali, though they may sometimes be more difficult to recognize—caught up, as they often are, in practices associated with the manipulation of intangible beings and forces.

The tension between these rival orientations would suggest that an instrumentalized conception of writing—understood either as a technology of communication or as a symbol of Balinese tradition—may be inadequate to the way *aksara* have figured historically in Balinese social life. Returning to Bagus's own analogy, oil lamps could be replaced by electric lights because the latter did the job better, and without remainder. But it seems—at least on Bagus's account—that the same cannot be said of Balinese script, for which roman transliteration would provide but a partial replacement. Put another way, in contrast to the oil lamp, there appears to be more to *aksara* than their linguistic instrumentality and cultural significance. One of my central aims is to explore the nature of this "surplus" and the conditions under which it might appear as such.

Prolegomena

In a manner similar to that of the apologia found in many palm-leaf manuscripts, Bagus stressed the preliminary nature of his remarks on *aksara*, insisting they were little more than a prolegomenon to more detailed study (1980, 5). My aim is to pick up where he and others have left off, to reflect further on Balinese uses of script and writing—and this with a similar acknowledgment of limitation. Given the complexity of the practices in question, the chapters that follow could not possibly provide a comprehensive account of how *aksara* are, or have been, used on the island.[7] Other considerations aside, the sheer breadth of historical, philological, and social issues in play would put such a task beyond the competence of any one scholar— let alone the scope of a single monograph. What I propose instead is to begin developing an ethnographic approach to Balinese uses of script and writing that is directed by a set of broader theoretical questions around the nature of communication, agency, and practice.

On the way to formulating these questions, it must be noted that, in the years following Bagus's inaugural address, there have been several studies that touch in various ways on the use of script and writing in Bali.[8] In her oft-cited book on the use of language in the Balinese shadow theater, for example, Mary S. Zurbuchen (1987) discussed a number of the more common diagrams and related configurations of *aksara* employed in the performance of ceremonial rites. Her approach was informed by Walter J. Ong's (1982) account of "religious literacy" and what he called "noetic economy"—the way a given society is seen to "shape, store and transfer information" (Zurbuchen 1987, 38). Working from a similar set of assumptions, Rubinstein's more closely focused study of poetic composition drew on the esoteric *tutur* literature to explicate, as she put it, "the religious context of literate activity in Bali" (2000, 65).[9] This included a series of nuanced reflections on Balinese conceptions of *aksara*, with specific reference to *kakawin* poetics as a form of "yogic" practice. Thomas M. Hunter (2007, 2016) has further developed this line of enquiry in a pair of studies that examine the historical and philosophical background of what he has described in terms of an "orthographic mysticism," in which Balinese have raised "the status of the written character as a medium of metaphysical energies to a level of prestige that in the South Asian tradition has generally been reserved for the enunciation of *mantra*" (2007, 272). Addressing a set of closely related issues, Andrea Acri (2016) has taken a more traditionally philological approach to the yogic "imposition of the syllabary" (S. *svaravyañjana-nyāsa*), as part of his broader effort to trace Indic textual precedents for present-day practices in Bali. More closely attentive to Balinese sensibilities, and the philosophical problems engendered by traditional philology, Annette Hornbacher (2014) has examined the pertinence of the esoteric *tutur* literature for contemporary practices of healing and sorcery. Meanwhile, David J. Stuart-Fox (2015) has written a book directed to a more popular audience that includes a series of "magical" drawings (B. *rarajahan*) incorporating Balinese script.[10] These he has contextualized with reference to the medicinal practices of Mangku Ketut Liyer, the Balinese healer made famous by the Hollywood film *Eat, Pray, Love*. The present study aims to build on this body of prior scholarship, albeit not uncritically.[11]

Regional Resonance

Stepping back from Bali, there is considerable scope for comparison with the wider scholarship on religion in Southeast Asia. Accounts of Buddhism in Thailand, Burma, and Cambodia describe in detail the powers attributed to inscribed amulets, tattoos, and related forms of writing.[12] Whether lifted directly from Pali *gāthā-s* or inspired by visions and dreams, these efficacious configurations of script and image are seen to enable the cultivation of personal empowerment and bodily protection—but also beauty, good health, prosperity, and eloquence. Earlier scholarship often looked down on these nonliterary uses of script, which it treated as either a non-Buddhist "cultural" accretion or the ignoble trappings of popular superstition. But, as more recent work has suggested, these judgments were based on a misleadingly idealized conception of Buddhism as centered on monastic practice and governed by the dictates of canonical scripture.[13] The upshot of this critique has been a series of studies exploring the purposes and presuppositions of popular practice, often with an emphasis on apotropaic uses of script and writing. Although Balinese *aksara* have received comparably little attention in the scholarly literature, this is not to say they are any less important for our understanding of day-to-day life on the island.

Turning to the region's Islamic traditions, we find both Koranic verses and the names of Allah and the Prophet used in a similarly talismanic fashion. Such usage has not gone uncontested, with reformers often decrying what they take for acts of heresy or even idolatry. But the historical and ethnographic literature offers frequent reference to inscribed amulets (e.g., *rajah* and *jimat*) making use of Arabic script and Islamic themes that may, for example, be carried for protection, inserted under the skin, posted over the entry to one's home, or ingested as a form of medicine.[14] Much like the *yantra*-bearing tattoos and jerseys worn by Buddhist soldiers on the mainland, efficacious configurations of Arabic characters and numerals have frequently been used as a form of armor (see, e.g., Ricklefs 2006, 87). As Christopher R. Duncan said of the pitched battles that took place in eastern Indonesia in the early 2000s, the "Christian fighters wore bibles or vials of water blessed by a minister," while those "on the Muslim side . . . wore headbands with verses from the Koran or carried pieces of paper with Koranic verses in their pockets for protection" (2013, 71).

As with similar practices in Bali, the use of these written instruments is not limited to Southeast Asia, but rather shows a marked affinity with trends in the broader Buddhist and Islamic traditions that link the region with other parts of Asia and the Middle East. The modern-day use of amulets and tattoos, for example, may bear a striking resemblance to older practices found in Indic and Arabic (or Persian) texts. But establishing provenance for a given practice may prove more problematic than it appears, and this for reasons that are at once evidentiary and theoretical. To cite a prominent trend in the current scholarship, many have drawn inspiration from Sheldon Pollock's (1996, 2006) notion of a "Sanskrit cosmopolis" to begin asking new questions about the region's historical and cultural relationship with the Indian subcontinent[15] and, by analogy, the Arabian peninsula.[16] Put very briefly, this is the idea that in the period between roughly 300 and 1300 CE, Sanskrit became the dominant idiom for articulating polity and power through a swathe of territory encompassing what we now call South and Southeast Asia (1996, 199). Clearly Pollock's analysis has provided new and wide-reaching insight into the historical interplay of the "cosmopolitan" and "vernacular" sensibilities at work in the region during the premodern period. And yet, given his argument's grounding in an understanding of philology as "the discipline of making sense of texts," there is some question as to whether this approach is suitable for thinking about nonliterary uses of writing.[17] Indeed, it may turn out that, having reflected on Balinese *aksara*, we will need to reevaluate our approach to those ostensibly "textual" objects that we have assumed were there simply to be read.

Toward an Ethnography of Script

Looking further afield, beyond Southeast Asia, it must also be noted that a sizable literature has grown up around the study of writing in other so-called traditional societies. Most recently this has included a range of closely observed historical and ethnographic studies,[18] as well as efforts to theorize a more general approach.[19] Though pulling in opposite directions, the emphases on local particularity and universal principles are driven by a common conviction that prior scholarship—and particularly the work of Eric A. Havelock, Ong, Jack Goody, and David R. Olson[20]—overstated both the "autonomy" of literacy as an institution[21] and what was often described derisively as a theory of "the great divide" separating oral and literate societies.[22] Closely allied to these criticisms have been accusations of "technological determinism." Put rather crudely, this was the idea that the invention of the "phonetic" alphabet—as a technology of communication—gave rise directly to the development of specific cognitive faculties and forms of social organization.[23] This would clearly have been a difficult position to defend. Yet it also appears to have been a charge more frequently made than substantiated. If one reads selectively, it is certainly possible to attribute such an argument to some of its alleged proponents.[24] And, to the extent they made unwarranted or exaggerated claims, or at times used infelicitous turns of phrase, their critics have been right to take issue.[25] But, at least on my reading, the central contention was not so much one of technology and determination. It was rather an effort to distinguish critically between differently mediated social practices, and the forms of *agency* and *collective life* that they enabled.[26] What I wish to suggest is that this relationship between writing, agency, and collective life—as intimated by some of the earlier scholarship—may warrant more careful consideration than its critics have generally allowed. But for this, I would argue, a new approach must be built up from rather different assumptions about the nature of writing as both medium and practice.[27]

To this end, what follows is a study of how script and writing have been used in a southern Balinese ward that I shall simply call Batan Nangka.[28] This is one of seven wards that make up the "traditional village" (B. *désa pakraman*) of Pateluan, itself also a pseudonym.[29] At the time of writing, the ward comprises 108 family households living in seventy-one houseyards, with a total reported population of around 480. In matters of marriage and inheritance, Batan Nangka is very generally similar to other southerly Balinese wards as described in the anthropological literature (see, e.g., H. Geertz and C. Geertz 1975; Hobart 1979; cf. Korn 1932). Although, strictly speaking, the *banjar* is not a territorial designation, the vast majority of Batan Nangka's houseyards occupy a continuous stretch of land measuring approximately eleven hectares. On the south and west, this central concentration of houseyards is bordered by rice fields and dry agricultural land. The easternmost houseyards abut a ravine through which a river runs from north to south; and the northernmost houseyards (with but a few exceptions) are situated along the southern side of a major road running from the semiurban village of Adan Palsu in the west (population approximately 5,500) to the main thoroughfare of Jalan Raya Kaneraka. The latter runs north to the comparatively rural administrative village of Mogbog Gdé and south toward the provincial capital of Denpasar. The economy of Batan Nangka is mixed, with most households generating a living from a combination of small-scale agriculture, informal labor, and salaried work. Although there is a limited number of "newcomers" residing in the community, the vast majority of those living in Batan Nangka are from extended families that have made their homes there for several generations. Many in the *banjar* community own and work rice land that is not directly contiguous with the area of Batan Nangka. Others own no rice land at all, having sold it (e.g., to pay debts incurred through gambling or the sponsorship of ceremonial rites) or given it up when moving to a new houseyard without rice land attached to it.

The methods employed in conducting this research were those generally associated with "participant observation," which included informal conversation, studying texts and transcripts, helping to prepare for temple festivals, and both producing and discussing video recordings of local events. But it additionally meant playing cards, taking trips to the market, fishing, and watching football—that is, the pursuits of day-to-day life in a small, semirural community. A formal survey was also conducted, documenting the use of Balinese script in each of the seventy-one houseyards that make up the ward. Although most members of the community had some—at least limited—facility with Balinese script, with but rare exception the use of inscribed ritual instruments required expert assistance. To enlist this assistance, members often drew on networks extending far beyond Batan Nangka and the wider Pateluan area. Those consulted included inter alia priests of various kinds, healers,[30] architectural experts,[31] and offerings specialists. The aim of the survey was to allow expert knowledge to emerge out of enquiry within the community and thereby avoid the otherwise arbitrary privileging of one expert account over another. If the houseyard survey itself was a first step in gaining a local perspective on script-related expertise, my subsequent work with the priests and other specialists employed in Batan Nangka was meant to gain an expert perspective on local practice.

A Customary Deferral

Unfortunately, the survey ran into trouble even before it began, and this for reasons that would prove instructive. As I had frequently done with new projects in the past, one of the first steps was to consult with a group of men and women who regularly congregated around a local coffee stall in the hot hours just after lunch. There, in the early afternoon, the shade of a large jackfruit tree offered a cool place to relax and chat over coffee before heading back out to work (see photos 1.2a and 1.2b). This was often a most congenial atmosphere for casual conversation. In the hope of eliciting some advice, I suggested to a couple of young men that I was thinking about visiting each of the ward's houseyards, with an eye to cataloging their books, manuscripts, and other script-bearing objects. And I wondered aloud as to whether this would be a good idea. My suggestion was met with nods and polite smiles, which usually meant there was something important I was missing. So I called over to Putu Subrata, with whom I had collaborated on much of my previous research in the community. I explained that I wanted to know how Balinese script was being used in Batan Nangka but was a little uncertain as to whether a survey of this kind was really the best way forward.

One of the older men, who had been quiet to this point, said he knew of several local families who had inherited palm-leaf manuscripts (B. *lontar*; *ental*), but that their owners probably never opened them.[32] His daughter, who was running the coffee stall, said she heard one of her neighbors owned a *lontar* inscribed with tiny letters, so small that no one could read them. Kak Peken, grandfather to the family with whom we were living, added that he had seen the manuscript and could not make out what it said. But he had been told that, if one were able to read it, this would confer special powers—such as the ability to fly. It was at this point that Putu interrupted to explain that I could not simply wander into people's homes asking after

Photos 1.2a and 1.2b. Women around the local coffee stall (*top*); a group of men sitting with their fighting cocks after lunch under the adjacent jackfruit tree (*bottom*).

lontar. Such an approach was too direct, or "raw." In the first place, there would be some question as to my motivation. Leaving aside the recent news reports of stolen heirlooms, one might be suspected of seeking out the knowledge—and so the powers—potentially embodied in these texts. Moreover, he said, if someone in the family were involved in (or even suspected of) sorcery, they would be unlikely to respond honestly to a "survey" of instruments commonly used for this purpose.

Perhaps seeing that I looked disappointed, Putu suggested we return to his house, where he would show me some of the *lontar* his family owned— adding quickly that he had nothing to hide. He explained that his father, now long deceased, had liked to read, and that as a child he would often accompany him on long bicycle rides to neighboring villages. There Putu would be left to amuse himself with the other children while his father helped local priests and healers decipher obscure passages in their manuscripts. Apparently he was seen as something of an expert. Putu went on to explain that, although his family's *lontar* were now only brought out of storage once yearly on *odalan saraswati*—a day devoted to honoring the instruments of writing and learning—one of his earliest memories had been of listening to his father sing poetry in the evenings.[33] He then added rather wistfully that he was embarrassed by the poor state of his family's *lontar* and

Photo 1.3. The northern pavilion (B. *balé daja*) in Putu's houseyard, where the family's *lontar* have been stored.

wondered whether the new project would afford an opportunity to find out more about these manuscripts—implying that I might be willing to hire in a bit of help to put "the family library" in order.

Later that afternoon, I walked over to Putu's house with a camera and a notebook. He showed me through to the compound's northern pavilion (B. *balé daja*), where he said the family stored their *lontar* (see photo 1.3). Historically the *balé daja* was often the only structure in a Balinese houseyard with four solid walls and a lockable door. So it was also a good place for keeping valuables, including unmarried daughters. But, in Putu's case, this was where his elderly mother slept—and so it was also used as a storehouse for the offerings she was continually preparing in anticipation of impending ceremonies. Inside, the furnishings were functional, if rustic, with pillows and rolled sleeping mats crowded in among baskets of offerings in various stages of preparation (see photo 1.4a). Suspended vertically from the rafters in the northeast corner of the room were a set of *lontar*, underneath which stood two large woven baskets filled with bound manuscripts and loose leaves, many of which looked as if they had been chewed by mice and insects (see photo 1.4b). Putu selected one of the smaller and well-bound *lontar*, which he carried outside into the sunlight for a closer look (see photo 1.5).[34] I could see, peering over his shoulder, that one of the leaves was etched with a

Photos 1.4a and 1.4b. Inside the northern pavilion at Putu's houseyard (*left*); *lontar* manuscripts suspended from the rafters in the northeast corner of the room, with baskets of manuscripts and loose leaves on the table below (*right*).

set of drawings of the sort one might use for sorcery or self-protection (which often amounts to the same thing).[35] At first Putu seemed as surprised as I was, and he asked his mother whether she knew who had made the drawings. She looked over, pointed to the short length of the leaves, and said it was probably just a set of notes his father had copied out from a borrowed manuscript—perhaps for use on a specific occasion. As I would later learn, this casual borrowing, copying, and returning (or, as often, "forgetting" to return) was an important part of how these manuscripts circulated among healers, literary enthusiasts, and others in and around Batan Nangka.

Looking over the assembled *lontar*, I noticed that they appeared to include a wide range of materials—from casual notes on healing and sorcery to Balinese short stories and Old Javanese court poetry. I told Putu I wanted to learn as much as I could about these manuscripts and how they ended up in his houseyard. But, given the state they were in—with, for example, many of the leaves badly damaged, and others loosely piled together in baskets—I also suggested we might need expert assistance. I had recently been working with members of the Proyék Tik (I.; typing project), a long-standing collaborative project run by European and Balinese scholars dedicated to copying and cataloging palm-leaf manuscripts. And I thought perhaps they might be of some help. In situations like this, the project frequently offers to clean, repair, and transliterate old or damaged manuscripts in exchange for an electronic copy of the transliteration. I pointed out that this might be an excellent opportunity for Putu if he wished to restore his family's collection of *lontar* and learn more about the history of its contents. But Putu politely refused, explaining that—despite my assurances—he could not possibly entrust family heirlooms (B./I. *pusaka*) to people with whom he had no standing relationship, let alone someone he had never met. If anything went wrong, he would be the one held responsible.

Thinking back, I recalled Putu mentioning on another occasion that he was on good terms with a man in the provincial capital of Denpasar who specialized in reading copperplate inscriptions and old manuscripts. So, as an alternative to the Proyék Tik, I proposed that we might pay his friend a visit, with an eye to enlisting his help. Putu seemed to think this was a good idea, so I left him to make the arrangements.

We had planned to meet up the following morning to discuss details and prepare for the visit. But Putu never showed up. When eventually I decided to give him a ring, he explained over the phone that Ngurah Wesi, a local

Photo 1.5. Putu carrying one of the *lontar* out onto the front porch.

healer, had arrived at his house early that morning asking to inspect his *lontar*. We had been to see him just a few days before, in order to examine a set of manuscripts and inscribed amulets that he often used in treating clients. According to Putu, 'Rah Wesi had come to see him on account of a dream he had the previous night, in which he opened one of Putu's *lontar* and recognized it as resembling one of his own. In relating the dream, he said 'Rah Wesi did not specify the nature of this resemblance but rather emphasized that the connection between their respective *lontar* meant that we had to be extremely careful—both for our own safety and to ensure that the powerful formulae and drawings inscribed in the manuscript would not be divulged to those who might misuse them.

When I asked whether 'Rah Wesi's warning would affect our plans to visit his friend in Denpasar, Putu did not seem particularly concerned. But neither did he propose any specific arrangements for the trip. In the following days and weeks, I made several attempts to follow up on our plans, and each time the visit was postponed—always for what seemed a good reason. It is, of course, possible that this was mere coincidence, and that Putu was still happy for me to examine his family's *lontar*. But I never saw the collection again. And, if prior experience is anything to go by, Putu's serial deferral was more likely the result of his having changed his mind—quite possibly on advice from 'Rah Wesi.

Getting Weird in Bali

It is impossible to know whether this was just a case of poor timing on my part or if Putu may have decided—for whatever reason—against my examining his family's *lontar*. But it seemed clear enough that neither Putu nor 'Rah Wesi took these inscribed leaves simply to be "manuscripts" (I. *naskah*) or "texts" (I. *téks*) in any straightforward sense. They were, in the first place, part of Putu's inheritance, and something that required special care. Despite their being allowed to rot, and become partially illegible, the *lontar* were hung in the northeast corner of the northern pavilion, the direction generally associated with purity, power, and status. They were moreover presented with special offerings annually on the day dedicated to honoring script and related instruments of knowledge and learning, *odalan saraswati*. Although no one in the family had expressed a particular interest in reading these *lontar*, it seemed they were in need of protection against both theft and improper use. 'Rah Wesi's dream, and his warning, would suggest that these inscribed palm leaves were taken to be powerful, and so potentially dangerous. But in what did their power, and this danger, consist? To what extent was it grounded in the specific inscriptions they bore? And how, if at all, might this be related to their being presented with offerings?

One might be inclined to see the potency attributed to *lontar* as parasitic on a more fundamental conception of the written word as something to be read for its "content." On such an approach, the caution with which Balinese have handled script and writing—as noted by Professor Bagus and exemplified by the story of Putu and 'Rah Wesi—could be set aside as a secondary accretion that obscures the true nature of the text as a medium for the expression and transmission of a conceptual message. This understanding would be in keeping with a philological sensibility long prevalent among students of Balinese literature. It would moreover find support in the broader propensity among scholars of Asian religions and cultures to reduce textual communication to an "expressive" conception of language (see Vološinov 1973, 84–85). With a few notable exceptions,[36] this approach has prevailed in the scholarship on Balinese letters. But on what grounds have we assumed the adequacy of this approach? And, in so doing, what might we be missing?

Although it may seem a rather distant comparison, juxtaposing Balinese textual sensibilities with those of the western academy brings to mind David

Halperin's remarks on the study of classical antiquity and its tendency to pass over the "weirdness" of Greek attitudes to sexual practice and pleasure. Here he put the matter succinctly:

> Everyone who reads an ancient Greek text, and certainly anyone who studies ancient Greek culture, quickly realizes that the ancient Greeks were quite weird, by our standards, when it came to sex. And yet, professional academic training in classical studies typically induces a kind of amnesia about the weirdness of the Greeks. The student of classical antiquity quickly learns to acknowledge, to bracket, and to screen out their erotic peculiarities, the cultural specificities in their experience of *erôs* that fail to correspond to any category or identity in modern bourgeois society. One simply acquires the habit of allowing for their differences, granting them the latitude to be weird, and then one turns one's attention to other topics of greater seriousness or philological urgency. (2002, 2–3)

Halperin goes on to reflect on the importance of attending to what prior scholarship has ignored in its pursuit of more conventional topics. Carrying forward broader trends in the historical study of sex and gender, his efforts were directed to revealing the historicity of ideas and ideals—regarding relations between, for example, bodies, pleasures, intimacy, and identity—that modern and broadly western society had incorrectly taken to be universal. Halperin's point of departure was "to ask what the consequences might be of taking the Greeks at their word when they spoke about sex" (2002, 3). As an exercise in historiography, this was directed to unsettling the complacency of classical scholarship regarding its understanding of antiquity. But, insofar as it revealed the cultural peculiarity of modern sensibilities, his excavation of Greek thought was also explicitly driven by a desire to open up new avenues for thinking differently—here and now—about how we inhabit our bodies and relate to one another.

Without wishing to draw the comparison too closely, I would like to propose a similar approach to Balinese uses of script and writing. Extrapolating from the critique of sexuality (e.g., Foucault 1990; Sedgwick 1990), could it be that the idea of "the text" and "its manuscripts" obfuscates the very practices that generated these inscribed objects in the first place? What would it look like to approach Balinese writing practices without recourse to a foundational conception of textuality? Or an understanding of communication that privileges reference and the indicative mood as the primary modalities of language? Returning to the vignette with Putu and 'Rah Wesi, what I am suggesting is that we take Balinese "at their word" when they speak of the power and efficacy of *lontar*. We might ask, for instance, To what do these objects owe their potency? And in what does it consist? How has it contributed to the ordering of activities and practices connected to writing, and other uses of Balinese script? What sorts of comparisons can be made with broader trends in Southeast Asia? And, as importantly, what might a constructive engagement with Balinese practices teach us about our own textual proclivities? With these questions in mind, I would like to turn briefly to a set of events connected to another set of *lontar* from Batan Nangka.

The Madness of Mbok Tut

Dédé and his wife, Mbok Tut, lived alone in a large houseyard across from the ward's central coffee stall—which made their comings and goings easily observable, and so a frequent topic of conversation. The couple were often said to be aloof in their dealings with the neighbors, and they were rarely seen to leave the houseyard. Most days a large metal sheet was set across the front doorway, blocking the entrance in a manner many took to exemplify their more general attitude toward the wider community.[37] Dédé insisted that he put it there to keep out wandering dogs. But, according to those who had been observing from under the jackfruit tree, his real reason for closing the entryway was to keep his wife inside. For, even standing out in the street, one could tell Mbok Tut was acting rather oddly. From beyond the compound's perimeter wall, she could often be heard singing in a strange voice for hours on end and shouting at people no one else could see. To her husband's dismay, she eventually took to slipping through the blocked doorway and wandering out into the community. If her escape went undetected, she would then frequently spend the rest of the afternoon eating and drinking at the coffee stall, commenting indiscreetly on passers-by. Quite apart from her excessive expenditures on food and drink, Dédé found her public comportment extremely embarrassing—sometimes going so far as to drag Mbok Tut forcefully across the street and back into their houseyard.

When I asked around for possible explanations for Mbok Tut's behavior, the initial responses were not especially informative. The men sipping coffee at the jackfruit tree mostly shrugged and said she was crazy (B. *buduh*; I. *gila*). The women at the coffee stall said it was "stress," a term increasingly used to cover a range of complaints—from headaches and anxiety to various forms of emotional instability. Some days later I raised the matter again with an old friend and neighbor, this time without anyone else in earshot. He said there was no way to know for certain, but that it probably had something to do with Dédé's involvement in a spiritual group (I. *aliran kepercayaan*), which he had also recently forced his wife to join. On my neighbor's account, the group forbade its members from making many of the more elaborate offerings ordinarily dedicated during temple ceremonies, and put strict limits on contributions to larger-scale festivals honoring the protective beings and forces associated with the larger village community. As Dédé and his wife had failed to "remember" (B. *inget*) these important obligations, he said, it was no wonder they were running into trouble now.

Some weeks later, the topic came up again during a conversation with Mén Dana, a middle-aged woman who ran a small convenience store at the other end of Batan Nangka. I had consulted with her in the past on other projects, and she wanted to know what I was working on this time. When I told her about my interest in script and writing, she suddenly became animated and started telling me the story of a set of *lontar* that were in the home of someone who had recently died. As the conversation wore on, I eventually worked out that there was a link to Dédé's houseyard.[38] I asked what sort of *lontar* these had been. She said the *lontar* that she had seen dealt with fighting cocks—recommending, for example, the best colors and varieties of cockerel to match up on specific days of the week. But she had also heard there were some *lontar* with instructions for developing "left-handed" capabilities (B. *pangiwa*)—a common shorthand for sorcery and related activities.[39]

Mén Dana went on to describe a stone shrine (B. *tugu*) at the center of the houseyard that had fallen into disrepair. Apparently it had originally been dedicated to the collection of *lontar* held by the family. She said that a member of the previous generation had been a powerful temple priest and a healer of some repute, adding that he was especially adept in the art of self-protection by means of preemptive attack. The shrine, she said, was associated with the storage of the family's *lontar* and may even have been the only place they could be opened and read safely.

She then went off on what I initially took for a tangent, telling me about a preparatory rite (B. *mawinten*) she had undergone in order to read a *lontar* containing the genealogy (B. *babad*) for her family's descent group.[40] This included a story about their forebears' having been assisted by a particular kind of fish, which they were now forbidden to eat. She said her cousin had been violently ill whenever he ate this fish; and, having read the *babad*, she now knew why. As the story unfolded, I realized Mén Dana was slowly working around to the idea that Mbok Tut's illness was likely a consequence of her husband's inattention to his *lontar* and the shrine that was dedicated to them. As with her family's debt to the fish, what she seemed to be saying was that Dédé had failed to honor his inherited obligation to care for these *lontar*.[41] So I mentioned that Putu had taken photographs of the *lontar* as part of our houseyard survey (which I had stubbornly insisted on carrying out, despite having been advised otherwise). And, indeed, Dédé's *lontar* were in a parlous state, stuffed into a pile of used rice sacks behind an old wall.

I asked whether Dédé's inattention to his *lontar* might be linked to the spiritual group he and his wife had recently joined. Noting the group had some rather stringent rules regarding offerings, I wondered whether something similar might be affecting Dédé's attitude toward his family's collection of manuscripts. Mén Dana said she could not say for certain, but that the group had a reputation for ignoring local tradition—particularly the offerings and other precautionary measures directed to placating potentially destructive beings and forces. She then added rather gravely that *lontar* of the "left-handed" variety, such as the ones that may have been held at Dédé's house, must be brought to life (B. *idupang*) in order to be effective—and this is often accomplished by offering them blood. Once this offering has been made, she said, they will from time to time want additional "wages" or "compensation" (B. *laba*). And then she began, "If these offerings aren't given to them . . . ," after which there was a long pause, and the sentence trailed off. I asked whether this might help to explain what had happened with Dédé's wife and suggested that perhaps she had been disturbed (B. *gulgul*) by the forces animating these ill-treated *lontar*. Mén Dana nodded and laughed nervously. She then abruptly changed the subject and offered me some biscuits.

Whatever was behind Mbok Tut's strange behavior, Dédé's *lontar* were seen as potentially embodying agency—and participating in relationships—in a manner incongruous with the textual sensibilities of western-style scholarship.[42] The question is how best to theorize this disjuncture. Are Balinese ideas about the power and efficacy of *lontar* additive to an underlying textual essence that may be extracted for purposes of philological analysis and translation? Or would this reductive presumption to scientificity obscure ontological and epistemological commitments that are no less contingent, and historically peculiar, than their Balinese counterparts? Recalling Halperin's approach to classical antiquity, this book sets out to explore the consequences of taking Balinese "at their word." What, for instance, did Mén Dana mean in saying some *lontar* must be "brought to life"? And how, if at all, was this related to the idea of inheriting an obligation to these objects? Professor Bagus's inaugural address stressed both the cultural importance of Balinese script and the inadequacy of an instrumentalized conception of writing for understanding its use. But, granted such an account, what precisely would we be in danger of overlooking? In my abortive encounter with Putu's *lontar*, these inscribed palm leaves were seen to be powerful and potentially dangerous. And now, in reflecting on possible causes for Mbok Tut's affliction, some aspects of that power are beginning to take shape. The following chapters carry this line of enquiry forward in an attempt to begin specifying what we may have missed in passing over Balinese self-understandings on our way "to other topics of greater seriousness or philological urgency." As with the Greeks, we may discover along the way that it is our own textual prudishness that is the historical anomaly.

Moving Ahead

It is at this point that authors often claim the chapters of their books may be read in any order whatsoever. And the same can be said of this book, at least to some extent. Each of the following chapters may be approached as a (more or less) self-contained exploration of script and writing, as taken in from a particular vantage—namely, with respect to religious and cultural complexity (chapter 2), Balinese ideas about "life" (chapter 3), theories of "practice" (chapters 4 and 5), and critical approaches to both "tradition" (chapter 6) and "translation" (chapter 7). Yet, when read sequentially, each chapter carries forward a broader argument for rethinking our approach not only to amulets and other forms of apotropaic writing but also to those more familiar objects we are in the habit of calling books, manuscripts, and inscriptions.

The reader will notice that several key terms and presuppositions transform as the argument develops, shifting away from commonsense usage to what I hope will turn out to be a more critical perspective.[43] The style of presentation is intended to reflect the nature of this transformation. So, for example, in examining local uses of writing in Batan Nangka, I shall begin by working from a relatively colloquial understanding of the term *practice*— suggesting something like "what people do" (in this case, with Balinese script). In search of further clarification, we will then turn to scholarly accounts of "practice theory," where the driving question will be, Under what conditions might we approach Balinese *writing practices* as an object of study? But, in returning to reflect more carefully on the ethnography from Bali, it will become apparent that the assumptions underpinning theoretical accounts of practice may require some rethinking. And, from there, the task will be one of building up a new approach based on different assumptions— a job that will require an analogous reworking of several related terms (e.g., *tradition, translation, religion,* and *way of life*).

This process is meant to exemplify a more general approach to anthropological enquiry—one that is grounded in a dialectical relationship between ethnographic encounter and theoretical reflection. On this approach, ethnography and theory are not kept apart as discrete lines of questioning (let alone as engaging different orders of reality), but are instead held together— in tension—as mutually constitutive aspects of a sustained line of *thought in motion.* This is an approach that, with any luck, will not end up in the same place that it started. Inspired by a nagging discomfort with received wisdom on issues of writing and textuality, I hope to avoid leaving things where I found them. So the aim is not so much to "apply" theory to a "given" set of ethnographic materials (as if such a thing were possible!) but rather to appropriate the often disconcerting experience of ethnography as a lever for unhinging recalcitrant assumptions—particularly those unthinking habits of thought that get in the way of a more open-ended engagement with the ways others have set about knowing, being in, and working to transform the world. In this respect, Balinese uses of script and writing have served as an important, if in many ways fortuitous, occasion for working through a set of broader problems in the philosophy of the human sciences. This includes perhaps most centrally a set of questions around what it might mean to engage critically with the practices that make up other people's lives. With this in mind, the following chapter begins by laying out some of the circumstances—in Bali and beyond—that gave rise to the questions I have pursued in this book.

For those who would like to review a chapter-by-chapter synopsis before carrying on, one is provided in chapter 8.

Chapter 2

Writing and the Idea of Ecology

Bahasa Bali dicintai UNESCO,
tapi tidak dihargai di negeri sendiri.
The Balinese language is loved by UNESCO,
but isn't appreciated in its own country.

—Protest banner

In 2012 the Indonesian Ministry of Education and Culture announced a new national curriculum that would greatly reduce the number of class hours devoted to the study of regional languages, such as Balinese. The announcement was met with public protests at universities and government offices across the island, with new developments featured prominently on local television and in the press. The demonstrations were just getting underway when I began research for this book. Much as Professor I Gusti Ngurah Bagus's lecture spoke to debates current at the time, my framing of the project was informed by these events. Taking the popular response to the new curriculum as a point of departure, this chapter develops a series of themes that were introduced in chapter 1—exploring the *potency* attributed to written letters and its transformation under the sway of a modernizing conception of *writing as representation.* One of the habits of thought I wish to query along the way is our tendency to reify language—both written and otherwise—as if it were an object that can be isolated and held up for inspection.

In the little shops that line Bali's ever more crowded roads, there is often a set of shelves devoted to the sale of locally produced books.[1] Alongside titles on religion, astrology, and traditional medicine are collections of folktales and booklets on various aspects of Balinese language and literature. A common title is I Wayan Simpen's ([1973] 1995) oft-reprinted handbook on Balinese script, which opens with an historical résumé of conferences and symposia dedicated to regularizing the conventions (B. *uger-uger*) for writing in Balinese. Each of the meetings recounted in Simpen's list, going back to 1915, was linked in one way or another to an educational initiative and often a wider program for social and economic development.

As one might expect, the perceived importance of the island's literary tradition changed with the times, reflecting current political circumstances and ideals. Simpen's handbook itself, for example, was the product of a "workshop" (B. *pasamuan loka karya*) organized in the early 1970s to normalize the romanization of Balinese script. This was one of several meetings directed to bringing regional languages—especially Javanese, Sundanese, and Balinese—into closer conformity with the national language of Indonesian (DPPD 1978), for which spelling reforms had recently been introduced in 1972. It was argued that a regular system of transliteration would help integrate Balinese language instruction within the state educational system; and this, in turn, would bring Balinese culture more closely into line with the ideals of national "Unity in Diversity."[2] Writing was thus bureaucratically harnessed to serve a centrally planned program for social and economic development.[3]

In more recent years, writing has remained a topic of interest to the state, but the situation has changed considerably. With the demise of former president Suharto's authoritarian "New Order" regime (1966–98), and the repeal of restrictions on the press (1999), there has been a proliferation of public forums for the discussion of social and political issues. On the op-ed pages, television talk shows, and news websites, it is now generally taken for granted that several decades of mass tourism, capital expropriation, and environmental destruction have left the island in a state of "total crisis" (I. *Kristal*, short for *Krisis Total*). Whatever Balinese may have thought in the past, government initiatives now rarely get a free pass—and questions of language and writing are no exception. The recent debate over changes to the national school curriculum provides a particularly illustrative example.

A Question of Curricular Reform

The initial protests took place in the Balinese provincial capital of Denpasar in late 2012 and ran through the first several months of 2013. Those assembled at the events included university lecturers and students but also community organizers, politicians, and others opposed to the national curricular reforms scheduled to take effect later in the year. Among the prospective reforms was a provision stipulating that instruction in regional languages, such as Balinese, was now to be incorporated into the module for local "arts and culture." As the protesters pointed out, the new provision would sharply curtail the number of weekly class hours devoted to the study of Balinese and so reduce opportunities for children to learn how to read, write, and speak their mother tongue—which is widely seen to be losing ground to the national language of Indonesian. It would moreover mean fewer jobs for certified language teachers, to say nothing of the future prospects for those presently studying for university degrees in Balinese language and literature.[4]

There was a certain irony in the new curriculum's marginalization of regional languages, given the wider push to decentralize governance at the national level. This had followed from the financial crisis of the late 1990s, when Indonesia was forced to accept a program of market deregulation, privatization, and austerity in exchange for economic stability in the form an IMF "rescue package." Following Suharto's resignation, legislation for regional autonomy (I. *otonomi daérah*) was implemented in 2001 in response to calls for greater transparency and reform.[5] Encouraged by the World Bank, and in accordance with the so-called Washington Consensus, the devolution of power to regional government was meant to mitigate against a return to the corruption and inefficiency associated with a regime widely criticized for its authoritarianism and predatory extraction of resources from the provinces. The image of Suharto's Indonesia was one of technocratic directives handed down from a Javanese center to the regional peripheries, while proceeds from the sale of timber, oil, and minerals retraced the route in reverse.[6] The Jakarta elite grew rich while the outlying regions suffered from ruthless exploitation and an often arbitrary "rule of law."

Regional autonomy was, at least in principle, supposed to change all of this. The new legislation afforded local governments greater control over their natural resources. But it also decentralized the administration and funding for a wide range of public services, including healthcare, infrastructure, and education. Although the curriculum for lower, middle, and high school was still centrally planned, class time had been set aside for the teaching of regional languages in recognition of cultural diversity and self-determination. But now, with the new curriculum for 2013, this would no longer be the case.

The problem was not so much that the devolution of educational authority had been a resounding success. Without centralized oversight, the teaching of regional subjects—such as language and, to a certain extent, religion—was subject to the vicissitudes of local politics. As a result, the teaching of these subjects has been in constant flux since the early post-Suharto years. Coupled with the privatized provision of school supplies, this has meant that— in addition to rising tuition and fees—parents are continually required to buy new schoolbooks to keep up with the changing curriculum, which many believe is deliberately manipulated to serve the interests of the publishing houses and their patrons in the local legislative assembly.[7] Under the circumstances, it is not difficult to see why Balinese might see the regional administration of education as something of a mixed blessing. The post-Suharto years of "reform" had promised much and delivered rather less. Now, as if adding insult to injury, the national curriculum of 2013 appeared to presage a sharp decline in the availability of teaching jobs.

While the threat to employment was a concern for many of those directly involved in contesting the curricular reform, this was not foregrounded in the public seminars and media outlets through which they made their demands. Rather, the language of protest emphasized heritage preservation and cultural diversity in a manner at once consonant with the ideals of international human rights and the Indonesian state bureaucratic model of national Unity in Diversity. The call to safeguard (I. *menyelamatkan*) Balinese tradition was lent a certain edge by the appearance of regional discrimination at the national level, deriving in part from the recognition that, unlike Balinese, two of the languages spoken on the neighboring island of Java were to remain as stand-alone subjects in the new curriculum.[8] Citing both local and national legislation, as well as the Universal Declaration of Linguistic Rights, protesters insisted that it was the government's "duty" (I. *wajib*) to protect Balinese language as an essential component of regional "identity" (I. *identitas, jati diri*).[9] It was argued in the op-ed pages of the local newspapers, and on protest banners, that Balinese provides "local content" (I. *muatan lokal*) within the framework of the national curriculum and acts as an important medium for the transmission and preservation of traditional values.[10] The protection of local language was in this way cast as a cultural bulwark not only to regional chauvinism on the part of the national government but also to the globalizing influence of the tourism industry and transnational media.

The Language of Protest

If language was seen as an important aspect of the island's cultural heritage, it may also have played a role in shaping the protest itself. For, even when expressed in Balinese, the call to defend tradition was couched more or less exclusively in terminology derived from the national language of Indonesian. There were several likely reasons for this.

Perhaps most obviously, the seminars, campus marches, and op-ed discussions were conducted through a series of public institutions (including, e.g., universities, local government, and the press) in which Indonesian has long figured as the primary working language.[11] But linguistic competence probably also played a part. As is often the case where bilingualism prevails, colloquial Balinese is today shot through with Indonesian phraseology and syntactic patterns, not to mention the ever-growing prominence of foreign loanwords picked up from films, pop music, and the internet. It is but rarely that one hears a conversation in Balinese that does not incorporate recognizably Indonesian elements, which themselves may be borrowed from elsewhere. This is no doubt in part due to the lack of indigenous Balinese terms for things such as motorbikes, citizenship, and draft beer. It may additionally be related to the tendency among younger Balinese to speak Indonesian as a means of avoiding the hierarchical distancing that comes with Balinese status markers and conventions of deference, on which more in a moment. But, significantly, the use of Indonesian may also reflect an increasingly prevalent inability among Balinese to sustain conversation wholly in Balinese—as one is expected to do, for instance, when engaged in bride negotiations, ward assembly meetings, and consultations with priestly patrons or one's deceased forebears.[12] As a local student of Balinese literature wryly remarked during one of the public seminars, many of the protesters would have been hard pressed to articulate their concerns in the language they claimed to defend.

Initially I took the student's remark to be little more than a snide jab at his classmates and professors. But, as I realized later, he may have been making a rather more subtle point regarding the fundamentally *Indonesian* character of the cultural ideal itself. Under the New Order, Balinese had been taught—particularly in school and on television—to recognize themselves as citizens of an organically integrated nation of discrete communities differentiated along lines of religion, culture, and language. This was the ideal that inspired the creation of such cultural monuments as Taman Mini, Beautiful Indonesia in Miniature—a theme park on the outskirts of Jakarta where visitors are invited to observe and sample the nation's many "traditional cultures," exemplified by local architecture, costume, food, and dance (Pemberton 1994). Calls for reform notwithstanding, in the early post-Suharto years it was precisely this understanding of national Unity in Diversity that informed the drive for regional autonomy and related efforts toward cultural revitalization in "traditional communities" throughout the archipelago (Duncan 2009; Hauser-Schäublin 2013). That Bali was no exception to this wider trend may be seen in the public campaign to defend the island's religion and culture under the aegis of Ajeg Bali (Schulte Nordholt 2007), a jingoistic catchphrase that has been variously glossed in English as "Bali standing strong" (Rhoads 2007), "Strong and everlasting Bali" (Picard 2008), and, perhaps most suggestively, "Bali erect" (Santikarma 2003).[13]

Promoted by local media mogul Satria Naradha and his Bali Post Media Group, Ajeg Bali has come to stand for a defiant—and at times militant—defense of Balinese tradition. Following the Kuta nightclub bombings of 2002, a precipitous downturn in the tourism market dragged many relatively affluent Balinese into poverty, crushing emergent aspirations for western-style luxury, higher education, and a more generally cosmopolitan way of life. Coming in the wake of an Islamist "terrorist" attack, it was Muslim "newcomers" to the island who were scapegoated for hardships that a more critical eye might have attributed to the inevitable collapse of an economy built on long-standing—and extractive—patterns of foreign capital investment and environmental destruction. Yet, parroting one of the island's leading celebrity priests, advocates for Ajeg Bali would complain of Javanese and other Muslims who had "invaded" the island and were "selling satay to buy Balinese land, while Balinese were selling their ancestral land to buy satay." Alluding to an ostensibly Islamic threat to local livelihood, the *Bali Post* and its affiliates called on their readers and viewers to reinvigorate the Hindu Balinese tradition that was seen to distinguish the island from the rest of Muslim-majority Indonesia.[14] Following years of indoctrination under the

New Order, this was a tradition now widely understood in terms of the Indonesian state bureaucratic articulation of religion, culture, and language (Picard 2008).

These were also the terms in which the protesters would formulate their opposition to the curricular reforms; and it appears their efforts may not have been in vain. After a series of consultations between representatives of the provincial and national government, it was announced in early April 2013 that—with certain administrative provisions having been met—the Balinese language would be allowed to join Sundanese and Javanese as a stand-alone subject within the new national curriculum. With the assurance of weekly class hours, the upshot was likely to include increased job security for Balinese language teachers and so a more stable intake of students for degree programs in Balinese letters. But what of the desired "cultural" impact? Given the politically fraught history of its foundational concepts, what critical framework and terminology are appropriate for evaluating this apparent victory for the preservation of Balinese tradition?

What I would like to suggest is that we step back from the immediate concerns of the public debate to consider a little more closely the nature of cultural preservation (I. *pelestarian budaya*) and the purposes it is meant to serve. As a first step, we might ask what precisely it is that Balinese stand to lose should they stop speaking their mother tongue; and, conversely, what it might mean to speak, read, or write Balinese in the absence of its traditional milieu. Does it matter, for instance, where or how one learns? And with whom? Or perhaps in what script the language is taught?[15] Assuming the curricular debate has been settled—which one hopes is not assuming too much—there is also the practical question of how one might set about "preserving" (I. *melestarikan*) and "protecting" (I. *melindungi*) a language such as Balinese.

Quite apart from those aspects of the language that are at odds with present-day ideals of social organization and political equality, to study a language in the classroom differs in several important respects from learning to interact "organically" through imitation, trial, and error—for example, within one's own household and its environs. We must also bear in mind that, historically speaking, Balinese was never subjected to the sort of grammatical standardization that facilitates classroom learning. As a result, Balinese not only varies regionally; but, in use, its syntax and diction are markedly situational, depending in large part on a highly localized form of shared prior understanding.[16] Arguably, to speak Balinese "by the book" is to fail to speak it competently, raising the question as to how classroom learning may end up transforming the skills and sensibilities that are acquired through more traditional forms of language learning.

Setting aside issues specific to Balinese, these are obviously questions of wider import. And they have accordingly been part of ongoing discussion in linguistic anthropology and related fields, particularly among those working with what are now conventionally described as "endangered languages." With over three million reported speakers, Balinese does not generally appear on published lists of languages under threat of impending disappearance. But I would like to suggest that a brief review of recent trends in the scholarship on language endangerment may have something to contribute to our assessment of the nature and purposes of "cultural preservation." This may in turn help to sharpen our focus on the contemporary significance of Balinese script and writing.

Endangered Liaisons

From the early 1990s the idea of "language endangerment" grew steadily in importance among both professional linguists and the development agencies that have helped to support their initiatives.[17] The sense of urgency was in part a response to statistical analyses that suggested global linguistic diversity was in rapid decline. It was argued that in traditional societies around the world, a younger generation, having been exposed to the influences of globalization and market capitalism, was opting for more cosmopolitan ways of communicating that promised increased access to such things as employment, social mobility, and entertainment. Promoted through formal education and related institutions, national and regional idioms were seen to be winning out over local dialects; and, as a result, it was feared the majority of the world's languages would soon die out, together with members of the older generations who spoke them.[18] As Nikolaus P. Himmelmann noted in a critical review of the field, "By the year 2000, language endangerment was firmly established as an active field of research in linguistics as evidenced by the usual indicators such as regular and manifold conferences, a steady stream of articles and books, new societies and funds dedicated to the documentation and maintenance of endangered languages, and a special mailing list" (2008, 340).

Alongside its rise to prominence within the academy, however, there has also been some suggestion that the basic premises underpinning the idea of language endangerment may require some rethinking. Several of those working in the field have highlighted the difficulty in defining endangerment and specifying its causes. Others have problematized established approaches to language as an object of study, calling into question such basic principles as the genealogical ordering of languages in terms of descent within linguistic "families" (e.g., Austronesian, Indo-European, and Sino-Tibetan).[19] Still others have noted the inconsistencies and unintended consequences arising from the rhetoric of advocacy (Hill 2002; Duchêne and Heller 2007). Meanwhile, it has become increasingly difficult to delimit language "itself" as a human capacity, with the broader sociocultural milieu figuring ever more prominently in scholarly accounts of language acquisition and use.

These and related challenges to the received notion of language as a uniform and bounded object of study are increasingly cited in support of an "ecological" approach to the analysis and preservation of endangered languages (e.g., Mühlhäusler 1992; Himmelmann 2008). Notwithstanding nuanced differences among its various proponents, the argument for language ecology has generally centered on redefining the object of study—namely, "language"—as being organically integrated within a wider and established, yet ever-changing, "way of life" (see, e.g., Woodbury 1993; Hill 2002).[20] This has been understood to encompass both cultural norms and the natural environment, with language performing a mediating role in the relationship between human beings and their surroundings.

The idea that language is somehow positioned "between" humans and nature has prompted some to argue for one or another form of linguistic relativism, for which Wilhelm von Humboldt and Edward Sapir are frequently if not always unproblematically cited as precedents. The case for relativism has most often been made in concert with a call to preserve linguistic diversity, arguing its merit through analogy to the benefits of biological diversity. But it is perhaps in drawing more directly on biology that the ecological metaphor for language has been deployed to greatest effect. As one of the early proponents of such an approach observed,

> Much of the literature on language preservation and maintenance is concerned with preserving the structures of individual languages. To me this is reminiscent of the following situation described in a textbook on biology

(Morgan 1969, 34): "In the laboratory it is possible (though not easy) to maintain a population of a single species of organism in a container, isolated from all other species, as a pure culture. But without the biologist who maintains it, the population could not survive for long. Thus only two species are related in this situation: man and the organism in the culture. However, under natural conditions, and even in most laboratory situations, the smallest part of the living world that we can conveniently study will consist of many interacting species." Preserving languages is often seen to involve putting them into man-made artificial environments such as grammars and dictionaries, high literature, or giving language kits to surviving speakers. Such measures are unlikely to yield success unless the question of language ecology is seriously asked. (Mühlhäusler 1992, 164)

So, in an effort to move beyond such a reifying conception of language, what would it mean to ask "the question of ecology" in a Balinese context? On even a quite conservative reading, it would likely entail broadening enquiry—and so efforts toward preservation—to include a much wider set of circumstances than linguistic study has traditionally encompassed.[21] In present-day Bali this would require, among other things, careful attention to the complex of relationships linking language, hierarchy, and exchange. We find, for example, that, when addressing a superior—and so, ideally, a patron—one is said quite literally to be "offering up" (B. *matur*) one's words. By contrast, when one's superior responds—speaking "down"—she or he may be said to bestow a gift of words (B. *mapaica baos*). This terminology parallels that associated with other forms of hierarchically ordered giving and receiving, in which clients offer up (B. *ngaturang*) their support both material and otherwise, while patrons bestow (B. *ngicén*) their beneficence in recognition of service and devotion.[22] To speak in a refined (B. *alus*) fashion, then, is not simply a matter of politesse; rather, it is the proper—and often strategic—positioning of oneself through speech, toward a specific end, in relation to others according to finely graded differences of purity and efficacy (Hobart 1979). The material nature of these exchanges—and their rootedness in a specific sort of social relation—becomes especially pronounced in the use of Balinese script and other forms of writing.[23] What I wish to suggest is that closer attention to orthographic practices may yield important insights into Balinese articulations of language and power, which, in turn, will have implications for how we think about the preservation of the island's cultural heritage, both linguistic and otherwise.

A Tale of Two Inscriptions

The first example I would like to consider is taken from a wedding ceremony that I attended in Batan Nangka in early 2011. It was a commoner couple in their early twenties who were getting married, and a brahmin high priest (B. *padanda*) had been specially invited to complete the ceremony, as is now often the case.[24] For this the bride and groom were seated on the eastern pavilion (B. *balé dangin*) of the houseyard compound, where many of the important life-cycle rites take place. There the *padanda* performed a set of ceremonial procedures, the culmination of which included inscribing a series of syllables in honey on the bodies of the bride and the groom—on their hands, shoulders, foreheads, and tongues, among other places.

The inscription took no more than a few minutes, and so it appeared to make up but a small part of the ceremony, which, in its entirety, ran to almost an hour. I was told by several of those in attendance that the inscription was no less important for its brevity. Yet, on enquiring, no one was able—or perhaps willing—to offer a more detailed explanation as to why it was necessary.[25] For at least some of those present, it seemed the inscription had something to do with purifying (B. *nyuciang*) the newlyweds. But the rationale for this explanation was vague at best. When I pressed the issue, it was pointed out that a similar act of writing on the body is performed on several other important occasions, including the consecration of priests (B. *madiksa*) and during preparatory rites (B. *mawinten*) for those wishing to embark on a new field of study. In these latter cases the inscription is sometimes said to effect a physical transfer of knowledge through writing on the tongue— quite literally a gift from Déwi Saraswati, the goddess of knowledge and learning. But why would one inscribe letters on the body during a marriage rite? What was the inscription meant to accomplish? And how? What was its purpose or its desired end—what in Balinese we might call its *tetujon*?[26] There are literary precedents for writing on the body in both Bali and Java; I shall return to consider one particularly apt example in just a moment. But first, for the sake of comparison, I would like to reflect briefly on a second use of Balinese script, this time from the newspaper.

On Sundays the island's leading broadsheet, the *Bali Post*, carries a section entitled Bali Orti, which might be translated as "Balinese news" or "The news of Bali."[27] In contrast to the paper as a whole, which is printed in the national language of Indonesian, the Bali Orti section is written exclusively

Photo 2.1. Inscribing the body at the wedding ceremony.

in the Balinese language, albeit largely in roman transliteration. In addition to local news articles and short stories inspired by the Indic epics, Bali Orti frequently prints poems and short stories addressing topical issues such as environmental pollution, interreligious marriage, and life in the modern city. Again, these are all written in Balinese and printed in romanized script. There is, however, one marked exception. And this is a more or less regular feature that centers on a brief literary passage that is printed in *Balinese* script, next to which a roman transliteration appears, sometimes together with a translation into vernacular Balinese or into the national language of Indonesian. As with the bodily inscription, the question is *why*? What purpose is served by this juxtaposition of Balinese script with roman transliteration and Indonesian translation? Is this simply a matter of providing parallel text for less educated readers, as one finds, for example, with dual-language editions of the Bible and the Qur'an?[28] Or might there be something more to this juxtaposition of scripts?

Here it is worth a wider look at the newspaper itself. Perusing the *Bali Post*, one often finds letters to the editor and op-ed essays lamenting the demise of Balinese language and literature. With the rise of state education and new media (initially radio and television but now cellphones, Facebook,

Photos 2.2a and 2.2b. The Bali Orti Sunday feature in the *Bali Post*, with detail of Balinese script (see next page). Reprinted by permission.

Ceraken

Kidung Gaguritan Burayut

Kaasuh olih I Gusti Madé Sutjaja

Ri tepengan mangkin anggé galah nembang miwah muruk nyurat basa Bali; mawit saking Perpustakaan Lontar Fakultas Sastra, Universitas Udayana.

	Bulun matané marabu,
	Alis tajep mabengad,
	Sing raras anggénya asin,
	Manglaliyer,
	Tan péndah bintang kartika.
	46. Nyamannyané né cenikan,
	Pat-pat pada bangkit-bangkit,
	lamiad-lamiad pada meros,
	Lanjar-lanjar ramping-ramping,
	Ules masawang gading,
	Nyambang nyampuah putih

Photos 2.2a and 2.2b. (continued)

Instagram, and Twitter), as well as the growing number of non-Balinese Indonesians who are currently living on the island, there has understandably been a shift toward the use of the national language in many forms of daily interaction. As with some adults in the capital city of Denpasar, it is not uncommon for Balinese children to grow up with little or no familiarity with what is notionally their mother tongue. It is with reference to these circumstances that the Sunday feature in Bali Orti might be interpreted as a call to tradition, encouraging readers to continue speaking, reading, and writing in Balinese.

The challenges facing *written* forms of Balinese were given special attention in a series of articles printed on the front page of the Bali Orti section in mid-April 2013 (see photo 2.3).[29] The spread included two photographs, one depicting a palm-leaf manuscript, or *lontar*, and the other showing a young man who appeared to be writing on just such a manuscript, probably as part of a competition. The lead headline at the top of the page read, "Palm-leaf books, a documentary compendium of Balinese culture" (B. "Cakepan lontar, sinunggil koléksi dokuméntasi budaya Bali"). This was accompanied by a second story, carrying the title "They Needn't Always Be Seen as *Tenget*" (B. "Nénten mesti setata katengetang," with *tenget* as inherently powerful and potentially dangerous). The latter piece cited an official from the Center for Cultural Documentation in the provincial capital, who encouraged Balinese not to be afraid to read *lontar* that were traditionally considered dangerous or inaccessible to the uninitiated. If the lead story made explicit the link between written language and culture, and the second aimed to alleviate traditional anxieties regarding the power of the written word, the third story confronted its readers with a call to action encapsulated in the headline, "Come let's preserve this cultural heritage of ours" (B. "Ngiring lestariang tetamian budaya druéné"). Opening on a didactic note, the article explained,

> The word *lontar* is derived from the words *ron* and *tal*, meaning palm leaves. The leaves come from the palm tree, and they are dried and used as the material on which Balinese characters [B. *aksara*] are written. These texts [I. *naskah*], or traditional books [B. *cakepan*], which are widely known as manuscripts [I. *manuskrip*], are made from palm leaves, and are treated as a source of historical information [I. *sumber informasi sejarah*] that is kept in museums and libraries. It would be a sad day indeed should the method of writing *lontar* be lost, overrun by our times and technology which are becoming ever more modern. Besides, there are but few among Balinese who wish to read *lontar*.
>
> As members of the community, we ought to embrace the contents of this culture of ours, through means such as writing the traditional script [B. *aksara*] on *lontar* leaves, or reading *lontar* together with other members of the community and those youths who have lost touch with [B. *sampun lali*, "already forgotten"] our culture. Such activities are well suited to wider use in the effort to preserve the existence of these *lontar*.[30]

Cakepan Lontar, Sinunggil Koléksi Dokuméntasi Budaya Bali

Nénten Mesti setata Katengetang

Bencingah

Mégasari

Ngiring Lestariang Tetamian Budaya Druéné

Kruna

BASA BALI	AKSARA BALI	BAHASA INDONÉSIA
Kruna basa Bali saré durung kauningin arcaryuréyé.	Sasuratan aksara Bali saking keuné-keuné melésa Bali	Kata berbahasa Bali yang belum dikenali artinya.
1. ayahan		1. kewajiban
2. besia		2. ikat
3. blabuh		3. capai terikat
4. botri		4. sandang
5. gaberg		5. regu
6. jaran		6. sementara
7. kabirawa		7. luar biasa
8. langgia		8. jahat, khianat
9. nylacet		9. melirik
10. pamebluh		10. produksi

The article called on readers to safeguard "this culture of ours" and to rekindle an interest in traditional literacy as a means of inspiring those who had lost touch with their cultural heritage. Here palm-leaf manuscripts are seen to provide access to important "historical information" while at the same time exemplifying local values and ensuring their preservation.[31] Such stark reification lines up neatly with the commodification of "Balinese culture" driven by the tourism industry. But it also raises the question as to whether the ideals of preservation are commensurate with those of its object. Put another way, cognizant of the transformations that have come with "touristification" (Picard 1996), we might ask: What happens to Balinese practices when they are rearticulated within the "discourse of preservation" (I. *wacana pelestarian*)?[32] It is with this question in mind that I would like to return to my earlier examples in order to compare the purposes of preserving Balinese script, as outlined in the newspaper, with the sensibilities underpinning other, older uses of writing in Bali, as exemplified by the bodily inscription. It is my working conjecture that these two uses of Balinese script are grounded respectively in quite different understandings of media, materiality, and what I shall provisionally call conceptions of the common good. But for this we must now return to the wedding.

It Is Alive!

It will be recalled that the bodies of the bride and groom were inscribed with a series of syllables; and the question I had asked was, *Why?* What purpose might this inscription have served? And how was it thought to work? Those with whom I had discussed the rite on the day were either reticent or unable to provide what I—or even they, for that matter—would consider a satisfactory answer. It must be emphasized that there are several possible reasons for such a response, not all of which would entail ignorance on the part of my interlocutors. Speaking the truth is traditionally thought to be efficacious; by the same token, to speak with undue confidence is to court disaster. To presume to comment on something for which one does not have ample evidence is to invoke—and so potentially risk offending—the forces at play, which, it seems, are not inconsiderable in the use of script and writing. So, in the absence of a readily available explanation on the occasion of the bodily inscription, I would like to take a slightly different tack and look to another common use of Balinese letters—namely, the little cloth amulets called *ulap-ulap* that one often finds affixed to newly constructed buildings and shrines.

These small sheets of white cloth, inscribed with various combinations of characters and images, are an integral part of the rites that must be performed before any new structure may be inhabited.[33] By local account, the rites themselves are meant to accomplish three things: the purification (B. *nyuciang*), fortification (B. *mamakuh*), and animation (B. *ngidupang*) of the building itself. It is to the third of these aims that I would like especially to draw attention—that is, to the idea of *animating* a building.

The crucial point is that Balinese buildings are said to be alive. They *maurip*, as one might say in Balinese. In order to begin work on a wooden house, one must first kill a tree. In the act of construction, then, one is working with dead tree matter. So, to inhabit a building before its rite of *reanimation* is often said to be like sleeping under a corpse. On this account, a dead building is taken to be inert and so incapable of defending itself. It is, in effect, open to all comers; while, by contrast, a living building can repel attack—much as a living tree can defend itself with its bark or even its thorns—and, when harmed, it may then repair itself through its inherent capacity for growth and self-transformation. So how are these little script-bearing amulets—the *ulap-ulap*—employed in the rites of animation? And, in turn, what might this tell us about the purposes of writing on the body?

The name of these little cloth amulets provides a first clue.[34] The base word *ulap* has many uses. To *ngulapin* is to call someone over, "to invite" or "to beckon." The accompanying gesture is one of waving with a single hand downward toward the body, much as one does in calling a taxi in much of Southeast Asia. Along similar lines, there is a set of rites called *(pa)ngulapan*, also derived from the base word *ulap*, in which one's "spirit" is called back either to the body, in the event of illness, or into a coconut, in the case of death, where the coconut then becomes a temporary vessel for transporting the vital essence of the deceased.[35] Here, too, the movement is a *waving in* toward the body, this time with both hands held out, one moving inward from each side. In Balinese this gesture is called *natab*, which is not only the name of the wedding rite performed by the high priest but also one of its recurrent features. That is to say, both before and after the letters were inscribed on the body, the bride and the groom were instructed to *natab*, or perform this *waving* or *wafting in*.

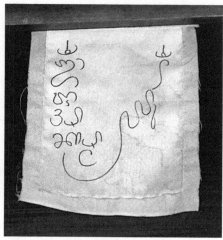

Photos 2.4a and 2.4b. An *ulap-ulap* over a modern garage, with detail. Variations on this configuration of *aksara*, known as the *dasabayu*, or "ten forces," frequently appear on *ulap-ulap* and other written instruments. But the method for reading and pronouncing this assemblage of syllables—and thereby activating it as an instrument—is not readily apparent without prior instruction. The ten characters may be read starting from the left side, top to bottom, and then bending up to the right as follows: ONG I A KṢA MA RA LA WA YA UNG (cf. Nala 2006, 31; Weck 1937, 75; Boeles 1947, 56). As one moves along the sequence, the shape of the *aksara* increasingly diverges from more-standard forms of Balinese orthography (cf. chapter 1, figure 1).

Returning to the rite of animation for a new building, it seems that it is the *ulap-ulap* that does the beckoning. It quite literally "calls in" (B. *ngulapin*) the forces that will bring the building—or perhaps its constitutive materials—"back to life" (B. *ngidupang mawali*) and thereby protect its inhabitants. Having told a local priest that I was having some difficulty in understanding the use of the *ulap-ulap*, he suggested that I think of them as working more or less like a satellite dish, channeling energy in "from on high" (B. *saking luhur*).[36] The physical manipulation of written script, he said, is a bit like "tuning the television." Use one set of syllables to reanimate a kitchen; use another for activating one's ancestral shrine. Changing the arrangement of characters on the cloth, he added, might be compared to changing the channel on the television. Different channel, different program. Different syllables, different energy. A given configuration might be appropriate for one sort of structure, but it would not have the desired effect on others.[37]

Curiously, the term that both he and others in Batan Nangka most commonly used in discussing this "energy" was the English loanword *énérgi*. I had initially assumed this usage must point to a relatively novel understanding of the *ulap-ulap*, perhaps one even specifically elaborated for my benefit. But, as I later learned, the more general idea of a "life force" at work in buildings, as mediated by writing, finds further support in the *aksara* themselves. To cite a particularly apt example, one of the configurations most frequently employed on the *ulap-ulap* in Batan Nangka is the series of syllables known as the *dasabayu*, or "ten forces" (see, e.g., photo 2.4b)—a sequence described by van der Tuuk (1897–1912, 2:456) as "the name of a life-restoring mantra" applied in times of weakness or ill health but also used for the "animation" of offerings and related instruments during ceremonial rites (Ottino 2000, 140).[38] Most in Batan Nangka would not readily recognize this arrangement of letters by this name (though many are familiar with the term *dasabayu*), let alone "dare" to read it aloud. But this understanding of the *aksara* and their potency accords well with the way they were being used— to invigorate, animate, and restore energy.[39]

Returning to the wedding rites, what I wish to suggest is that a similar *restoration of energy* may have been the aim of the high priest's inscription on the bodies of the bride and groom.[40] By having a series of syllables placed at specific points on the body, one might absorb their energy—perhaps a specific capability or faculty—much as the *ulap-ulap* help to channel the forces of animation that bring a newly built house "back to life." It is perhaps telling in this respect that in some parts of the island, a newlywed couple—before this rite has been performed—is called a "living corpse" (B. *bangké idup*).

Power and Precedence

If the link between writing and power is left unstated elsewhere, it is made explicit in traditional accounts of literary composition, where Balinese letters not only *channel* energy but are themselves said to be *alive*—much like trees, human beings, and buildings. That is to say, they have the power to transform both themselves and the world around them. Commenting on a related link between writing and power, Rachelle Rubinstein noted in her study of *kakawin* composition that "the association of spelling with life and death . . . is more than [mere] convention. It signifies a belief . . . that letters have a divine origin, are invested with supernatural life force, and are a powerful weapon that can be employed to influence the course of events." She went on to suggest that "to write and spell properly is to preserve that life force and, conversely, to make errors is to eliminate it—it is to kill letters. . . . [This] also implies that letters are powerful weapons and that the poet's manipulation and the scribe's copying of them is comparable to engaging in battle" (2000, 194; cf. Hunter 2007).

On this account Balinese orthography is not merely the graphic representation of sound, or of meaning, but instead participates in bringing about willed changes in the world. As living things, but also as weapons, letters have a dangerously ambivalent power of their own. This may help to explain why Balinese children in previous generations were warned to be careful when they wrote. They were told not to study haphazardly (B. *Eda ngawag-awag malajah!*). For to read and write Balinese characters without the requisite preparation can render you emotionally unstable or make you "stupid" (B. *belog*). It might even drive you crazy (B. *buduh ing sastra*). It is rather like giving a small child a set of sharp knives as a plaything. A good knife is no doubt a useful tool in the kitchen if one knows how to use it. But, when mishandled, Balinese characters—like knives—can cause serious damage. This is one of the reasons why only certain types of people are thought capable of safely and effectively handling the ambivalently potent configurations of script that can animate buildings and confer energy on people during life-cycle rites, such as we saw with the wedding.[41]

Although things may have been different in the past, in present-day Bali the person most consistently consulted for this purpose—that is, for the handling of letters—is a high priest from a brahmin house to whom one's family owes fealty, through a patron-client relation that usually extends back several generations.[42] The power of writing and the transformative potency of letters are closely linked both to their material form and to a *localized* sense of place. I would moreover suggest that this linkage of matter, place, and power only makes sense in the context of a very specific kind of social relation—such as those we find in Bali's overlapping networks of patrons and clients (Hobart 1975), clans and wards (Korn 1932; Hobart 1979), temple congregations (H. Geertz 2004; Stuart-Fox 2002), and extended families (H. Geertz and C. Geertz 1975). These are relations of but loosely calculated giving and receiving that are sustained through time. But they are also, significantly, relations that are closely tied to particular places and objects—such as rice land, rivers, and trees but also temples, palm-leaf manuscripts, cloth amulets, and heirloom daggers. These objects, like the letters that may be inscribed on them, are very much alive—which is again, at the very least, to say they can effect change in the world (see chapter 3). And their potency is inseparable from the ways in which writing may be controlled and deployed to localize and materialize relations of power and patronage.

In the Sunday Papers

Recalling the discussion of language ecology, and its broadening of the field of enquiry, I would argue that it is on precisely these three points—namely, those of materialization, localization, and power—that the practice of writing on the body may be contrasted with what we saw in the Sunday newspaper, where the power of script seemed not so much to be immanent in its material presence. Instead, its power—if indeed it had any—consisted in its ability to point beyond itself. The Balinese characters appearing in the special feature on the Bali Orti page "stood for"—as opposed to embodied (B. *maraga*)—an ideal of cultural identity and tradition; and, crucially, this broadly cultural ideal transcended any one of its material instantiations. Unlike the cloth amulets, or *ulap-ulap*, the newspaper can be printed over and over again and yet still remain "the same newspaper"—something that cannot be said for these small, script-bearing amulets with their aura of singularity.[43] So it seems we may be dealing with two quite different sensibilities regarding Balinese script. One is resolutely immanent, the other representational. Before proceeding to the broader questions this raises, it is worth first reflecting briefly on the preconditions for the latter—that is, for the use of Balinese script as it appears in the newspaper.

Recent estimations would suggest that Bali is home to some four million people, approximately 85 percent of whom are formally registered as adherents to the state-sanctioned form of Hinduism, *Agama Hindu*. Here it is important to bear in mind that, although a majority on the island itself, Balinese Hindus are nationally a minority, making up less than 2 percent of Indonesia's population of some 250 million.[44] In the early years of the republic, it was in part this sense of numerical disadvantage that drove certain among the urban intellectual elite to seek formal state recognition for Hinduism.[45] It was feared that, without formal recognition, Balinese would be seen as backward tribalists who had "not yet" embraced a world religion; and they would consequently become targets for conversion at the hands of the country's larger and institutionally established Islamic and Christian communities. The Ministry of Religion had stipulated certain criteria to qualify for state recognition—namely, a belief in one God (I. Tuhan), the testimony of a prophet, the possession of a holy text, and a community of adherents that extended beyond the boundaries of a single ethnic group (Pitana 1999).

As we have seen, traditional uses of Balinese script—such as the *ulap-ulap* and writing on the body—help to anchor an important series of social relations in both matter and place. The act of writing may be seen as momentarily fixing these relations within a particular locale, thereby securing the transfer of power and efficacy that they embody. By contrast, the need to constitute a religious community extending not only beyond the immediate locale but indeed beyond Bali itself required an account of community that transcended the sort of localizing solidarities characteristic of the island's long-established forms of social organization. The requirement for a canon of sacred scripture further called for an account of "the text" that, unlike older ideas of script and writing, transcended the bounds of matter and its physical presence. So what we have, it seems, are two parallel sets of relations. On one side, there is a materially immanent theory of writing and power linked to a localizing form of social organization (exemplified, e.g., by the *ulap-ulap* and writing on the body). On the other, we have a displaced and dematerializing theory of writing linked to translocal forms of solidarity associated with the postcolonial nation-state (exemplified, e.g., by the newspaper and the idea of canonical Hindu scripture). Put another way, there appears to be a link between Balinese *practices of script and writing*, on the one hand, and broader *styles of practical reasoning*, on the other. By *practical reasoning* I mean to suggest, in the first instance, those forms of deliberation through which means and ends are evaluated and decisions to act are taken. But this is also meant to point, more generally, to the ways in which people set about embodying, cultivating, and contesting shared ideals of agency, community, and the common good—themes that will be developed further in subsequent chapters.[46]

Returning to the curricular debate, the possibility of a disjuncture between styles of reasoning raises a series of difficult questions around the relationship between language and cultural preservation. First, with reference to these shifting sensibilities regarding script and writing, how are efforts toward preservation most likely to transform their object? That is, in what ways will "preserving Balinese tradition" (I. *melestarikan tradisi Bali*) change the nature of traditional Balinese practices? The Greek ancient, Heraclitus, is frequently cited as having said one cannot step into the same river twice. Yet, on the face of it, this is often precisely what cultural preservation programs set out to accomplish. Meanwhile, the invocation of timeless ideals—"culture," "heritage," "values," and so on—is rarely accompanied by a clearly stated account of how their preservation relates to the wider form of collective life that such efforts aim to bring about. Here I am thinking of those aspects of community commonly understood under the rubrics of economy, law, and politics. It is important to bear in mind that, were Balinese able to "preserve" their traditions wholesale, we would be looking at a return to farming, fishing, and high "Indic" culture but also to slavery, internecine warfare, and bride capture (B. *malegandang*), which often began with what is perhaps best described as a period of community-sanctioned rape.

Clearly, cultural heritage is a selective business.[47] But what are the criteria for choosing those aspects of Balinese tradition suitable for preservation? And whose interests are to be given priority? It is important to recognize there is no neutral ground here. For example, the desire to reduce status markers in the language (starting, e.g., with the *sor/singgih* distinctions for condescension and deference) serves a particular vision of collective life based on the articulation of equality with a specific understanding of the common good.[48] These ideals obviously differ from those of the opposed argument for retaining "language levels" that would register distinctions of relative purity and efficacy between, for example, *anak jaba* (commoners) and *triwangsa* (gentry).[49] To adjudicate between these rival visions of collective life is to upgrade a particular political project to the status of universal wisdom—a hegemonic substitution of part for whole (Laclau 2005). What is the upshot of all this? Decisions regarding preservation are directed toward a specific purpose (B. *tetujon*), even when this purpose is not clearly stated. So perhaps we may need to reflect a little more carefully on the purposes of cultural heritage. What have they been in the past? And what ought they to be now, with reference to the kind of polity Balinese wish to cultivate for the future? It seems the protests against the 2013 curricular reform averted one sort of disaster. But their success has given rise to a whole new set of challenges that ought to be recognized as no less formidable. Looking to the future, one hopes the protesters' success in opposing the new national curriculum is not ultimately a case of *ngelidin sétra, nepukin sema*—"avoiding the cemetery only to wind up in the graveyard."[50]

Lines of Enquiry

Pulling back from the curricular debate, these reflections on cultural heritage also suggest a series of wider, and more theoretically oriented, questions regarding language, script, and writing. By expanding the scope of enquiry beyond the narrowly instrumentalist notion of language as "a means of communication," it is possible to see how, in Bali, both speaking and writing are inextricably tied up with practices that at once materialize and localize hierarchical relations of exchange and patronage. This link between language and a broader array of practices is, I believe, quite close to what linguists and others have often meant by *language ecology*—the need to understand language in relation to its "surroundings." One might see in this an affinity with Wittgenstein's aphoristic suggestion that "to imagine a language is to imagine a form of life" (2009, § 19). Yet taking a "form of life" as one's object of study, or perhaps as a frame of reference, would raise several questions of its own.

There is first the question of complexity. It was noted that colloquial Balinese is today strongly inflected by Indonesian speech patterns and lexical borrowing. But what of the practices—and "form of life"—within which these utterances take place or of which they are a part? Can we extrapolate from the internal complexity of language-in-use to a similar argument regarding the wider conditions of collective life? (Note how difficult it is to avoid reification—for instance, through spatializing and totalizing metaphors such as "internal complexity" or being "within"—or "a part of"—something such as a "form of life.") The examples from Bali were meant to exemplify the incongruities between two rival conceptions of agency, materiality, and what it means to be "alive." But things are rarely so tidy. To argue for discrete theories that map onto corresponding practices would be to elide the indeterminacy of those practices for which competing interpretations are available. For instance, was the bodily inscription at the wedding an act of purification informed by the Hindu monotheism taught in schools and broadcast on television? Was it alternatively a rite of protection, performed in recognition of the newlyweds' vulnerability to attack? Could it have been both? Or maybe neither? The answer would likely depend on whom one asked and under what circumstances. And, to complicate things further, it is difficult to know what would constitute falsifying evidence against any given account. But this ought not to be mistaken as grounds for a simple perspectivalism. For competing interpretations are often premised on incommensurate understandings of the world and the conditions under which it may be known and acted upon. If, as Alasdair MacIntyre put it, "a viable tradition is one which holds together conflicting social, political and even metaphysical claims in a creative way" ([1979] 1998, 67; see chapter 6), then it behooves us to attend more closely to the ways in which writing and script articulate points of tension between rival ways of being, and acting, in the world.

There is then the "ecological" relationship to consider. Common turns of phrase include the "rootedness," or "embeddedness," of a language within the practices that make up a particular way of life. It has been suggested, for example, that "when a language dies, a culture dies" (Woodbury 1993)[51] and that efforts to protect endangered languages ought to focus on the preservation of their ecology, understood as the "home" in which a given language can survive (Mühlhäusler 1992). Taken together, these arguments would appear to suggest a relationship of mutual dependence, an idea now widely recognized as an important corrective to the assumption that language can be isolated for analysis like bacteria in a petri dish. But, beyond its mutuality, is there anything further we can say about this relationship between language and a way (or "form") of life? What exactly does it mean to describe the relation as *ecological* in nature? And as opposed to what?

The more cautious accounts of language ecology tend to stress that "ecology" is but a metaphor, implying that a more literal representation of the relationship between language and its "environment" is—at least in principle—a possibility. Such statements might lead us to wonder what a less figurative account would look like. But I suspect this would turn out to be a red herring.[52] For, on a closer reading, the insistence on metaphor appears—as much as anything—to betray a certain ambivalence in the articulation of language as an object of study. On the one hand, the idea of ecology appears to acknowledge the tension between the grounding presuppositions of linguistic analysis and a growing body of contradictory evidence (see earlier in this chapter); yet, on the other, were it taken "literally," the implications of an ecological understanding of language would potentially threaten to undo the field. For example, were we to assume that the sense of a given language derives from its use within a particular form of life, and that this form of life is only properly intelligible in terms of its indigenous language, we would be left with some rather awkward questions regarding the translation between potentially incommensurate frames of reference. It is not so much that the "gaps" would be "unbridgeable" but that there would be a degree of indeterminacy (Quine 1960) in the translational movement between languages, and so forms of life (see chapter 7). Significantly, there is no self-evident reason to think this would apply any less to the language of scholarly enquiry in its efforts to analyze a foreign tongue. What are we to do, for instance, when the form of life under scrutiny has its *own* theory of language (see, e.g., Hobart 2015)? Given their differing ecologies, one would presumably need a third (ecologically neutral?) language to describe the disjunctures between the language of scholarly accounts and the language these accounts take as their object. And this, at least on the face of it, would give way to infinite regress.

Though the problems may be daunting, they are not unique to the idea of language ecology. One finds similar difficulties emerging from other forms of "ecology" (see, e.g., Bateson 1972; J. Gibson 1979; Ingold 2000; Postman 2000), as well as from that congeries of publications lumped together under the sobriquet of "practice theory" (Ortner 1984)—a label meant to cover the likes of Pierre Bourdieu, Marshall Sahlins, Anthony Giddens, and a rather attenuated Michel Foucault, among others (see chapter 5).[53] Speaking very generally, it is my sense that the trouble originates from a conflict between theoretical desire and the force of disciplinary habit. Having sensed the problems they engender, we set out to unsettle such vexing dichotomies as structure/agency, body/mind, langue/parole, medium/message, and nature/culture. But it is not long before we run up against our established practices of enquiry, which are themselves rooted in precisely the dichotomies we wish to transcend—and much jargon ensues. Put another way, and despite protestations to the contrary, it seems the day-to-day practices of critical enquiry all too often exempt themselves from the "theory of practice" they intend to foist on Others. One of the central aims of this book is to work out some of the implications that follow from taking a stronger line on practice—one that endeavors to recognize its own susceptibility to the sorts of questions that it is in the business of asking its Others.

Among the challenges in pursuing this line will be the need to counter-act the immobilizing and reifying tendencies of our received terminology, which predispose us both to freeze what is in motion and to treat events as if they were objects. Our critical arsenal consists of such terms as *identity, subject positions, society, social structure, culture, cultural formation, media, text, object of study, meaning, logic, materiality, locality, ontology,* and *power.*[54] With the use of each of these terms, we are often substituting a noun for a verb—a stationary and perduring object for a directed yet evanescent event. (Here the reification of *discourse* in pop theory—e.g., "the discourse on X"—is espe-cially ironic, given the etymological sense of *discourse* as "running to and fro" or "away.") A stronger theory of practice would entail attending to the direc-tionality and evanescence of its "object." But what would it mean to take such an approach to practices of writing? In the coming chapters we will ask neither about their logic nor their structure. Rather, we want to know what sorts of worlds they are trying to call into being. What projects of transfor-mation do they carry forward? What countervailing forces are they meant to forestall? And, not least, what instabilities do they aim to secure? We will be less interested in pursuing "the materiality of the written word" and more so in asking, Who *materialized* what through an act of writing? What does Balinese script *do*? And to what end? Under what conditions? And with what consequences, both intended and otherwise? It may be recalled that Balinese children were admonished in the past not to study haphazardly, a warning meant to fend off the unintended effects of materializing the po-tentiality embodied in Balinese script. The following chapter examines this potentiality in further detail by asking what it means when Balinese say written letters are "alive."

Chapter 3

The Meaning of Life, or How to Do Things with Letters

Scholars of Balinese letters have often noted in passing that the characters, or *aksara*, employed to write Balinese texts are taken to be "alive" by those who use them—an idea we have also encountered in Batan Nangka.[1] This is arguably one of the more remarkable ways in which Balinese understandings of writing differ from their Euro-American counterparts. But what does it mean to say that Balinese letters are alive? It is all too clear that our received accounts of "life" (Thacker 2010), and of "writing" (Derrida 1974, 1981), engender considerable ambiguity. Might attention to Balinese practices help us to think more clearly about the use of letters and perhaps even what it means to be "alive"? In this chapter I offer some provisional reflections on these questions. I shall begin where we left off in the previous chapter, with the idea that contemporary uses of *aksara* are caught between two conflicting conceptions of writing, each allied to a different articulation of agency, life, and matter. The aim will be to examine more closely the character of these two ideals and the styles of reasoning through which they have been pursued. Recalling the critique from ecology, the ambiguities and disjunctures that we meet along the way will help in starting to develop a more critical orientation to "practice."

On Life

Let us begin with life. The idea of *life* is as slippery as it is consequential. Decisions regarding things so important as our care for the unborn and severely disabled entail judgments as to when life begins, ends, and is "worth living." Yet even cursory reflection on limit cases—say, the "life" of viruses or the idea of "brain death"—would suggest our conventional terminology is rather too blunt an instrument for the questions we have allowed it to define. Looking to the historical and ethnographic record, we find others have had quite different ideas about life and what can—and ought to—be done with it. For the ancient Ionians, for example, nature (φύσις) was itself alive, as evidenced by its movement and capacity for growth and self-transformation. Whereas, by contrast, the modern world is one in which nature has been reduced to a "standing reserve" (*Bestand*), as the later Heidegger so bitterly complained, ready and waiting for exploitation by humanity in its "technological" quest for progress. Certain trends to the contrary notwithstanding, it seems even our desires for environmental "preservation" are guided by this logic of utility and the graded order of life that it presupposes. Given the entrenchment of these ideas, is it even possible to think otherwise than exploitation? Or is the very idea of an "alternative" mode of thought always already a standing reserve, which, rather like Luke Skywalker in his struggle with the Dark Side, becomes ever more thoroughly coopted the harder we fight? It is with an eye to these and related issues that I propose we examine the various linkages between life and writing.

A Note on Terms

When it comes to *life*, the key Balinese words are *urip* and *idup*. As one might expect, we find the most elaborate treatment in van der Tuuk's

Kawi-Balineesch-Nederlandsch Woordenboek (*KBNW*; 1897–1912). Consonant with both the later lexicography (e.g., Barber 1979; Kersten 1984;
Warna 1990) and present-day Balinese usage, the *KBNW* describes *urip* as
the "high" (*hoog*) or refined form of *idup*, for which "life" or "to live"
(*leven*) is offered as a simple equivalent. Under each term—*urip* and
idup—is provided a series of cognates in other regional dialects, together
with numerous examples of usage. These include words derived directly
from the root form (e.g., *ngurip*, *humurip*, *murip* as "bringing to life" [*in
het leven brengen*]), as well as phrases that make use of the root and its
derivatives (e.g., *toja pangurip-urip* as a kind of life-giving water [*het levend makend water*]). As in the *KBNW* more generally, examples are drawn
from both literature (e.g., the Tantri stories) and colloquial speech (e.g., an
exclamation made following earthquakes). Yet, despite these numerous
examples, the *KBNW* gives no clear indication that the use of these terms
might be anything other than equivalent to Dutch, or more broadly European, ideas about "life."

This would perhaps pose less of a problem were it not for the fact that
Balinese attribute "life"—that is, *urip* or *idup*—to things that most modern
Europeans and Americans would consider "dead matter."[2] As Leopold
E. A. Howe observed in an early essay on Balinese architecture, "All buildings
are considered to be 'alive.' All temples, houses, meeting places, shops, offices, factories and indeed all important constructions, whether permanent
or temporary, are 'brought to life'" (1983, 139).[3] But it is not just buildings that are said to be alive, or to *maurip*. On enquiring, one finds, for instance, that many ritual instruments, heirlooms, stone and copperplate
inscriptions, palm-leaf manuscripts, and social collectivities—such as the
village and local ward—are also possessed of, or characterized by, "life." So,
what does it mean to be alive in Bali? As it turns out, the written characters
of the Balinese alphabet offer a surprisingly helpful way forward. What I
wish to propose in general terms is that we approach "life" as that which
"living things" are said to do. And, more precisely, my aim is to specify
what it means to say that letters are alive by asking in what ways letters act
in the world.[4] It will be in reflecting on the answer to this question that we
may gain some insight into what it means to attribute life to other ostensibly
"inanimate" things (such as houses, heirlooms, and funeral biers), but also
how these animating sensibilities are transformed through their relation-

ship with different, and often incongruent, ways of articulating agency, life, and matter.

Doing Things with Letters

Enquiring into the uses of Balinese letters in Batan Nangka, I found there to be considerable variation in opinion—both among expert consultants and between them and their clients. But there was also a great deal of regularity, which I would attribute—at least in part—to the sedimentation of these uses of script and writing in wider-reaching practices of social organization and collective labor. I had suggested that we approach the meaning of life through an account of what living things do. And, as we have seen, Balinese letters—or *aksara*—are said to be "alive." So what is it that these *aksara* do? To summarize schematically: in Batan Nangka, Balinese letters were predominantly seen to (1) represent cultural identity; (2) embody and transmit knowledge (= efficacy); (3) purify; (4) animate and enable; (5) render things usable and so nameable; (6) protect; (7) attack; (8) turn on their user; and (9) both incur and pay debts. In many cases these modes of agency and instrumentality were explicitly attributed to Balinese letters, as, for instance, in explanations proffered for the use of an inscribed amulet. But at other times the associations were left implicit—as, for example, with decorative (B. *uparengga*) uses of *aksara* to exemplify the "traditional" character of a wedding or cremation. So, although this résumé of "uses and acts" is the product of observation and discussion in Batan Nangka, and each of its members was recognizable to those with whom I discussed it, I wish to stress that this schematization does not reflect a local typology or system of classification.

It must also be emphasized that these nine uses and acts of *aksara* do not hang together naturally as elements of a unified "scriptural culture." Nor do they individually comprise the collective representations of an organically integrated "literary community." Rather, I found these uses and acts to be variously articulated through practices that at times incorporated incongruous ideals of agency, community, and the common good. Bearing this in mind, I would like to consider each of these uses and acts in turn—with an emphasis on the conditions under which they occurred and the ways they were related to one another.

Transcending Letters

The first three uses of *aksara* are closely aligned with the state bureaucratic articulation of "Hindu religion" as a universalizing monotheism grounded in "sacred scripture" (see chapter 2). Initially promulgated through programs for national development, this state-sponsored form of Hinduism has been subsequently redeployed in support of a particularist identity politics under the aegis of Ajeg Bali but also in more dispersed, and less deliberately organized, efforts to "defend Balinese tradition."[5]

AKSARA REPRESENT CULTURAL IDENTITY

On T-shirts, bumper stickers, and storefronts, Balinese letters figure as a badge of authenticity and guarantor of continuity with an idealized vision of the island's Hindu history. This graphic assertion of cultural identity is pitted against a perceived encroachment of Islamic sensibilities—thought to be led by the Javanese but increasingly national in scope. Here *aksara* stand opposed to Arabic script in a series that pits pork against goat meat; Balinese "traditional attire" (I. *pakaian adat*) against the *jilbab* and *kopiah*;[6] both *pasantian* reading[7] and the *Tri-Sandhya* mantra[8] against the call to prayer (I. *azan*); and the neo-Sanskritic greeting *Om Swastyastu* against the traditional Arab greeting *Assalamalaikum*.[9] During wedding celebrations, for instance, it is not unusual to find *Om Swastyastu* emblazoned in Balinese script on a brightly colored Styrofoam sign suspended over the front gates of the houseyard hosting the ceremony (see photo 3.1). Similar signs may be found at the entrance to gas stations, restaurants, and shopping malls, as well as on banners displayed prominently during major temple festivals. It is in this way that *aksara* have come to exemplify the very idea of "tradition" (I. *tradisi*; see chapter 6).

As an exemplification of tradition, the reading and writing of *aksara* are taught in school and cultivated through competitions (I. *lomba*), poetry clubs (B. *pasantian*), extracurricular programs (B. *pasraman*), and art exhibitions (I. *paméran*). These events are often covered in both the print and electronic media as expressions of local genius and as efforts toward the protection (I. *perlindungan*) and preservation (I. *pelestarian*) of cultural heritage—as we saw in the previous chapter. There, as on the Styrofoam signs and bumper stickers, the power of script was seen to lie in its ability to point beyond itself

Photo 3.1. *Om Swastyastu*, now taken to be a "traditional Hindu greeting," painted
in Balinese script on a carved Styrofoam board, set over the front gateway
to a houseyard celebrating a wedding; detail inset (*upper right*).

to an ideal of cultural identity commensurate with the state bureaucratic
model of national Unity in Diversity. This articulation of Balinese letters and
their efficacy has entailed a transformation of earlier ideals of script and writing, which linked *aksara* to the particularities of matter, place, and person.

AKSARA EMBODY AND TRANSMIT KNOWLEDGE (= EFFICACY)

Balinese letters are also seen to mediate the transfer of traditional knowledge
through palm-leaf manuscripts, inscriptions, and printed books. In so doing
they appear to link two frames of reference that are not entirely commensurate. As we have seen, this includes a broadly modern understanding of
representation and textual transmission, on the one hand, and an older orientation grounded in the pursuit of potency and protection, on the other.

In the first instance, the written word is widely taken to comprise a form
of documentation (I. *dokumentasi*), providing access to information (I. *informasi*) pertaining to religion (I. *agama*), culture (I. *budaya*), and history (I. *sejarah*).
Efforts to preserve the textual record are channeled through initiatives such
as the Cultural Documentation Center (Pusat Dokumentasi Kebudayaan,
or Pusdok), which has very generally aimed to pick up where earlier Dutch

programs left off. But the documentary ideal is also evident at a more popular level in the use of printed books containing metrical compositions, such
as *kakawin, gaguritan,* and *kidung.*[10] To be sure, the recitation of this traditional literature (I. *kesusastraan*) is procedurally important—that is, as one of
the "five songs" or "sounds" (B. *panca-gita*) essential for the completion of
major rites.[11] But, as cultural documents, these books and their contents are
also understood to provide a window onto life in "former times" (I. *jaman
dulu*)—envisaged as a mélange of high Indic culture and Balinese bucolics.

In addition to these printed books, at least eleven of Batan Nangka's
seventy-one houseyards possess one or more *lontar,* which—as we have
seen—are looked after with varying degrees of care. These are generally
valued as a form of inheritance (B. *tetamaan, tetamian;* I. *warisan*), though—
with but one or two notable exceptions—they are not known to be read.
Although the manuscripts are regularly presented with offerings on the
holiday of *odalan saraswati,* their owners are often reticent to handle—let
alone open—them, for fear of upsetting the forces that potentially reside in
such "powerful" (B. *tenget;* I. *keramat*) objects.

If the use of Balinese letters in ceremonial contexts appears nowadays to
pull in the direction of heritage and cultural identity, the prevailing attitude
of caution in handling manuscripts suggests there is also another, seemingly
older force at play. Here knowledge (I. *ilmu;* B. *wruh, kaweruh*) is less a form of
abstract "information" and more a kind of power, or potency (B. *kasaktén*).
But it is also—at least sometimes—a substance; and this substance is drawn
to (B. *arad*), and may become concentrated in, the figure of Balinese letters
and so the objects on which they are inscribed. In both rites of passage and
those of initiation, one inscribes the body—and especially the tongue—in
order to effect a transfer of this efficacious substance.[12] The healing and restoration of the body and its faculties, then, may be similarly effected by inscribing the appropriate combination of letters and images—physically or
otherwise—on the afflicted organ (see the discussion later in this chapter).
The crucial point is that—on this understanding—the "knowledge" embodied in letters not only *is* power but is *primarily* a form of power. Put another way, letters transfer knowledge, but this *transfer of knowledge* is itself
a subset of a more fundamental, and inclusive, *transfer of efficacy.*

AKSARA PURIFY, BUT . . .

The use of *aksara* is also frequently associated with the idea of purity. This comes most visibly by way of a series of procedures organized around the loosely Sanskritic trope of *suci*. In very general terms, this ideal is cultivated through the removal, or mitigation, of those ostensibly "polluted" states (B. *leteh, sebel, cuntaka*) that are seen to result from contact with death, disease, and various forms of disintegration (e.g., corporeal, social, or political).[13]

We find this ideal of purity linked, for instance, to the configurations of *aksara* inscribed on ritual instruments (B. *upakara*), such as the *belakas pangentas*—a heavy cleaver used to cut open the layers of cloth and palm-fiber matting that encase a corpse prior to its cremation.[14] The link between writing and purity appears more explicit with the *banten suci*, a composite "offering" that incorporates—among other things—the *jajan sara(s)wati*,[15] a small rice-flour cake bearing the written *Ongkara* syllable (see photos 3.2a and 3.2b). Employed during cremations and temple anniversaries, this *banten suci* is commonly understood to assist in purifying (B. *nyuciang*; I. *menyucikan*) the location of the rite and those involved in performing it.

Aksara may also be linked less directly to the ideal of purity through their appearance on the *ulap-ulap*. These are the script-bearing cloth amulets that we saw in the previous chapter, which are affixed to new buildings and other

Photos 3.2a and 3.2b. *Banten suci* offering (*left*), with detail of a freshly made *ongkara*-bearing *jajan sara(s)wati* (*right*).

structures during a sequence of rites often simply referred to as *mlaspas*. I suggested earlier that these amulets were used to channel energy that would animate new structures. But that is only part of the story. For, when asked directly about the purpose of these rites, those I consulted—both common-ers and gentry, laypersons and priests—would usually begin by saying they are directed to purification and that the script-bearing *ulap-ulap* is in some way implicated in this process. It was here, and in related contexts, that I most frequently encountered the neologism *huruf suci*, or "pure letters." Yet a closer look at the rites of *mlaspas* themselves may give reason to question not only this specific example but also the more general association of writ-ing with purity. To appreciate the wider significance of this point requires a brief digression.

As a first step we may note the prevalence of synecdoche in Balinese hab-its of naming and reference. For instance, when men gather to prepare meat and spices for a coming ceremony, this is commonly called "chopping," or *mébat* (I. *mencincang*), even though the act of chopping is but one of several tasks carried out at the time. (Here one might compare any number of En-glish phrases, such as "having a barbecue" or "going for a drink.") In a sim-ilar fashion, the *mlaspas* is but one of several procedures carried out in the series of rites popularly known by that name. In Batan Nangka this series is understood to include, in addition to the *mlaspas* proper, at least two further rites or procedures, called *makuh* and *ngambé*.[16]

If the term *makuh* suggests a strengthening of the structure (from *bakuh*, meaning "strong" or "sturdy"), the *mlaspas* proper involves a separation (B. *malasang*, from *palas*) and rejoining (B. *masang*, from *pasang*) of various ele-ments. This is often described as removing (B. *ngelus*) what is "bad," or even "ugly" (B. *jelé*), from what is "good" (B. *luung*) and so correct (B. *patut*) and fitting (B./I. *cocok*) for the structure in question. As a removal of what is "bad," one can see how this *mlaspas* might be construed as a "purification." Yet it is crucial to note that the inscribed amulet—or *ulap-ulap*—is not actually part of the *mlaspas* rite itself, in the narrow sense. Rather, the script-bearing *ulap-ulap* is affixed during one of the other procedures within the series, known as *ngambé*—which might be glossed as "to summon" or "welcome." This lines up neatly with the name for the amulet itself, the *ulap-ulap*, a term that suggests a "calling in" or "beckoning" (B. *ngulapin*, also from *ulap*). And, indeed, as we have seen, there appears to be a sort of energy, or vital-ity, that is "called in" (B. *ulapin*) to the building through the medium of the script-bearing *ulap-ulap*. According to local accounts, the written letters themselves channel that energy and provide it with a seat (B. *palinggih*), or place of concentration—an issue to which I shall return in just a moment. But, if this were the case, why all the talk of purity?

In my conversations with Balinese—both in Batan Nangka and elsewhere—the invocation of purity was usually accompanied by a shift in language from Balinese into Indonesian. When I realized this was happening, I asked one of my older, and better-educated, consultants why he thought the shift in register was so common. He explained (in Indonesian) that, when speaking Indonesian, one is inclined to provide clear answers that are easily received (I. *diterima*) and understood (I. *dimengerti*). Such explanations (I. *pengertian*) are concise (I. *singkat*) and help to "close the discussion" (I. *menutup diskusi*). By contrast, conversation in Balinese tends to be more detailed (I. *mendetail*) and often somewhat ambiguous (I. *saru*), requiring further discussion and specification. Here it seems the Indonesian language facilitates a crucial substitution. One can speak specifically (e.g., about God, the remembrance of ancestors, purity, spiritual balance and harmony, personal salvation, and the like) without having to refer with any specificity to the sort of ambivalently powerful beings and forces at play—such as those activated in the use of script and other forms of writing. This is not to suggest that the trope of *suci* is irrelevant to Balinese handling of *aksara* but rather that the ideals and sensibilities it embodies may not always be quite what they appear. Such play between languages raises an important question regarding what the act of translation is meant to accomplish, an issue to which we will return in chapter 7.

Being Written: Materializing and Localizing Power

Notwithstanding a degree of ambiguity in the ideals of "knowledge" and "purity," the first three acts and uses of Balinese script predominantly exemplify a representational understanding of writing—for which *aksara* point beyond themselves to a transcendental realm of language, meaning, and cultural identity. By contrast, the remaining six are explicitly oriented to bringing about change in the world and to actualizing goods of a more imminent nature.

AKSARA ANIMATE AND ENABLE

In the first of these latter uses, we find *aksara* deployed to animate and so enable such things as bodily organs, ritual instruments, houseyard structures, and shrines; but they also may be brought to life in their own right.[17] At a most fundamental level, writing is animated by affixing (B. *masang*) consonants and vowel elements together to form pronounceable syllables. Although the written characters themselves may be seen as inherently powerful, the life of letters is said to be closely—and even causally—tied to the breath (B. *angkih*) that passes through the mouth and nose to produce the spoken word (B. *raos*). In this regard, writing is curiously analogous to both houses and human bodies—which are similarly construed as composite entities assembled by affixing elements together in a manner specific to their function (I. *fungsi*) or use (B./I. *guna*). The life of a bamboo hut, for example, is in part the product of rejoining elements that had previously been configured differently and so enjoyed a different sort of life—namely, that of the bamboo plant from which its posts and beams were cut. (It is for this reason that, strictly speaking, the *mlaspas* complex is said to bring about a "*re*animation" [*ngidupang mawali*]; see the foregoing discussion.) Along similar lines, the composite nature of human beings is perhaps most readily apparent in ideas about the body as being composed of disparate parts that are liable to disintegrate, and to go their own way, in the absence of trained attention. This may be found both in the disciplined movements associated with dance (cf. Hobart 2007, 122) and in Balinese demonology, where body parts are seen to roam about on their own (see C. Hooykaas 1980; Lovric 1987; cf. Addams 1964).

In this respect, both human bodies and buildings are construed as jointed (B. *mabuku*) structures whose life is generated and maintained by the fluid movement of wind (B./I. *angin*), water (B. *yéh*), and vitality (B. *bayu*) through their junctures, channels, and apertures—which themselves must be kept clear and free of obstruction.[18] Though I do not wish to draw the analogy too neatly, there appears to be a similar set of relations at play in the emergence of life through the purposeful and ordered linkage of consonants and vowels. Yet some of the most powerful arrangements of letters are those that, on the face of it, appear unpronounceable. In Batan Nangka these are generally (and somewhat indiscriminately) called *tastra* or *sastra*, and sometimes *modré*.[19] These arrangements of script and related elements (such as extended lines and patterns) are in themselves said to be "dead" (B./I. *mati*), but they may be activated or animated (B. *idupang*) by those who know how to read (B. *maca*) and pronounce (B. *ngucap*) them.[20] It is through this activation that they are deployed to specific ends—such as healing, protection, and attack.

A respected local healer, for example, was known for his use of a wooden manuscript describing the *sastra* located on various parts of the body (e.g., liver, heart, and lungs).[21] When one of his clients was afflicted, he would reaffix the appropriate *sastra* in order to recall—or make present—its "energy" (I. *énérgi*) and thereby bring about his client's reinvigoration, refortification, and recovery. According to the healer, each bodily organ is possessed of its own "spirit" or "soul" (B./K. *atma*),[22] which may flee when one is startled or attacked. He added that one might carry additional *sastra*—in the form of a *bekel*[23]—which afford their user enhanced capacities—for strength, agility, potency, confidence, protection, or heightened sense faculties. Put another way, the written syllables and related figures are means (B./I. *sarana*) of instilling task-specific energy and efficacy—such as hearing, sight, and movement but also invincibility and dominance over others (cf. Connor 1995; H. Geertz 2005).

AKSARA RENDER THINGS USABLE AND SO NAMEABLE

The acts of both writing and naming appear to be linked to the very *being* of certain objects, perhaps especially human beings and newly constructed buildings. More specifically, it seems that to name something is to affirm its existence, which is equated with its efficacy or utility. For example, in preparing the *ulap-ulap* for rites of animation, it is often said that the inscription of a simple *Ongkara* syllable will suffice for any building or shrine. But some in Batan Nangka have been instructed by their priestly patron (see the later discussion) to employ specific designs for particular kinds of buildings. For it is by virtue of the rite in which the *ulap-ulap* is affixed that an unnamed structure becomes, for instance, a kitchen, a shrine, or an office building— that is, as opposed to something else. Here, *naming* and *utility* are closely related. It is in a similar vein, I think, that Balinese often refer to these rites— when speaking Indonesian—as "inaugurating" or "making official" (I. *meresmikan*) the structure's status as the sort of building it is meant to be. Before this rite has been performed, the structure is not fit for its purpose (e.g., as an ancestral shrine), and so it cannot bear that name (B. *adan*).

The association of naming with being is more readily apparent with the use of writing in several of the life-cycle rites, particularly those of name giving and death. It is here that the body is respectively integrated and disintegrated—both within itself and in relation to the broader collectivities in which it takes part. Rites of name giving may include the inscription and burning of palm-leaf name cards to determine a fitting appellation for the child. H. I. R. Hinzler observed in her detailed study of these rites that, "according to the texts on ritual and to the majority of the brahman priests, a personal name should be given to a child only on the occasion of a first birthday, when the child is 210 days old," explaining that "it is believed that only after the first birthday does the child become a real human able to bear [a] name" (1988, 142). Although things in Batan Nangka are not so clearly or consistently defined, ideas about naming appear to be organized around a similar set of sensibilities, linking acts of writing with ceremonial procedure (B. *upacara*), name bearing (B. *maadan*), and being, or becoming, human (B. *dadi manusa*).

Special forms of writing also figure in rites of death and cremation. This may be seen most prominently in the *kajang*, or shroud(s), inscribed (B. *karéka*) with an arrangement of *aksara* and other figures specific to the descent group (B. *dadia, kawitan*) or "caste" (I. *kasta*) of the deceased. This is often popularly analogized to the government-issue identity card (I. KTP, for *kartu tanda penduduk*) as directing one's soul or spirit to "the right place"— whether construed as a heavenly hereafter (e.g., I. *swarga*; B. *kadituan*) or as reincarnation (e.g., B. *numitis*; I. *lahir kembali, réinkarnasi*) in a subsequent generation of the patrilineal family.[24]

During cremation rites, the name of the deceased also appears in writing— often in Balinese script and traditionally on a short piece of palm leaf— affixed to the complex of ritual instruments that act as a physical support for the soul during the cremation of mortal remains. While still alive, one avoids using one's own personal name within the confines of the cemetery and its environs, for fear of rendering one's name (and thereby oneself) known, and so vulnerable, to Ida Batara—here an elliptical reference to the overlord of the cemetery, who holds command over (B. *ngamong*) the souls of those who are deceased but not yet cremated. By the same token, the name of the deceased *must* be used—preferably in written form—in order to specify the soul that Ida Batara is to release for the final rites that will allow it to be freed of any remaining material ties, and so to depart—and eventually

Photo 3.3. Rewriting the human body from the ashes of a cremated corpse.

return again.[25] It is in aid of ensuring bodily integrity on return, then, that the ashes are brought together and "written" (B. *karéka*) into the form of a human body (see photo 3.3). Summing up, one might say that writing is instrumental to naming, which both affirms and helps to form a sort of being that is itself determined by its utility or efficacy.

AKSARA PROTECT

Aksara are also employed in various procedures directed to the protection of the body.[26] This may involve either surrounding oneself with powerful beings and forces or entreating them to reside on or within the bodily organs themselves. Common tropes encountered in this connection include the four—or sometimes six—"spiritual siblings" (B. *kanda mpat*),[27] as well as the ten forces or capabilities (B. *dasabayu*), which are often associated with an efficacious configuration of ten syllables (B./K. *dasaksara*)—and their corresponding divinities, colors, weapons, and so on.[28] It is by inviting (B. *nuur*), or drawing in (B. *ngarad*), and surrounding oneself with their life-enhancing energy that one hopes to be protected from attack.

I found, for example, that, in addition to his more straightforwardly curative work, the local healer that was mentioned earlier is also known for using *aksara* in aid of "opening *cakras*" (I. *membuka cakra*), the subtle physiological points, or nodes, at which vitality (B. *bayu*) is thought to concentrate and through which it may be caused to flow. According to the healer, this opening of *cakras* results both in an increase in the person's general efficacy and in the generation of a force field of sorts, which surrounds the body and prevents the intrusion of malevolent beings. One of his clients, an educated man in his late forties, described this as "walling up the body" (B. *magehin awak*)—rendering one invulnerable to attack, which he construed in terms of being "penetrated" (B. *tumbakin*). He recounted having expressed some incredulity when the healer declared his *cakras* open, to which the latter replied by grabbing two copper wires, which he then proceeded to thrust toward the body of his client. To the client's surprise, he said, the wires bent around his body as if compelled by some unseen force—which he interpreted as evidence of his newly acquired imperviousness to attack. This opening of the *cakras* was accomplished, he explained, with the aid of a mantra-infused glass of water, which he was instructed to drink. As he understood it, this helped to affix the requisite *aksara* onto the pertinent organs of his body. Through their intensification of the body's capabilities, he said, the letters themselves functioned as a wall or fortification.

Whatever relationship it may bear to textual tradition, the client's account of opening *cakras* brought together three sets of ideals that seem more generally characteristic of Balinese techniques for self-care and protection—namely, fortification, fluidity, and equanimity.[29] Albeit ultimately directed to the same end, these ideals correspond to tactical, physiological, and temperamental registers, respectively, each of which is cultivated through its own complex of techniques. If "walling up" is directed to preventing penetration, the opening of *cakras* was said to increase the fluid movement of one's life force, or vitality (B. *bayu*), as it courses through the channels of the body (B. *uat*; I. *urat*).[30] As indicated earlier, the obstruction of these channels corresponds to illness, impotence, and absent-mindedness—all of which are states associated with a loss of efficacy.

A generalized state of equanimity mediates this relationship between the fluidity of bodily energy and invulnerability to attack. It is impassivity in the face of sudden, or what would otherwise be startling, events that prevents one from being opened up to malicious penetration. For instance, one will not be *makesiab-kesiab*, which is to be thrown off kilter by an unexpected or surprising event—a condition that, again, might leave one vulnerable to attack. Neither is one *anak geleh*—that is, one prone to outbursts of emotion in response to unexpected stimulus, be it pleasant or otherwise. It seems that ideally the relationship between invulnerability and equanimity is recursive: invulnerability gives rise to equanimity, from which one gains greater invulnerability, thereby developing still further one's capacity for equanimity, and so on. My sense is that practices of self-protection—such as the directional positioning of *aksara* and the powers they embody—are often directed to initiating this cycle and carrying it forward.

Here the analogy between houses and human bodies comes once again to the fore. When a house has been "brought to life"—through the script-enabled calling in (B. *ngarad*) of protective beings and forces—it can repel or turn away an opposed and potentially malevolent force (B. *nulak bala, nulak ané sing demen*). It seems that it is through a similar set of procedures that one both energizes one's bodily organs and surrounds oneself with a wall of power, in order to further the mutually fortifying relationship between invulnerability and equanimity. One might compare this to the *aksara*-bearing sash, or *sabuk*, worn around the waist for protection.[31] To be effective, these too must be brought to life through a *pasupati* rite—after which, it is said, the sash will protect against all comers; it will give one confidence and strength in addressing others, who will in return admire the one who wears it.

AKSARA ATTACK

Self-protection is no doubt important. But the best defense is often a good offense. And, rather like certain kinds of offerings (see Fox 2015), the deployment of *aksara* can be an expedient means to this end. Some configurations of script and image are said to serve as weapons of attack that, once "brought to life," can travel afar under their own direction in search of their victim.[32] The examples I was shown in Pateluan were inscribed in palm-leaf manuscripts and copied onto either paper or small copper plates—though I was also told that, for those with the requisite skill and experience, the support of such a coarsely material form was usually unnecessary. It is often said the *aksara* themselves may be inverted—literally "stood on their head" (B. *sungsang*)—for the purpose of attack. Script-bearing objects may also be used as weapons, as in the case of those beings that embody the entrail-devouring demonic form of *rangda*, with her *tastra*-bearing cloth—the *rurub* or *kekereb* (closure)—with which she strikes those who dare to attack her, sending them into fits of self-stabbing (B. *ngurek*). The latter may be

similar to the cloth wielded by the sorcerer's students (B. *sisya*) in performing *Calonarang*, the dramatic enactment of which reaches its climax at mid-
night in the cemetery. Here *lontar* manuscripts themselves may appear as
the weapon employed by the fearsome widow of Dirah.[33] Given such popular associations with sorcery, I was told many Balinese conceal their possession
of palm-leaf manuscripts—which others, not knowing their contents, might
construe as means to malevolent ends.[34]

As with skill in the use of other weapons, many of those adept in the
handling of *aksara* are also known for having an aggressive, and even pugi-
listic, temperament—whether presently or in the past.[35] This seems to play
on the more general association of knowledge with efficacy and of efficacy
with the domination of weaker wills. More specifically, I think we are dealing with a variation on a certain character type—recognized by Balinese—
that often, if not always, brings together prowess in the use of physical force
with sexual conquest, success in gambling, and eloquence in oratory. This
may be seen quite clearly among some of the healers and others from whom
those in Pateluan would request assistance in defending against attack or
mounting retaliation. However, these associations are not limited to those
recognized for their skill in the black arts. Many of those now known for
their bookish learning and "spiritual" accomplishment as high priests (B.
sulinggih)—that is, *padanda, rsi bhujangga*, and others—were in their youth
known as street toughs, gamblers, and thugs. For them, if *aksara* are seen to
channel vitality, and this vitality is a means to the mastery of oneself and
others, then the manipulation of *aksara* is at once a form of spiritual exercise
and a martial art.

AKSARA TURN ON THEIR USER

The potency embodied in *aksara* is not only morally neutral but also liable
to turn on its user. Like other forms of efficacy, the power of letters is as
likely to *possess* the one who wields it as it is to remain under their control. It
is for this reason that one must undergo certain forms of preparation, most
commonly centered on the rite of *mawinten*. This is often described as a rite
of "purification" (see the earlier discussion). But, again, purification is but
one aspect of a broader series of procedures directed to empowerment and
self-protection in the face of those beings and forces (embodied, e.g., in writing)
that one wishes to handle and potentially deploy. Those trying to read or

otherwise work with written materials for which they are ill prepared report feeling confused (I. *bingung*; B. *paling*), sick (I./B. *sakit*), or disoriented (B. *punyah*, "drunk"). In extreme cases this may result in prolonged illness and even death. I was told by a local actor, for example, of the dizziness and headaches he experienced when trying to read a palm-leaf manuscript containing instructions for achieving release (K./B. *moksa*) from the cycle of death and rebirth. He took his symptoms to be a sign (B. *cihna*) of his unreadiness for the text and decided to stop reading for fear of the possible consequences. A more serious case was reported by a local priest, who told of a young man—quite likely his own nephew—who had been studying, with a teacher (B./I. *guru*), the methods for affixing *aksara* on various parts of the body. When the young man's teacher died unexpectedly, he nonetheless carried on independently with his studies—that is, without anyone to guide him. But, in the absence of supervision, he began placing the *aksara* on the wrong parts of his body. And it was not long, said the priest, before he fell gravely ill and died—yet further evidence of the ambivalently powerful nature of Balinese letters.[36]

AKSARA INCUR AND PAY DEBTS

As ritual instruments (B. *upakara*), *aksara* have traditionally circulated through networks of patronage. These networks are grounded in hierarchically ordered relations of giving and receiving, through which clients offer up (B. *ngaturang*) their fealty and material support to powerful patrons who, in exchange, bestow (B. *mapica*) gifts of spiritual sustenance and protection. The latter include various kinds of "holy water" (B. *tirtha*) and "offerings" (B. *banten*). But of equal importance is the bestowal of speech (B. *baos*)—in the form both of mantras and other formulae used to complete important ceremonial rites, as well as expert advice (B. *pitutur*) regarding such things as the organization of domestic space and the maintenance of bodily well-being.

Perhaps the most visible of these relationships is that which obtains between high priests (B. *sulinggih*) and their constituents, or "pupils" (B. *sisya*), for whom the former complete (B. *muput*) ceremonies requiring the safe and effective handling of ambivalently potent forces—such as those that are channeled through *aksara*. It is often from a priestly patron that one requests (B. *nunas*) the script-bearing instruments employed in the inauguration of new houseyard structures and shrines. In return, when ceremonial work

(B. *karya*) is performed at the home of one's priestly lord (B. *siwa*), it is expected that his constituents will present themselves (B. *nangkil*) and render service (B. *ngayah*) in the form of labor and material contribution.[37] In my experience, Balinese tend to resist characterizing this exchange as one of debt (B. *utang*) and repayment (B. *panauran*). Yet, when relations between lord and pupil go sour, the reciprocal give-and-take at the center of their relationship can become quite pronounced.

This may be illustrated by way of a brief anecdote, in which a certain well-established priestly house (B. *griya*) lost several of its pupils to one of its younger, subsidiary branches. The occasion for this transfer of allegiance came when the sitting priest in the former house was said to have refused to complete ceremonies for those of his constituents planning to vote for the "wrong" candidate in the coming gubernatorial elections. The priest's behavior was widely condemned as an inappropriate mixing of religion (I. *agama*) and politics (I. *politik*). Yet the most damning criticism centered not so much on this as on his failure to honor a standing obligation to act with generosity (B. *pasuécan*) toward his clients. Without referring specifically to the case at hand, his own brother pointedly characterized this sort of behavior as that of one who only enjoyed receiving (B. *demen ngidih*), while others referred to his actions more directly as miserly (B. *cupar*), greedy (B. *demit*), and overly proud, or arrogant (B./I. *angkuh*)—all terms frequently used in reference to other, more readily acknowledged relations of reciprocity, such as those that obtain between neighbors, members of the ward assembly, and other collectivities.

Significantly, the first act performed by those switching priestly patrons was the dedication of an offering of sincerity (B. *ngaturang banten pajati*). The presentation of this offering is, more generally, the initial step in opening up a relation of exchange. The exchange may be, as here, carried out with a priestly patron. But the *pajati* offering also figures as an expression of sincerity at the opening of bride negotiations, when one visits the home of another family to request a woman for marriage. Similarly, relations of exchange may also be contracted with nonhuman agents, such as the banyan tree from which one requests freshly picked leaves for use in postcremation rites (B. *nyekah, maligya*).[38] An exchange of sorts may analogously figure in one's relationship to the written word itself. Just as an offering of sincerity works toward establishing a tie of reciprocity with a priestly patron, a *pajati* may also be dedicated before opening up a palm-leaf manuscript or setting out on a new course of study. This offering may be dedicated explicitly to Déwi Saraswati as the goddess of learning and the divine embodiment of letters.[39] But, in the case of reading, the expression of sincerity may also be directed to the text itself—as an entity that is both named and alive and so potentially capable of entering into a relationship of reciprocal obligation.[40]

The link between life and reciprocity is an issue to which I shall return in just a moment. But first, recalling the earlier anecdote, if the prospective pupil's offering of sincerity is directed to initiating a relationship of patronage, it is the priest's bestowal of a shroud (B. *kajang*) in the event of his or her pupil's death that marks the end, or closure, of their relationship. It may be recalled that many in Batan Nangka understood the *kajang* as an identity card of sorts that ensures the safe passage of one's soul to the hereafter or its rebirth within the correct family line. But this inscribed length of white cloth is also seen, at least by some, to embody a final gift (B. *paica*) of knowledge that ensures the priestly lord remains in no way indebted (B. *mautang*) to his or her dead pupil.

Taken together, these examples trace the contours of a network of circulation, through which *aksara* and *aksara*-bearing instruments move in relations of hierarchically ordered giving and receiving. When juxtaposed with the initial sections—on cultural identity but also transmission and purity—it would appear these traditional forms of reciprocity are increasingly butting up against, and being transformed by, the emergence of new networks—such as those associated with mass tourism and formal education—which may be characterized by quite different forms of both solidarity and exchange.

The Meaning of Life

> Well, that's the end of the film, now here's the meaning of life.
> —Lady Presenter, *Monty Python's The Meaning of Life*

Balinese have traditionally attributed "life"—in the sense of *urip* or *idup*—to things that in a broadly modern idiom are thought to consist of "dead matter." My question was how it could make sense to say that things such as kitchens, cars, and consonants are alive. Working on the assumption that "life" is what "living things" do, I proposed that we look to contemporary uses of Balinese script, as these letters seemed to be a particularly dense point of transfer for ideas about agency, life, and matter. In a word, the ensuing discussion was meant to answer the question as to what Balinese letters *do*.

The results of enquiry in Batan Nangka would suggest that, when it comes to script and writing, there are at least two very general and opposed forces in play. On the one hand, we have the idealizing articulation of letters as a medium of representation and transmission. Here power is dematerialized; it resides in the ability of the written word to point beyond itself—to sounds and information but also to cultural identity and heritage. Of letters we might say, in this first case, that *life is elsewhere*. On the other hand, there is another set of script-related ideals and sensibilities that materialize the power of writing in particular localities. Here *aksara* mediate the transfer of efficacy and vitality between people, places, and things.

It is in following this latter line of reasoning, and extrapolating from the ethnography, that I would like to suggest we find "life" (B. *urip*)—as attributed to bodies, buildings, and so on—where there is an ordered yet contingent linkage of constituent parts, resulting in a complex and potentially tenuous entity that can bear a name, that has the ability to transform both itself and others, and with which, or whom, one might enter into a relation of ongoing reciprocal obligation, as embodied in a form of solidarity-through-exchange.[41] By way of conclusion I would like to consider briefly each of these aspects in turn. My argument is that, from the vantage of many traditional practices, these attributes of "life" are as fitting of funeral biers, agricultural knives, and ward regulations as they are of farmers, buffalo, and jackfruit trees.[42]

An Ordered Yet Contingent Linkage of Constituent Parts . . .

Both written syllables and buildings are formed by "affixing" their constituent parts to one another in a manner conducive to a specific use. We have seen that, in a similar fashion, one affixes the configurations of *aksara* proper to the movement or capability associated with the joints and organs of the body.[43] This ordered linking up of constituent parts may be altered in various ways, but not without consequence. Much as there are standardized conventions (B. *uger-uger*) for the combination of *aksara*, so too are there guidelines for the layout of living space and the construction of buildings. Posture and bodily movement are analogously ordered with an eye to health but also to etiquette (B./I. *tatakrama*) and so one's relation with others.

Resulting in a Complex and Potentially Tenuous Entity . . .

The resulting entity is both internally complex and prone to disintegration. Put another way, unity and stability—whether orthographic, corporeal, architectural, or political—are tenuous achievements that must be articulated and rearticulated through the calling in and binding of disparate forces that would otherwise tend toward dissipation (H. Geertz 1994, 95). It is perhaps for this reason that so many Balinese life-cycle rites—coming at moments of integration and so potential disintegration—entail an intensification of the body and its faculties. This is accomplished through contact with, and ingestion of, various substances; but it is also manifest gesturally in the wafting in (B. *natab*), drawing in (B. *ngarad*), and calling in (B. *ngulapin*) central to the restorative *upacara (pa)ngulapan* and the *mlaspas* complex (see the earlier discussion)—but it also, potentially, may be seen in the dedication of those "chthonic offerings" (B. *caru*) often explained in terms of "purification" (I. *menyucikan*) and the "making benevolent" (B. *nyomiyang*) or "neutralization" (I. *menetralisir*) of demonic forces (B. *butakala*).[44] Here the inscription of *aksara* would work to fix this dynamic potential on, or in, the body or building where it might be put to a specific use—an issue to which we shall return in the next chapter.

That Can Bear a Name . . .

If living things are brought into being through an ordered joining of parts, the act of naming is itself an affirmation of their existence and quite often their utility—a point that may be related to the prevalence of agentive nouns (e.g., *refuser, closer, hardener, life helper*) as designations for those powerful— and "living"—formulae and instruments employed in healing, sorcery, and the performance of ceremonial rites. An analogous sensibility may be seen in the colloquial understanding of the *mlaspas* rites as "making official" a given structure's status as the kind of building it is meant to be. Before these rites have been performed, the building is neither alive nor fit for its intended use, by virtue of which it would bear its proper name. In this regard it appears that *to be* is *to be nameable*. As Mark Hobart noted in a related connection, "The [Balinese] word for proper name, and class name, is *adan*," explaining that "Balinese sometimes argued that the etymology was from *ada*, to exist, the genitive suffix '-n' . . . making it 'the existing/existence of.' In that case to name something would be to affirm its existence" (2015, 8).

That Has the Ability to Transform Both Itself and Others . . .

Essential to the concept of vitality is that of efficacy. To be alive is to have an effect on both oneself and the surrounding world. Balinese differentiate between the various forms of life with reference to their relative capacity for movement or force (B. *bayu*),[45] speech (B. *sabda*), and thought (B. *idep*)—a series known collectively as "the three faculties" (B. *tri-pramana*).[46] It is often said that plants, animals, and human beings have one, two, and three of these faculties, respectively. Although less commonly discussed in these terms, the life of such things as weapons and houseyard structures may also be characterized, on reflection, as possessing a certain capacity for movement or the exertion of force. Some heirloom *keris* daggers, for example, are thought capable of moving under their own direction. At the same time, in almost Newtonian fashion, architectural features such as supporting beams and walls are seen to exert a force equal and opposite to the weight they carry—or, when under attack, the powers they repel. In this regard, potency and dynamism are the very stuff of life.

And with Which, or Whom, One Might Enter into a Relation of Ongoing Reciprocal Obligation, as Embodied in a Form of Solidarity-through-Exchange

Ideally, the relationship that obtains between living things should be one of reciprocity through exchange. The ordering of this exchange may be hierarchical, instrumental, and even exploitative—and it may appear differently to all those involved. But there is as much give-and-take at play in the use of a broom, or the herding of ducks, as there is in the expression of one's fealty to a king or high priest. Much of Balinese "ritual" life is devoted to maintaining these relationships of but loosely calculated giving and receiving, through such things as the *jotan* or *saiban* offerings dedicated each morning to the instruments employed in cooking and household chores (e.g., sink, stove, chopping block, water container, and mortar and pestle).[47] Meanwhile, the solidarity established with things such as plants, draft animals, and buildings is evident in the idea that the traditional polity, or *gumi*, includes not only its human subjects but also the plants, animals, and living objects (e.g., books, shadow puppets, and gamelan instruments) that are provided periodically—for example, at the various *odalan* and *tumpek* holidays—with offerings and entertainment. We see, for example, that many a masked dance-drama performance (B. *topéng*, *prémbon*) turns on a ruler's loss and reappropriation of power, as embodied in the well-being of his realm. When the performance of ceremonial rites breaks down, the land and its resources dry up (B. *sangar*) and the realm itself descends into a melee of disorder and chaos (B. *uug gumi-é*). Maintaining the life of the realm is a collective endeavor, which—like assembling letters, buildings, and bodies—entails a purposeful linking together of parts that might otherwise be inclined to disintegration. It is through reciprocal exchange and obligation that these elements are tied (B. *kaiket*), one to another, thereby ensuring their collective well-being (B. *rahayu*).

A Few Questions

These reflections on the meaning of "life" raise a number of issues warranting further consideration. There is first the question of competing accounts. While the five-part description of where we find life in Bali may help us to make sense of "living" buildings, texts, and ritual implements, it is also sharply at odds with the ideals and sensibilities that have driven Indonesian national development and the commodification of Balinese culture—most notably in the interest of tourism. The latter center not on relations of solidarity-through-exchange but rather on the management of culture as "capital" (I. *modal*) and both human beings and nature as "resources" (I. *sumber daya manusia/alam*) for exploitation in aid of "progress" (I. *kemajuan*). It is difficult to imagine a starker example of Heidegger's "standing reserve." In my experience, the problem is not lost on Balinese. As many have recognized, the island is beset by an environmental crisis that may be irreversible. In an attempt to address the issue, some have looked to the past, arguing for a return to "traditional ideals" rearticulated in terms of *Tri Hita Karana*, a neo-Sanskritic formulation of humanity's various dependencies (viz., with itself, with God, and with nature). But it seems unlikely that such (often well-intended) moralizing will produce its desired result without a fundamental transformation of the institutions and practices through which these virtues are cultivated, embodied, and contested. Other difficulties aside, this leaves us with the question of how to theorize the relationship between competing accounts of specific practices—such as those we have encountered in reflecting on Balinese *aksara*.

Second, we are faced with a couple of potentially important questions regarding the nature of "the text" as a topic of scholarly enquiry. Clearly, philological analysis is well suited to answering certain kinds of questions. Its findings are historical in their own way; and, when it comes to accounting for events on the contemporary scene, the textual record may have much to contribute to our understanding of the emergence and relative stability of certain ideas and styles of reasoning. As recent scholarship has shown (Rubinstein 2000; Hunter 2007; Fox and Hornbacher 2016), there are important literary parallels for many of the uses and acts of *aksara* that I found in Batan Nangka. But the question of how contemporary practices are related to accounts found in palm-leaf manuscripts is just that—a question. There is also the question as to how philological enquiry is related to the practices—for example, of composition, copying, and performing—that ostensibly generated its object of study. For now it should suffice to recall that Balinese have traditionally made rather different presuppositions about the nature of agency, life, and matter—things that are, as we have seen, of direct pertinence to the handling of letters. So how, if at all, should this apparent disjuncture inform our approach to "the text"? There are both ontological and epistemological issues in play. But there may also be an ethical question as well. Rachelle Rubinstein argued that "*kekawin* philology as practised to date undermines the religious beliefs and values upon which *kekawin* composition has been based" (2000, 225). If this were really so, it may be worth reflecting a little more carefully on the foundations of our work and its consequences—both intended and otherwise.

There is third a question of translation. Many of the key terms we have encountered in Balinese and Indonesian appear to be caught between competing understandings of human agency and collective life. How, for example, is one to translate a term like *suci*, which seems to point simultaneously to ideals of purity and power? Can we assume this is simply a matter of Balinese *linking* a pair of ideals we are in the habit of *separating*? Alternatively, might this be a case of overdetermination, in which multiple and potentially conflicting goods and virtues are working themselves out through one and the same set of actions? And, were this the case, could we distinguish these factors without at the same time reifying them? These are difficult questions, and we will be returning to consider them more closely in chapter 7.

In the meantime there is also the closely related question of cultural complexity. Students of Southeast Asia have long recognized that unifying terms such as *Hinduism*, *Buddhism*, *Tantrism*, and *animism* do not adequately reflect the heterogeneity of the region's history and culture. Yet prevailing attempts to account for this complexity—in terms of "great and little traditions," "syncretism," "hybridity," and so on—often do little more than defer the moment of essentialization. And, as a result, their approaches often appear as uncritical as the oversimplified terminology they wish to call into question.[48] Engaging the later work of Alasdair MacIntyre, my aim is to begin developing an approach to complexity centered on the analysis of rival *styles of practical reasoning*—with an emphasis on competing articulations of agency, community, and the common good (cf. final section of chapter 2). The approach I am proposing will require an account of practice that can accommodate the sort of complexity we encountered in the uses and acts of *aksara*. This will be the central task for the following two chapters.

Chapter 4

Practice and the Problem
of Complexity

For all its seeming importance, *writing* has proven difficult to pin down, let
alone isolate as an object of study. It was partly in recognition of this difficulty that the critique from ecology argued in favor of approaching "writing
practices" as embedded within a broader "way of life" (chapter 2). Provisionally
following this line of enquiry, we examined some of the ways that Balinese
script was used in the semirural ward of Batan Nangka (chapter 3). However, instead of finding a unitary and practice-grounding "way of life," what
we found were two contrasting styles of writing, each embodying a different
articulation of agency, matter, and what it means to be "alive." One of these
sets of ideals was broadly congruent with a modern, Euro-American model
of representation, in which written script points beyond itself to such things
as information, meaning, and identity. The other linked up with older ideals of efficacy and human flourishing as pursued, for example, through sorcery, healing, and architecture. In commenting on the latter, I employed the
phrase "uses and acts of *aksara*" to draw attention to the way Balinese often
attribute both life and agency to letters. Developing this line further, and

recalling the critique from ecology, this chapter and the next ask what it would mean to approach these uses and acts of *aksara* under the description of "practice."

To this point I have used the term *practice* somewhat indiscriminately to suggest something like "what people do."[1] The aim of this provisional usage was to shift our attention away from the scholarly abstractions of "literacy" and "language," and onto historically situated uses of script and writing. But, on reflection, such casual recourse to practice raises a few questions of its own. How, for instance, are we to differentiate *practice* from specific acts or activities? Procedure? Or process? Can all human action be understood as practice? And, if so, in what ways is "practice theory" preferable to other forms of interpretation, such as those associated with historical hermeneutics or structural analysis? Alternatively, if practice cannot be so broadly generalized, what is there to distinguish it from other acts and actions, not least those attributed to nonhuman agents? To the extent that scholarship itself may be seen as a practice, we must also ask what claim, if any, we can make to a privileged outlook on the practices of others. Does practice theory require, for instance, that we consider the Balinese "life of letters" on equal footing with Noam Chomsky's generative grammar or the deconstructive critique of logocentrism? And, if so, given their apparently conflicting claims, according to what criteria are we to assess their respective ontological and epistemological commitments?

These and related questions will be explored through the analysis of a ceremonial rite known as *Caru Rsi Gana* (CRG), which was performed in one of the houseyards of Batan Nangka during the course of my fieldwork. A rite of this kind employs a complex sequence of verbal formulae (K./B. *mantra*; B. *sasonténg*) and hand gestures (K./B. *mudra*), as well as thousands of intricate offerings and related instruments, many of which would potentially warrant monographs in their own right.[2] I hope it is needless to stress that, even were it possible, an exhaustive enumeration of these elements would take us far beyond the questions this book aims to answer.[3] What had initially drawn my attention to the CRG was the use of several *aksara*-bearing objects that were buried in the floor of the family temple when the rite was complete. In working toward an account of practice, I would like to begin by trying to understand how the burial of these objects and their inscriptions were related to the wider purposes of the rite.

The Rite Occasion

The CRG was performed as part of a ceremony for the family temple of a neighboring houseyard held every six months. The houseyard belonged to Dong Tawang, a local offerings specialist (B. *tukang banten*) who had moved to Batan Nangka with her husband some twenty-five years before.[4] The CRG is one of the more elaborate, and costly, of the many forms of *caru* enacted in connection with the establishment and regular maintenance of spaces that are to be inhabited or otherwise used by human beings—including houseyards and temple grounds but also office buildings, storehouses, and schools.[5]

Although Dong Tawang suggested in conversation that a CRG ought to be done once every twenty-five years, this did not appear to be the most pressing factor in her family's decision to sponsor the rite.[6] Rather, it was in response to a series of what she described as "strange occurrences" (B. *ané aéng*). Dong Tawang's husband, a farmer and occasional stone carver, had recently injured himself with one of his chisels, an unusual event that came but shortly after a large coconut tree had inexplicably fallen over in their garden. As Dong Tawang's son later confided, the family was also experiencing financial difficulties, and one of his children had been uncharacteristically ill tempered, frequently troubled by fevers and diarrhea. Coupled with a more general sense of unease, these events were taken to suggest things were somehow amiss (B. *sing patut*). Having consulted with both their priestly patron and a spirit medium of some repute, the Batan Nangka branch of the family requested financial assistance from their relations in a neighboring ward to perform the CRG at the next regularly scheduled temple anniversary.[7]

A rite of this kind is not undertaken lightly. Families will often sell, or pawn, ancestral land holdings—historically a guarantor of sustenance and of more general well-being—in order to cover the expense.[8] Beyond the usual outlay in time and materials for an ordinary temple anniversary, which already entails a substantial investment, the performance of a CRG requires the preparation—and often purchase—of additional offerings and related ritual instruments, as well as the assistance of multiple specialists, all of whom must be fed and paid an honorarium.[9] So what is the CRG? What exactly is it meant to achieve? And how might burying a set of script-bearing objects help in bringing this about?

Some Terms, Classifications, and Procedures

By name and classification, the CRG is a *caru*, a term often locally etymologized with reference to Sanskrit *cāru*, suggesting beauty or comeliness. On these grounds it is frequently said that the aim of the rite is to "make beautiful" the place in which it is performed—rendering it peaceful, safe, and prosperous (I. *damai, selamat dan sejahtera*; B. *rahayu*).[10] *Caru* are also generically described as a form of *bhuta yadnya*, one of the five classes into which ceremonial rites are now routinely categorized.[11] The distinction drawn between these classes is made with reference to the relationship the rite is meant to mediate—namely, with coarse or "demonic" forces (*bhuta*), human beings (*manusa*), ancestors (*pitra*), holy people (*rsi*), and divinities (*déwa*). Understood as a form of *bhuta yadnya*, then, the CRG is often seen as a *caru* specifically directed to maintaining relations with the coarse and potentially unruly spirits of a particular place.[12]

Another term commonly used in reference to the CRG is *upacara*, which is frequently glossed in English as "ritual." But, in modern Indonesian usage, this designation also objectifies the rite as a particular class of event associated with state-sanctioned forms of "religion" and "traditional custom."[13] This understanding of *caru* as *upacara* is pervasive in popular representations of Hindu religiosity (e.g., on television, the radio, and the internet). Yet, in less publicly oriented discussion, one more commonly encounters the practical term *gaé* (or *karya*, in the formal register), which points to the collective "work" of preparing for and carrying out such rites. So, for instance, in referring to a forthcoming ceremony, it is often simply said that one "has work" to do (B. *ngelah gaé*; *madruwé karya*). We might be tempted to pull these terms together and say that, as a *caru*, the CRG is a type of *bhuta yadnya*, which figures as a component of an *upacara* (ritual) that is carried out collectively as a form of *karya* or *gaé* (work). But in ordinary conversation it would be unusual to find these terms juxtaposed in this way, for they tend to be used situationally, as opposed to forming a classificatory system.[14]

As to procedure, Dong Tawang's CRG figured as a preliminary stage in the performance of a temple anniversary called an *odalan*. This six-monthly ceremony culminates in a hierarchically ordered exchange between the current residents of the houseyard and their deceased forebears, who are sometimes described as "deified ancestors."[15] The well-being sought in this periodic exchange is effected through a series of stages that include readying the location and participants, summoning the pertinent beings and forces, entertaining them, presenting an offering, making a request, witnessing the exchange, and sending them off again.[16] Yet these stages are not so much a linear sequence as they are a scale of forms (Collingwood 2005, 54–91), mediating a set of overlapping relationships with various intangible beings and forces, each of which embodies the potential for both benevolence and harm. Taken under the rubric of *bhuta yadnya*, the CRG may be understood to mediate one such relationship—specifically with those powerful yet intangible beings whose dominion overlaps with that of the houseyard. Until it can be ensured that these relatively coarse spirits of the place will not interfere with the proceedings, it is impossible to secure relations with the comparatively refined—and generally more powerful—beings who have been called down to take up their "seats" in the houseyard temple for the *odalan*. So, as an act of readying, the *caru* figures as *part of* a wider sequence of procedures; and, at the same time, it appears to proceed on a smaller scale through these same stages.

In Preparation

A month or so before the rite was to be performed, Dong Tawang's family began assembling materials—including bamboo for temporary structures and dried cakes and rice cones for offerings. If a neighbor or associate happened to have items required for the rite—for example, a chicken of the right color or recently ripened bananas—these were requested or given preemptively, on the assumption that the favor would be returned when the need arose. In this respect, the performance of ceremonial rites helps to forge and perpetuate the relations of debt and repayment constitutive of the ward community—an issue to which we shall return in the next chapter. Through boxed offerings delivered up (B. *maaturan*) to various local temple complexes, these occasions also contribute to the maintenance of the houseyard's relationship with the often overlapping constituencies of the village and descent group, as well as any number of local irrigation societies and other congregations to which the family is "tied" (B. *kaiket*).

When it comes to performing the rite itself, the sequence of procedures is sufficiently complex to require extensive preparatory advice from an offerings specialist and, on the day, detailed instructions from the officiating priest, usually as relayed by an assistant. Decisions regarding funds and logistics are often made in family meetings held some weeks prior to the ceremony. But ordinarily it is not until two or three days before the event that the houseyard is overtaken with preparations. It is at this time that women from neighboring houseyards are expected to visit in the evenings to help cut and sew together the elaborate palm-leaf offerings and adornments for which the island is well known (see, e.g., Stuart-Fox 1974; Fox 2015). Their husbands (or sons) also pay a visit, though usually at a different time, to assist in butchering a pig purchased for the occasion and to arrange the meat offerings. The character and duration of such neighborly assistance (B. *ngoopin*) are often prescribed in the written ward regulations, which tend to be followed rather loosely—with some neighbors helping more than is required, others less.[17]

On the morning of such a major ceremony, the houseyard is usually bustling with family and neighbors rushing about, trying to get everything in order before the arrival of the officiating priest—for whom they may then be left waiting for hours.[18] But, due in part to Dong Tawang's experience as an offerings specialist and her working relationship with the local priests, preparations on this particular morning went unusually smoothly, and things were mostly ready ahead of time.

The items assembled were both those generally associated with the houseyard temple anniversary as well as more specialized paraphernalia for the CRG. The latter notably included a tall bamboo shrine (B. *sanggah tutuan*) erected at the northeast end of the temple; a set of four "brooms" (B. *sapat*) composed of cuttings taken from different plants; a torch made of dried leaves (B. *prapat*); a palm-branch club (B. *kaplugan*) to be beaten on the ground; a bamboo slit-gong (B. *kulkul*) paired with a wooden mallet; and an earthenware bowl (B. *paso*) inscribed with an *ongkara* syllable that would later be filled with a mixture of black sand, sea water, and uncooked rice of five colors. There was also a collection of colored flags (B. *kobér*) marking out the points of the compass. These were affixed to a set of temporary shines (B. *sanggah cucuk*) stuck into the ground on thin sticks of bamboo, encircling the complex of offerings and instruments that had been laid

Photo 4.1. The layout of a five-chicken *caru* (K./B. *caru panca-sata*), with its directional shrines, flags, and related accouterments (NB, this was taken at a separate CRG).

out on the temple floor (see photo 4.1). At the base of each flag was a differently colored dead chicken, which had been splayed out "as if alive" (B./K. *winangun urip*) and surrounded with other cooked and uncooked offerings. As with such rites more generally, these items were laid out in accord with the colors, weapons, and numbers associated with their directional orientation (see table 4.1).[19]

Inscribing a *Caru*

When all of the offerings and related paraphernalia had been assembled, the family awaited the arrival of the *rsi bhujangga*, who would "complete" (B. *muput*) the rite with the assistance of his wife. The *rsi* brought with him a number of additional items, including an assortment of bells, drums, and conches to be sounded at specific points in the proceedings. After he and his wife were formally greeted and offered refreshments, they ascended a temporary platform erected in the houseyard's central courtyard, from which

Table 4.1. Directional colors, divinities, syllables, numbers, and weapons

Direction	Color	Divinity	Syllable	Number	Weapon
East	White	Iswara	*Sa*	5	Thunderbolt (*bajra*)
South	Red	Brahma	*Ba*	9	Club (*danda*)
West	Yellow	Mahadewa	*Ta*	7	Serpent noose (*nagapasa*)
North	Black	Wisnu	*A*	4	Discus (*cakra*)
Center	Multicolored	Siwa	*I*	8	Lotus (*padma*)

Note: The scheme is often expanded to nine to include the four ordinal directions, or eleven, with zenith and nadir.

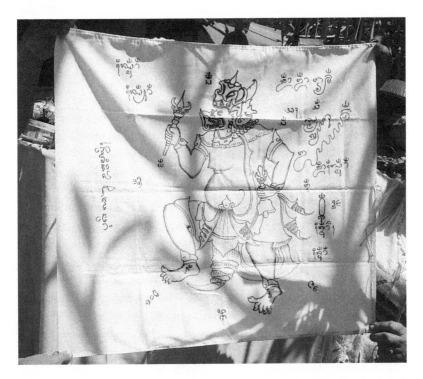

Photo 4.2. The flag for the CRG, with configurations of *aksara* surrounding a line drawing of the elephant-headed deity, Ganapati, wielding a thunderbolt bell and club; also see photo 4.8.

Photos 4.3 and 4.4. Ida Rsi inscribing the rice flour on the banana leaf with an eight-petaled
lotus and its directional syllables (*left*); an alternative method, in which the
rice flour is laid out and inscribed on the ground (*right*).

they would conduct the performance of the CRG. In addition to their personal assistant, Ida Rsi and his wife were also attended by several of the local temple priests, who had come at Dong Tawang's request.

The *rsi* began by inscribing a series of objects for use in the rite. He was
first brought an oval cutting from a banana leaf containing dirt from
beneath the temple floor, which had been covered over with a smooth layer
of rice flour. He sprinkled the flour with energized "holy water" and then
inscribed it with a directional configuration of syllables (B. *aksara pangider-
ider*) set within the outline of an eight-petaled lotus (see photo 4.3). Next he
was brought a set of nine leaves from a *nagasari* tree (Lat. *Mesua ferrea*), on
which he used white lime to write the syllables of a mantric formula that
read *om am r-si ga-ṇé-bhyo na-maḥ* (see figure 4.1). What was the inscription meant to accomplish? In their magisterial collection of *Stuti and Stava*,
Teun Goudriaan and Christiaan Hooykaas have glossed this formula as "OM
AM Honour to the Group of Seers!" (1971, 159–60). Yet, while the rendering
may be "accurate" from a philological perspective, it is worth pausing briefly
to reflect on what the translation of mantric formulae entails. One might
begin by noting that Balinese tend to associate the phrase *rsi gana* with a
priestly manifestation of the deity Ganapati (see photo 4.2), as opposed to a
group (S. *gaṇa*) of seers (S. *ṛṣi*). But, moreover, as Goudriaan and Hooykaas

Figure 4.1. The mantric syllables *ong ang rĕ si ga ne byo na mah* (oṃ aṃ r̥-ṣi ga-ṇe-bhyo na-maḥ), as inscribed on the *nagasari* leaves laid out under the white duck, which had been splayed out "as if alive" (see the earlier discussion).

themselves made clear, this formula was never simply an expression of praise reducible to its eulogistic "content." In the version they cited, it was instead directed to the efficacious imposition (S. *nyāsa*) of these syllables onto the body "in order to be protected by means of the names of the group of the seers" (S. *gaṇa-r̥ṣi-nāma-rakṣaṇe*; 1971, 160).[20] We shall return in chapter 7 to consider more closely the problem of translation. But, in the meantime, the question is whether a similar desire for protection may have been at work in the CRG.

When the *rsi* had finished inscribing the leaves, his personal assistant placed them onto a woven tray containing a set of rice cones and related offerings resting underneath the specially prepared carcass of a white duck.[21]

Photos 4.5 and 4.6. Laying the *banten caru* complex in the hole prepared in the temple floor (*left*); the *banten caru* complex in the ground, with the CRG flag on top (*right*).

This was in turn set atop the banana leaf with the *aksara*-bearing dirt and flour, which was then covered over with a white cloth bearing a second drawing of Ganapati, this time surrounded by the weapons of the five directions (see table 4.1).[22] Once assembled, the complex of offerings and inscribed objects was then carried to the northeast corner of the houseyard and carefully laid into a hole that had been opened up in the temple floor (see photos 4.5 and 4.6).

This complex is often simply called *banten caru*. And, in this configuration, it is one of the instruments unique to the CRG. But its composition and accompanying procedures vary to some extent with the inclinations and background of the officiating priest. So, for example, at another CRG performed in Batan Nangka, the priest insisted that the offerings complex be dedicated above ground (against the wishes of the local offerings specialist) and only interred afterward. In addition to the *nagasari* leaves, he also included a set of nine *aksara*-bearing banyan leaves. And, instead of using a banana leaf, the eight-petaled lotus was drawn directly onto a layer of rice flour spread out on the temple floor (see photo 4.4). There were several other differences besides, and in my experience this is anything but unusual. Yet, such variations aside, the rite for Dong Tawang's family more generally proceeded through each of the stages—from readying, summoning, and entertaining to offering, requesting, witnessing, and sending away again. However, as with *caru* rites more generally, the order was modified—with the main request and witnessing performed after the invited beings and forces of a coarser nature (viz. *bhutakala*) were asked to depart.

Each of these steps was enacted through a specific combination of mantric formulae and hand gestures, accompanied by offerings and related instruments. In many cases their names appear to suggest their purpose. So, in readying the houseyard for the CRG, there were instruments directed, for example, to "cleansing" and "purification" (B. *pabersihan, panglukatan*), as well as the dispelling of both ill will (B. *tebasan durmanggala*) and other destructive forces (B. *pabiyakaonan*).[23] Fitted with incense and small pots of fresh water, these instruments were "brought to life" through the *rsi*'s utterance of the apposite formulae. They were then carried around to specified locations in the houseyard temple and later the wider compound, where their effects were distributed by wafting their incense and sprinkling the water.

With these preparatory measures having been taken, the location was ready for the summoning, offering, and sending away. Each of these steps was marked by the roar of bells, drums, and conches, set against a repetitively percussive tune banged out on a small gamelan orchestra that had been assembled off to one side.[24] To a casual observer the acts of summoning and offering might be difficult to distinguish, as both were accompanied by a similarly boisterous explosion of sound. But the send-off was characteristically distinctive. Having dedicated the complex of offerings arrayed on the houseyard temple floor, participants in the rite were instructed to walk around the temple perimeter in a counterclockwise direction (B. *prasawiya*) while manipulating one of the assembled instruments and making as much noise as possible (see photo 4.7).[25] Marching circularly, and in single file, there were four people sweeping (B. *nyampat*) the floor with the various brooms, one making a similar gesture with the burning palm fronds—first along the floor and then against low cement walls and surrounding structures. Meanwhile, another member of the family banged on the ground with a palm-branch club, and another hammered away at the slit-gong. Still others blew on the conches and manipulated hand drums and bells, while the gamelan carried on with its droning and heavily percussive tune.

Photo 4.7. Circumambulating the houseyard temple for the send-off at a *caru* rite,
with burning palm fronds, conch, and drum.

The group was then instructed to march out of the temple and into the wider houseyard, where they continued the sweeping and noisemaking. They stopped briefly to circumambulate two other spots where smaller, less elaborate *caru* offerings had been dedicated. The parade then proceeded out to the front gate and into the street for one last burst of conches, bells, and noisemaking. After that they returned to the houseyard and everything went quiet. The CRG came to a close with the family "praying" (B. *muspa*, I. *sembahyang*) in the houseyard temple—offering fealty to, and requesting the beneficence of, their forebears and protectors, but also in the name of Rsi Gana. A separate offering was then dedicated by a single member of the family as witness (B. *pasaksi*) to the event.[26]

A Few Questions

As a preparatory stage in celebrating a temple anniversary, the CRG was meant to ensure that the events of the following day would go smoothly. This was to culminate in a communicative exchange between the family and its departed forebears, in which fealty and material gifts would be offered up in exchange for safety, sustenance, and well-being. Seen as a form of *bhuta yadnya*, the CRG might be understood as an effort to placate potentially destructive forces and prevent them from interfering in this process—which, on the face of it, seems a reasonable interpretation and one for which we would find ample support in the published scholarship.[27] But it also suggests a few questions. Precisely how, for instance, would the rite's various instruments and procedures be effective in preventing undue interference? What was the purpose of all the sweeping and noisemaking? And how, if at all, was this related to the burial of the script-bearing *caru* complex? We might also wish to ask how the CRG, as an act of "readying," was related to the "strange happenings" that occasioned the performance of the rite in the first place. Dong Tawang and her family had suffered a series of mishaps, and the decision to perform a CRG was driven at least in part by a desire to set things aright. So how were the purposes ostensibly served by the rite *in general* related to its performance *on this particular occasion*?

There are several ways we might set about trying to answer these questions. We could begin, for example, by looking to the palm-leaf manuals that Balinese recognize—at least in principle—as authoritative statements on the proper performance of ceremonial rites. Given historical ties with ancient Java, and ultimately South Asia, we might then seek evidence of Indic precedent in the form of rites employing similar paraphernalia, procedures, and terminology. Such recourse to textual precedent has figured prominently in the scholarship on Balinese religion and culture, as this often appears to provide a degree of certainty and order that has otherwise proven elusive. But, before turning to examine one of the texts associated with the CRG, I would like to begin by reflecting on a series of conversations I had in the days following the ceremony.

In Conversation

The first was with Dong Tawang herself, together with her husband and their son, who was in his early thirties at the time. I had taken the family a set of photographs and a DVD that I had made of the ceremony, and asked whether they might help me to understand what I had seen. Dong Tawang dominated the conversation, with the other two only periodically interjecting on specific points. Each time I enquired as to why a certain offering or instrument was employed, she would begin by enumerating its elements. If I repeated the question, she would usually explain either where the item was to be placed or when it was to be used. When I pressed the issue, clarifying that I wanted to know the "purpose" (B. *tetujon*) in using a given item or "why" it was used in this way (B. *ngudiang kéto*), her response was consistently the same: "Well, that's just how it is" (B. *'nak mula kéto*). This phrase, commonly encountered by scholars asking questions of this sort, is usually taken as evidence that Balinese do not understand the reasons for their ostensibly "ritual" labors, or that their efforts exemplify an implicitly slavish (if as often romanticized) devotion to "tradition." But was this the case with Dong Tawang? Could such a highly experienced offerings specialist have really been ignorant of the purposes served by her expertise?

When I asked about the aims of the CRG more generally, Dong Tawang described it in broadly apotropaic terms, as a measure directed to preventing further ill fortune. Reflecting back on my earlier line of questioning, she added that this was the point of the sweeping (B. *nyapat*). Here she used the term *nyomya*, a Balinese verbal construction suggesting transformation into benevolent form (K. *somya*). Encountered frequently on the now ubiquitous television "dharma talks" (see Fox 2011), this understanding of *caru* as *nyomya* appears to be a relatively recent conception, though it plays on an older notion of transforming coarse and often malevolent forces into their more refined counterparts.[28] But, when I asked what specifically she meant by *nyomya*, Dong Tawang glossed her remark by saying this is done "so they go home" (B. *'pang ya mulih*), so we will no longer be disturbed (B. *'pang sing gulgul*).[29] Her son added that this was so things would be "clean" (B./I. *mangda bersih*), an idea with which she seemed to agree. When I queried the congruence of these various terms, and the differing aims (B. *tetujon*) they seemed to imply, there was a long pause and then laughter. Evidently I had missed the point. Then, as she had already done a couple of times before, Dong Tawang apologized for being unable to answer my questions. She offered by way of explanation that she was illiterate (I. *buta huruf*), implying that my line of questioning was better directed to someone with a knowledge of letters, and perhaps more specifically a priest.

The following afternoon I went to see the *rsi bhujangga* who had officiated at the ceremony. I have worked with Ida Rsi on other projects in previous years, and our conversation took much the form it had often taken in the past. We sat opposite one another on the veranda where he ordinarily received his clients. And, after some brief talk of family and common acquaintances, he asked how he could be of help. We spoke in a mixture of formal Balinese and Indonesian, as I had often seen him do with his younger petitioners. In response to direct questions, and when I seemed to be having trouble understanding, he would begin again slowly, frequently prefacing his remarks with the phrase, "According to the beliefs of the Hindu religion . . ." (I. "Dalam kepercayaan Agama Hindu . . ."). Although the *rsi* was apprenticed to a traditional patron and preceptor (B. *nabé*) from within the family's priestly line, he had also completed a course on Hinduism at the Indonesian Hindu University in Denpasar. Accordingly, his remarks on the CRG reflected the complexity of his background, bringing together the sensibilities of state bureaucratic Hinduism with older ideals of efficacy and authority.[30]

In responding to my questions, Ida Rsi's commentary moved along three rather different lines of interpretation. The dominant line was that of transformation. This was the idea that the rite, as "payment" (B. *panauran*), would encourage potentially destructive *bhutakala* to return to their benevolent form—an idea familiar from my earlier conversation with Dong Tawang. The second line was that of "purification"—evident, for instance, in his passing remark that "the meaning of *caru* . . . is to cleanse in a manner that transcends the senses."[31] Finally there was the idea of doing battle—a notion the *rsi* seemed intent to suppress but that was nonetheless implicit in much of what he said. One could see this, for instance, in the emphasis he placed on the use of the various inscribed instruments for "calling" (I. *memanggil*), or "drawing in" (B. *ngarad*), powerful forces that might be employed to fortify the houseyard and its inhabitants against attack.

The tension between the ideals of "fortification" and "transformation" was most readily evident in Ida Rsi's explanation for the noisemaking and sweeping. This came in response to my asking why one needed to blow the conch in the course of concluding the rite. He explained there was a story in the Mahābhārata in which Prabu Duryodhana called on the goddess Durga and her minions, the *bhutakala*, to assist him in attacking the Pandawas. To defend against the onslaught, he continued, the gods bestowed on Arjuna a special conch shell called Déwadatta. At the end of the sentence, he added the term *nyomya*—as something of an afterthought—seemingly suggesting that the effect of the conch would be one of transformation into benevolent form. Yet he then carried on with the story, switching back into Indonesian to explain that the Pandawas prevailed in the end because *bhutakala* "cannot stand to hear" the conch (I. *tidak tahan mendengarnya*). Given that the story was unambiguously one of battle, centered on repelling an overwhelming enemy, I asked whether I had understood correctly—that the *bhutakala* would indeed be "driven away" (I. *diusir*) by all the noise and commotion, much as Durga's retinue was repelled by the sound of Arjuna's conch. He said this would certainly be a "natural" (I. *alami*) way of understanding the story and so the rite; but, "philosophically speaking" (B./I. *cara tatua filsafat*), he insisted it was still more properly understood in terms of a "change in character" (I. *berubah sifat*).

As with Dong Tawang, it seemed Ida Rsi's commentary brought together a series of tropes that were not self-evidently compatible. These included paying off (B. *panauran*), purification (I. *menyucikan*, B. *nyuciyang*), transformation into benevolent form (B. *nyomya*), chasing away (I. *mengusir*), and engaging in battle (I. *memerangi*).[32] The question is whether the rite can be all of these things at once—and, if so, how these seemingly incongruent ideals can be related to one another. Is there, for instance, a narrative account that might pull them together into a cohesive whole? Alternatively, could they be interpreted as differing "perspectives"? Or perhaps as metaphors? Or even as hierarchically ordered "levels of truth," as the *rsi*'s invocation of "philosophy" might be taken to suggest? Then again, there is always the possibility that Dong Tawang and Ida Rsi were simply confused or ill informed. But, if this were so, where might we look for a more reliable account? And in exactly what sense would it be more reliable?

It was with these questions in mind that I went to visit a brahmin high priest, or *padanda*, who acted as spiritual patron and adviser to several families in Batan Nangka. Ratu Padanda is known through much of the island for his regular appearances on television and especially for his learned, yet pragmatic, approach to the preparation of offerings and the performance of ceremonial rites.[33] As I had recently consulted with him on a related matter, he was familiar with my current project and the kinds of issues I was hoping to discuss. Befitting his status, the *padanda* answered each of my questions with unwavering certainty, speaking down to me from his chair on an elevated platform. He listened closely to what I said, and responded with care, checking frequently to ensure I had understood him. Yet, despite my several attempts to shift the conversation into Balinese, he addressed me almost exclusively in Indonesian.[34]

Having reviewed a couple of issues we had discussed on a previous visit, I raised the question of the CRG and the seeming incompatibility of its various aspects and interpretations. I cited the term *nyomya* by way of example, asking how the ideal of transformation was related to procedures—like sweeping and shouting—that seemed directed to other purposes, such as cleansing and chasing away. He began by noting that *nyomya* is formed from the Old Javanese base *somya*, which he said could be taken to mean "clean" (I. *bersih*) in the sense of "rounding off" or "perfecting" (I. *membulatkan*). He went on to link the notion of cleanliness to "good character" (I. *sifat baik*), explaining— briefly in Balinese—that by transforming the character of *bhutakala*, we en- sure "they won't cause trouble" (B. *mangda tan ngarabéda*). Mentioning that I had heard something similar from a friend in Batan Nangka, I asked how this was linked to the idea of payment (B. *panauran*), as seemingly im- plicit in the offerings of meat and liquor spread out on the temple floor. He laughed and said that dedicating *caru* offerings was rather like buying pro- tection from a local tough or a thug. If you give them a little something, they are less likely to bash up your car—or, as in this case, your houseyard. Providing them with sustenance (B. *manyuguhan*) changes their demeanor.[35]

Recalling Ida Rsi's story from the Mahābhārata, I asked whether this "buy-off" could in turn be linked up with the conch—perhaps as a means of chasing away any recalcitrant *bhutakala*. But the Padanda said no. The sound of the conch, like the other noisemaking, was a form of entertainment (I. *hiburan*)—calling in the *bhutakala* to enjoy their meal, and celebrating the success of the ceremony. But, significantly, this was not to suggest protection was unimportant. Returning to an earlier theme, I enquired as to how the provision of offerings and entertainment might be related to the script- bearing instruments buried in the floor of the temple.

Self: With the ritual instruments buried and uh . . . in-
            scribed . . . inscribed with those syllables . . . are those . . .
            like the *ulap-ulap* [used in rites of establishment for new
            buildings], can they also be used to call . . .

Padanda: To call in? No. Not to call in.

Self: No?

Padanda: Nope. They're different. The *ulap-ulap* are just . . . these
            here are what we call *ulap-ulap* [pointing to an *ulap-ulap*
            on the edge of the roof].

Self: Yes.

Padanda: It's not like those [*ulap-ulap*]. That's what's called
            marajah. It's different.

Self:	Oh, no no. What I meant was . . . Is its purpose the same as that which is used . . .
Padanda:	No, no. It's different.
Self:	Different?
Padanda:	So for instance . . . the one inscribed with the *nawasanga* [i.e., the nine directions of the compass lotus] . . . on the rice flour . . . requests of the *nawasanga* divinities that the perimeter be firmly guarded.
Self:	Firmly guarded?
Padanda:	Yes, firmly guarded . . . so negative elements are no longer able to enter.
Self:	Like a fortification?
Padanda:	It's a fortification. It is indeed a fortification. The Balinese term is *tumbal* [protector, guard].
Self:	*Tumbal?*
Padanda:	It's a *tumbal*. The Balinese term is *tumbal*. Or *pangijeng*. It's a *pangijeng*, to put it more crudely. The Indonesian term is *penjaga* [guard, watchman].[36]

Here the *padanda*'s remarks differed somewhat from those of both Ida Rsi and Dong Tawang. Perhaps most significantly, his reference to burying a "guard," or *tumbal*, tied the purposes of the CRG to themes—and tactics—more commonly associated with sorcery and the cultivation of occult powers.[37] Although these associations may be at odds with publicly prevailing understandings of Balinese ritual and religion, they are anything but unusual. Going back a couple of generations, the father of one of Batan Nangka's largest landholders is thought by many to have accrued his wealth and power precisely through the intervention of a *tumbal* that he had buried just outside the front walls of his family compound. No one could say for certain what the object was, though there was some speculation that it was a still-born fetus that he had brought back to life and to which he made regular offerings in exchange for protection and support. So to what extent was Dong Tawang's CRG playing on similar sensibilities? And how might this be related to the other ideals in play?

It is not difficult to see how the rite might be interpreted as a form of payment-for-protection, resulting in the transformation of potentially malevolent forces, leaving them well disposed to the interests of the houseyard with which they share a domain. Such an account might also help to reconcile some of the incongruities both within and between the commentaries given by the offerings specialist and the two priests. But we would still be left to account for the ideals of cleanliness and purification, not to mention the pervasive use of inscribed instruments, which do not seem so readily assimilable to the aims of buy-off and protection.[38] It must also be borne in mind that this would introduce a degree of order and consistency that was absent from the commentaries themselves, and that was even resisted at various points by those who offered them. So was this simply a case of incoherence? Perhaps a form of analogy? Or might these seemingly incongruous accounts be reconciled through recourse to a higher principle or authority?

Textual Precedent and the Problem of Complexity

In the course of conversation, both the *rsi* and the *padanda* cited a *lontar* called *Bhama Kertih* (*BKh*; other spellings abound, such as *Bhamakretih* or *Bama Kerti*), which addresses the construction and maintenance of domestic space, including sections that deal specifically with various forms of *caru*. Although both men seemed to recognize the *BKh* as bearing some authority, they mentioned the text but in passing—and, in the *rsi*'s case, only in response to my asking whether he knew of a *lontar* that dealt with the CRG.[39] As neither priest reported having a copy on hand, I was unable to consult the *BKh* at the time. But later I examined several versions of the text, including two manuscripts from the Hooykaas-Ketut Sangka Collection (HKS 7480 and 7769) and a printed edition with an Indonesian translation (Suhardana 2009).[40] Setting aside the Indonesian translation for the moment, the general tenor of the *BKh* seemed otherwise to be generally consistent across the three Kawi-Balinese versions. Most importantly for present purposes, they each included a section bearing the label *kaputusan sanghyang reṣi gaṇa* (KSRG), which is basically a set of instructions for performing the CRG.[41]

Read as a ritual manual, the text of the KSRG section describes the circumstances in which the rite ought to be performed, providing lists of the requisite instruments, procedures, and verbal formulae. It also gives descriptions of the script-bearing implements—such as the *nagasari* leaves and the eight-petaled lotus written in rice flour (see photos 4.3 and 4.4). It further entreats its reader not to err or skimp (K. *haywa korup*; *haja nglongin*) in laying out the meat and cash prescribed by the text. Interestingly, its style of exposition has a certain resonance with Dong Tawang's responses to my questions, in that it emphasizes the content and quantity of various elements employed in the rite. Much as the great chef Auguste Escoffier assumed his readers already knew how to cook, the *BKh* similarly presupposes detailed knowledge of houseyard layout and the preparation of offerings and related instruments. However, beyond a statement of the rite's specific utility, the text offers neither theological interpretation nor any additional information. In effect, its form is that of notes for a performance.[42]

The opening line of the KSRG describes the rite itself as a "purifier of a terrifying houseyard" (K./B. *pamarisuddha ning karang angker*)—a description that appears to entail a mixing of registers, bringing together the tropes of "purification" and "fright."[43] As with the oral commentaries in Batan Nangka, my sense is that the ideal of purification here similarly rearticulates a more general preponderance of threat and affliction. We find, for instance, that the phrase *karang angker*—which I glossed as "a terrifying houseyard"—is qualified as "including when there is a hot houseyard, a bad death, one run amok, struck by lightning, or when the householder is in danger."[44] In such a predicament, "it is said this rite is to be done" (K. *kojarana caru iki gelarakna*).[45]

By contrast, the commercially available Indonesian "translation" of the *BKh* introduces several novel elements, effectively aligning the aims of the CRG with the state bureaucratic articulation of Hindu religiosity. These include such things as expressing one's devotion to God (I. *Tuhan*) through "praying," and "cleansing" the houseyard by sweeping with the various brooms. On my reading, there is little to suggest these themes in the Kawi-Balinese terminology employed in the KSRG, where the more readily apparent aim is to send destructive forces away.[46] Both the "screaming and shouting" (K. *surak awu*) and final mantra, for instance, are described explicitly as "removers of destructive forces" (B. *pangihid bhuta*). One of the mantras is even called a "grand repeller" (B. *tatulak agung*).[47] How do these aims articulate with the ideal of "purification"? The juxtaposition is too common to be but fortuitously coincidental. Could it simply be a case of metaphor? Or, again, a form of analogy? Alternatively, might "purification" say something important about the procedures that make up the rite and the purposes they ultimately serve?

Phrased in this way, the question may be unanswerable. Whether we look to the palm-leaf manuals or to local commentary, the purposes of the CRG appear caught between ideals of battle, exchange, transformation, and cleansing. Much the same may be said for the written instruments buried in the temple floor. And, at least starting from Batan Nangka, there is no self-evidently nonarbitrary means of reducing this complexity. The point is not so much that it would be impossible to formulate a consistent interpretation but rather that doing so would introduce a form of coherence recognized neither by the ritual manuals nor by those performing the rite. So what does this mean for our account of the CRG?

It may be recalled that we came to this rite by way of the uses and acts of *aksara* encountered in Batan Nangka. I had wanted to know what it would mean to approach writing in terms of "practice," as recommended by the critique from ecology. But, whereas the latter seemed to suggest a degree of coherence and uniformity (i.e., in a "way of life"), what we have found in the CRG is—once again—a multiplicity of apparently incongruous aims and ideals. The question, now more pressing, is what it would mean to approach this multiplicity in terms of "practice." We will turn in the next chapter to consider whether "practice theory" may offer a way forward.

Chapter 5

Maintaining a Houseyard
as a Practice

The preceding chapter ended with an unresolved question regarding our critical orientation to *practice*. The central issue was that of *complexity*. The *Caru Rsi Gana* (CRG) was seen to involve the production and use of several script-bearing instruments. And, reflecting on local commentary, it seemed the performance of the rite—and the use of these instruments—brought together rival conceptions of human flourishing and conflicting judgments about the means best suited to its cultivation. Was the CRG's organizing principle that of battle, exchange, transformation, or cleansing? Were the *aksara* themselves to be understood as amulets, weapons, satellite dishes, or "pure letters"? And, as importantly, what might the multiple incongruities in play tell us about the "way of life" out of which they emerged? The difficulty is that these competing ideals were not simply espoused by differing factions or individuals. Instead they often appeared to coexist alongside one another, impelling one and the same act.[1] Recall, for instance, Dong Tawang's rapid movement between tropes of cleanliness, transformation, and banishment; or Ida Rsi's account of the CRG's engagement with the *bhutakala*—namely, as variously directed to paying off, purifying, chasing away, and engaging in battle. One can certainly imagine an overarching conceptual framework that would render these ideals compatible with one another. And yet, as we saw, this would introduce a degree of coherence that was not only absent from the commentaries themselves but also resisted by many of those who offered them. The question is whether we can find—or perhaps formulate—an approach to *practice* that can accommodate this multiplicity of apparently incongruous aims and ideals.

Theories and Practices

Beyond the critique from language ecology (chapter 2), the idea of practice has figured prominently in recent debates both within and between a range of disciplines, from anthropology and sociology to history, philosophy, and media studies. There has been no little contention over the concept and its application. But arguably the discussion has as frequently foundered on misunderstanding among its participants as it has led to new insights. It would appear that, much as George Bernard Shaw reportedly said of Britain and the United States, practice theorists are prone to separation by a common language. We find, for instance, that the idea of practice has underwritten such disparate projects as an explanatory sociology inspired by the work of Pierre Bourdieu and Anthony Giddens; a vaguely Geertzian cultural hermeneutics by way of Sherry B. Ortner; a philosophically inflected genealogy for the human sciences from Ian Hacking; and a historically grounded virtue ethics associated with Alasdair MacIntyre. To add to the confusion there is a good deal of cross-fertilization among their followers, not least in the younger (anti-)disciplines of cultural studies, comparative literature, religious studies, and queer theory. Some more or less regular points of contrast may be discerned among them. But even to speak as if there were schools of thought would probably be to overstate the coherence of enquiry into practice as a critical concept, a point already recognized by Ortner in the early 1980s.

The genealogy for practice is complicated. Its proponents commonly lay claim to the mantle of Aristotle, Marcel Mauss, and Ludwig Wittgenstein. But they tend to understand these authors in quite different ways. A second cluster of regularly professed allies includes Friedrich Nietzsche, Charles Sanders Peirce, Antonio Gramsci, Mikhail Bakhtin, Willard van Orman

Quine, Michel Foucault, and Gilles Deleuze—a rowdy bunch if there ever was one. But, again, the significance of their respective contributions may be seen to differ from one "practice theorist" to the next. To trace the history of these lines of thought and untangle their various trajectories would require a quite separate study; and, if previous efforts in this direction are anything to go by (e.g., Ortner 1984; Schatzki 1996; Turner 1994; Postill 2010), it is not altogether clear this would bring us any closer to a coherent account of practice. So, what is this thing called practice? In what do disagreements over its nature consist? And, looking back, how might it help us in thinking about the CRG, and so the uses and acts of *aksara*?

It should be noted from the outset that disagreement between rival "theories of practice" cannot necessarily be decided through recourse to empirical evidence. For there can be no "evidence" prior to the asking of a question (Collingwood [1946] 1993, 485–86). And, to the extent that rival theories answer questions riding on incongruous presuppositions, there can be no theory-independent assessment of "the facts" (see, e.g., Quine [1951] 1994; Kuhn [1962] 1996; Feyerabend 1975). Put another way, competing theories may on closer inspection embody answers to differing lines of enquiry, which themselves constitute what we take to be "the empirical data" differently. To cite a favorite example from the history of science, "the movement of heavenly bodies" does not mean the same thing as one shifts from a geocentric to a heliocentric cosmos. The upshot is that observations recorded under a Ptolemaic research program (Lakatos 1970) cannot be unproblematically incorporated within its Copernican successor—despite many of the descriptive terms appearing much the same.

One might wish to raise doubts at this point that such lessons in the translation between theories can be exported so easily from astronomy to practice theory. But, fundamental differences between the *Natur-* and *Geisteswissenschaften* notwithstanding, the more general point appears to hold for social theory: just because two "practice theorists" share a vocabulary, this does not necessarily entail the commensurability of their statements about an ostensibly unitary object. By examining carefully the questions driving enquiry into *practice*, and the presuppositions on which they are based, we find that "disagreement" is not always what it appears. On closer scrutiny, the grounds for debate often dissolve—not on account of a higher synthesis or previously unrecognized common ground but, rather, because it usually turns out the proponents of rival "theories of practice" are trying to answer different kinds of questions, based on incongruous presuppositions regarding the nature of the world and the conditions under which it may be known and transformed.[2]

Differing in Practice

Considering the obstacles to a positive account of practice, one might begin to wonder whether the project was doomed from the start. Is it possible the very idea of a "theory of practice" is somehow confused or contradictory? Or, taking a slightly different tack, might it be that the idea of practice is at its best when deployed in aid of critique—that is, when demonstrating the limitations of more conventional theorizing, without necessarily offering an alternative? We will need to return to this line of argument, even if it ultimately proves unsatisfying. But first I would like to consider whether we might yet find reason to prefer one of the going accounts of practice over the others. As recourse to "the facts" cannot alone provide grounds for such a judgment, I propose we take a somewhat different route and compare briefly the central questions, presuppositions, and projects of transformation embodied in the work of two prominent social theorists—namely, MacIntyre and Bourdieu. A comparison of other theorists on the question of practice (say Foucault or Judith Butler) would offer different and equally important insights. But, for reasons that will become apparent, the contrast between MacIntyre and Bourdieu is particularly instructive for present purposes. Although MacIntyre is a philosopher by profession, and Bourdieu was a sociologist, they have both been influential far beyond their respective disciplinary specialties, with commentators and acolytes in a diverse range of fields. And they each exemplify the ideals of a different critical tradition. Albeit but a thumbnail sketch, this comparison will help to frame a series of questions we may then bring to bear on the CRG and, by extension, the other uses and acts of *aksara* encountered in Batan Nangka.

The fundamental question for Bourdieu, as for Louis Althusser (1971) before him, was how to account for the reproduction of a class-stratified society (see, e.g., Bourdieu 1977, 1984, 1990, 1993; Bourdieu and Wacquant 1992). In his estimation, the two prevailing theoretical options of his time were inadequate to the task. Neither structuralist "objectivism" (e.g., 1990, 26–27) nor what he called the "subjectivism" characteristic of both existentialist philosophy and rational actor theory (e.g., 1990, 46–47) could account for the way in which people were more or less consistently inclined to act contrary to their own interests. Bourdieu was critical of structuralism for mistaking *statistical regularity* for *regulation* (1990, 39), as if social structure were totalizing, while the actors themselves were devoid of any capacity for self-determination. But, on the flip side of the coin, he also criticized rational actor theory for overvaluing agency by abstracting "decisions" from their rootedness in time—and particularly from their indebtedness to constraints established by an ongoing process of socialization.

In place of these mistaken theorizations, Bourdieu developed what he described as a more scientific account of practice. He accepted both structure and agency as given but felt they were inadequately theorized in accounts that took action to be wholly determined by one, to the exclusion of the other. In short, he wished to argue that individuals are indeed the *agents* of human action, but they do not act freely. The driving theoretical question, then, was how best to account for this unfreedom.[3] Bourdieu argued that the constraints that come with the structuring of action are explicable with reference to a class-specific habitus, which he famously described as the totality of a group's "durable dispositions." He saw these dispositions as being transmitted through social norms of the group, as "inscribed" on the body of its constituents—through such things as habitual posture and bodily comportment, the routinized division of labor, and the organization of domestic space. This "structuring structure," as he called it, was at once the *product* of prior actions and the *precondition* for new ones. The individual agent, or "organism," may strategize to maximize access to various forms of "capital" in a given field of practice, but these strategies are not one's own. For it is the class-specific habitus that conditions—and, at least on my reading, *determines*—both one's desired ends and the means employed to achieve them, as adjusted to the objective conditions of production.

Whatever else Bourdieu may have accomplished, in setting social structure against individual agency, his account of practice replicated modern sociological "common sense."[4] This is probably one of the more important reasons for his enduring popularity, as Bourdieu's "theory of practice" can be "applied" without calling into question the received wisdom of both one's precritical social ontology and scientistic epistemology.

The idea of practice has been important for MacIntyre too, but for different reasons. As with Bourdieu, MacIntyre's work addresses issues of social injustice. But his account of practice emerged in response to a rather different line of questioning. While Bourdieu's point of departure was the reproduction of social inequality, MacIntyre asked on what grounds we are justified in making moral judgments in the first place. Although this question appears to have driven MacIntyre from the start of his intellectual career, it was only with the publication of *After Virtue* ([1981] 2010), and his adoption of an Aristotelian ethics, that his response required such an explicit formulation of practice as a critical concept. Having concluded that liberalism in its various forms had failed to provide nonarbitrary grounds for moral judgment, he had come to see that the prevailing alternatives—and particularly the Marxism of postwar Britain—had fared no better. MacIntyre argued that the source of the problem was "the Enlightenment project" and its desire to decouple human reasoning from the authority of tradition—and, more specifically, from an Aristotelian conception of moral teleology and the virtues. In the absence of an agreed-upon telos for human life, and criteria for judging what constituted the good life, modern moral valuations could be nothing more than expressions of personal preference—a position MacIntyre described as "emotivism." His work has since been devoted to developing a line of moral enquiry within the broadly Aristotelian tradition, which he has more recently qualified in explicitly Thomist terms.

In MacIntyre's original formulation, practice figured as the first of three stages in a progressive reconstruction of virtue, the subsequent steps including the narrative unity of a whole life and one's situation within a moral tradition ([1981] 2010, 186–87).[5] In beginning with practice, the aim was to ground his account of the virtues both historically and sociologically, but without recourse to metaphysics—a position he would later modify. In a frequently cited passage, he explained, "By a 'practice' I am going to mean any coherent and complex form of socially established cooperative human activity through which goods internal to that form of activity are realized in the course of trying to achieve those standards of excellence which are appropriate to, and partially definitive of, that form of activity, with the result that human powers to achieve excellence, and human conceptions of the ends and goods involved, are systematically extended." He went on to specify that "tic-tac-toe is not an example of a practice in this sense, nor is throwing a football with skill; but the game of football is, and so is chess. Bricklaying is not a practice; architecture is. Planting turnips is not a practice; farming is. So are the enquiries of physics, chemistry and biology, and so is the work of the historian, and so are painting and music" (187). Participation in a practice so construed is ordered by rules. But, on MacIntyre's account, rules may be improved as the practice itself progresses—as we see with his examples from gaming and sports but also science, agriculture, art, and architecture. Crucially, this progress is the product of collective endeavor—and often reasoned deliberation—on the part of a community at once engaged in and constituted by such a practice.[6] The goods "internal" to the practice are its end and organizing principle, which in subsequent formulations MacIntyre would call "goods of excellence." These are the abilities and accomplishments—such as becoming an outstanding chess player or a great chef—that one can only achieve through participation in the practice. It is through the pursuit of such shared goods that practitioners cultivate excellence of character, or virtue.

Here the constructive aspect of MacIntyre's account comes to the fore, as reflected in a pair of distinctions that highlight potential conflicts threatening the development of character and community through a given practice. The first distinction is between practices and the institutions that support them, the interests of which may come to be prioritized over those of the practice itself. Here one might think of the privileging of finance over the traditional goods of scholarship in contemporary institutions of higher learning, or perhaps the way team profits and product endorsements have taken precedent in professional sports. A closely related distinction is drawn between "goods of excellence" and what MacIntyre has called "goods of efficiency"—such as money, fame, and enjoyment—which may be accrued by excelling in the practice but may also be acquired by other means. This distinction points up the conflict that may arise between a desire to excel in the practice and a wish to enjoy the material wealth or admiration that is a by-product of one's achievement. As with institutions and practices, privileging such goods of efficiency over those of excellence entails mistaking for *ends in themselves* things more properly understood as *means*. For MacIntyre this valorization of means is particularly pronounced in the managerialism and bureaucratic rationality characteristic of contemporary capitalism. On his account, practices that are "in good working order" militate against these socially corrosive forces by developing personal character and community as the proper ends of human life. Although some have seen this as a fundamentally conservative—and even retrograde—project (e.g., Nussbaum 1989; Nagel 1995), his more nuanced commentators have described his efforts as directed to explicitly "revolutionary" ends (Knight 2007; cf. Lutz 2004, 2012).

A more detailed reading would reveal further, and arguably more profound, differences between the accounts of practice given by Bourdieu and MacIntyre. But, even on such cursory examination, some important contrasts emerge. We have seen that, for Bourdieu, practices figure as those mechanisms through which social inequality is perpetuated. On his account, practices perform this function (a term I use advisedly) to the extent they remain *inaccessible* to critical reflection and collective reasoning. Sociological analysis, then, is directed to revealing the workings of practice and thereby undercutting its ability to perpetuate injustice-through-obfuscation, understood as the undue encroachment of the group on the individual's right to the pursuit of self-interest.[7] As one of Bourdieu's leading commentators, Loïc Wacquant, remarked, "The more scientific sociology becomes, the more politically relevant it becomes, if only as a negative tool—a shield against forms of mystification and symbolic domination that routinely prevent us from becoming genuine political agents" (Bourdieu and Wacquant 1992, 51; cf. Wacquant 2014, 122–23).

Meanwhile, for MacIntyre, practices are the foundation on which shared goods and virtues are cultivated within a community. Yet, crucially, the community is not a sociological datum but rather is itself constituted—and continually reconstituted—through those very practices. In contrast to Bourdieu, MacIntyre's practices are effective to this end precisely insofar as they remain *accessible* to critical reflection and collective reasoning. On such an approach, the pretense to a neutral account of "the group"—or of "society"—à la Bourdieu is revealed as a sleight of hand directed to naturalizing a particular vision of collective life—namely, that of "social science methodology," which MacIntyre ([1979] 1998) tellingly has described elsewhere as "the ideology of bureaucratic authority."

These contrasting accounts of practice may at first appear to be little more than differing perspectives on one and the same thing. And this might lead us to think we can reduce the ostensible disagreement between them to an *empirical* difference of opinion as to the effects of critical self-awareness or, alternatively, a *moral* difference as to the value of authority as against freedom. This, however, would be to elide the foundational differences between their respective social ontologies and critical epistemologies. In short, to proceed with Bourdieu would entail an a priori privileging of western social science over all other ways of construing the world. On such an account, Balinese practices might be *explained* through reference to the interests they serve and the forms of social inequality they naturalize. But at no point would Balinese be taken seriously as offering rival accounts of the world and the conditions under which it may be known and transformed.[8]

MacIntyre, by contrast, takes precisely this conflict between traditions as his point of departure, a position he has further developed in his subsequent work (e.g., 1988, 1990). On this approach, Balinese uses and acts of *aksara* might be seen as a potential rival to modern Euro-American understandings of script and writing. Significantly, the emphasis on conflict not only parallels certain prevalent strands in Balinese ways of thinking but is also particularly well suited to the complexity of the contemporary Balinese scene, where acts of writing are caught between competing styles of reasoning about human flourishing and collective life.

Returning to the CRG, then, the question is whether this rite might be interpreted as a "practice" in something like MacIntyre's sense. The simple answer is probably no. The CRG is complex, and it is directed to achieving specifiable ends. But, as we have seen, prevailing accounts of these ends are not self-evidently coherent. Moreover, as they may be achieved by other means, the ends of the CRG are not properly "goods of excellence," which, for MacIntyre, are the sine qua non for practice. But that does not necessarily make MacIntyre's account irrelevant to the interpretation of the rite. For it may be recalled that, although throwing a football is not a practice, the game of football is. So might the CRG be seen as *contributing to* a practice in something like MacIntyre's sense—as, for example, bricklaying contributes to architecture? Here I think we may be on somewhat stronger footing.

The Practice of Maintaining a Houseyard

As a provisional first step, what I would like to suggest is that we return to consider the CRG as one of a series of regular activities that make up the practice of maintaining a houseyard (B. *pakarangan*). We have seen, for instance, that the CRG is included in any number of the palm-leaf manuals enumerating rites, routines, and methods for establishing and maintaining domestic space. It also figures in more recent accounts of the domestic rites performed in "the Hindu home" (I. *rumah tangga Hindu*)—for example, in elementary school religious education and on television. So, what are the goods "internal" to the practice of maintaining a houseyard—that is, its "goods of excellence"? How are they ordered? And in what way does the CRG contribute to their pursuit?

The answers to these questions are complicated, in that—like acts of writing but on a larger scale—the CRG brings together at least two rival conceptions of the goods and virtues in play. Recalling the critique from ecology (chapter 2), we might say that the rite provides an occasion for conflict between competing "ways of life," each of which envisages and pursues the good of the houseyard in a different fashion—a point perhaps best shown by way of example. Events surrounding the death of a local businessman in Batan Nangka illustrate this well.

Bli Agem died unexpectedly. As a successful real estate agent, and something of a loan shark, he was relatively affluent and widely respected for his generosity in supporting community initiatives. But he also had a reputation for abruptness of character and impatience for what he took to be the backwardness and irrationality of his fellow villagers. One day Agem had gone to a neighboring ward to act as spokesman for his nephew in bride negotiations. But, just as he was about to begin speaking, his body slumped to the side, and shortly thereafter he was pronounced dead.[9]

Several explanations were given for Agem's untimely demise. Although he was energetic and comparatively youthful for a man in his late forties, he was also known to suffer from a heart condition. Many assumed this to be the proximate cause of his death. But, as is often the case, there were other factors to consider. In addition to accusations of sorcery, it was said that recent renovations to his houseyard may have played a role in his illness. Although the compound itself was relatively small by local standards, Agem's financial success had allowed him to improve several of the buildings, adding a modern kitchen and a number of nicely tiled individual bedrooms. The symmetry and precision of the new structures gave the houseyard a modern and tidy feel; and, for convenience, Agem had joined the roofs of the main northern and western pavilions, so one might pass between the two buildings without getting wet during the rainy season. A priestly adviser to the family had warned him not to make a permanent link between the two structures, as this would potentially become a point of congestion (B. *embet*)—blocking the free flow of wind and water but also of the intangible forces that are thought to pass regularly through the causeways and passages of Balinese houseyards. There was apparently a similar problem with the positioning of the doors to the new bedrooms. And it was pointed out that the eastern pavilion would also need to be expanded, so the relative dimensions of the compound's various structures would be kept in proportion. Agem was warned not to let his desire for utility and style cloud his judgment. But, according to the neighbors, he carried forward with his plans, discounting the advice he had been given as little more than village superstition.

Whatever other factors may have been involved in his death, this was now widely thought to have been a mistake. As the priest wryly pointed out, the kitchen may have looked neat and modern (I. *rapi dan modéren*), like the ones "in the television adverts." But, as a consequence of his temerity, Agem was no longer around to enjoy it.

Unfortunately, this was not the end of the family's troubles. In life Agem had been strict with his children, insisting on obedience at home, diligence at school, and conscientious service to the community. Following his death, his elder daughter carried these ideals forward in pursuing an advanced degree at one of Indonesia's leading universities, returning home for major holidays and community events. By contrast, her younger brother was widely thought to have lost his way. Fulfilling regular family obligations in a most desultory manner, he also seemed to lose interest in school. Much to the consternation of his neighbors, he used his inheritance to make highly visible purchases, including a top-end motorcycle and a pure-bred pit bull, which within a couple of months had already killed several of the other dogs in the village. Despite growing discomfort at this behavior, his arrogance was said to have made it difficult for the wider family to offer him any advice.

Following Agem's death, the houseyard stood empty most days. His widow left early each morning for work, his daughter was at university, and his son was usually off cavorting with his friends. As the compound was situated along a major thoroughfare, and relations with at least some of the neighbors were becoming strained, an effort was made to ensure the front gate could be securely locked against intruders. The protection of valuables has long been a concern for Balinese, with the northern pavilion commonly used as a storehouse. Yet a locked and empty houseyard is more commonly associated with those "newcomers" to the area who lease or purchase land for a villa and commute daily to the city for work. In place of their contribution to community service, these newcomers are expected to pay the ward a monthly fee. But they are not entitled to the same support that comes with full membership in the ward—which, significantly, includes immediate assistance in the case of theft, fire, or threat of violence.[10] In addition to such assistance, full participation in the ward also ensures one's family can count on the support of its neighbors during major life-cycle rites and temple anniversaries. As one might expect, these privileges are not equally distributed; one tends to receive in proportion to what one is seen to give. So, unsurprisingly, with the son's growing disregard for the surrounding community, this became something of a concern. With each passing temple anniversary, the extended family had to provide an increasing amount of help with the preparations—and this despite the fact that, as members of the same extended lineage, they too were conducting the same rites, and making the same preparations, in their own houseyard. This meant more work for everyone, a problem that some linked to Agem's ill-fated plans for houseyard renovation.

Local commentary on these developments within Batan Nangka would suggest that Agem's houseyard was not being maintained properly and that this had consequences far beyond his individual fate. Pulling back from the vignette, this appeared to be based on the idea that a well-maintained houseyard would be one that was inhabited, enclosed, free of congestion, ordered, and in good standing with respect to a series of ongoing relations of mutual obligation that "tie" it to various intangible beings and forces but also to its neighboring houseyards and the overlapping forms of institutionalized collectivity that support them. It must be emphasized that these ideals do not go uncontested, as evidenced by Agem's willingness to disregard admonitions from his priestly adviser in favor of modernizing his home. But, before turning to this conflict of ideals, I would like to reflect briefly on each of these aspects of what is taken to be a well-maintained houseyard.

Inhabited, Enclosed, Uncongested, Ordered, and Tied

The situation following Agem's death points to the importance of one's houseyard being inhabited and so lively, or *ramé*, a point that has often been cited in the scholarly literature.[11] This ideal extends beyond the houseyard to temples during festival times; and it is especially important in the home of the recently deceased, when refreshments and gambling are provided to keep the space bustling with activity through the night. A common phrase employed to describe the stillness of an empty houseyard is "as if a corpse had just been carried out" (B. *cara umah kalain watangan*)—evoking the "creepy" (B. *aéng*) emptiness of the deceased's houseyard when all her friends and relations have vacated the compound and left for the cremation grounds. The boisterousness of the recently departed funerary procession contrasts palpably with the stillness it leaves behind.[12]

A houseyard must also be enclosed for protection. Near the front gates of many, especially older, houseyards in Batan Nangka stand two stone shrines that are called *tugu apit lawang*—"gate-pinching shrines"—commonly said to prevent malevolent beings from proceeding farther into the living space of the houseyard. Moreover, for those compounds abutting a crossroads or T junction, a special shrine—often called a "road piercer" (B. *panumbak jalan*)—is erected along the outer wall. Although this shrine is understood in various ways (Fox 2015), for many it is conceived as a "weapon" (B. *sanjata*) directed to discouraging passers-by from entering and interfering in the domestic life of the houseyard. As a middle-aged farmer put it, these shrines work "like a fortification" (B. *sakadi bénténg*); the farmer explained that "the houseyard itself will be pierced if it doesn't have a road-piercer" (B. *pakaranganné 'kal katumbak yan panumbak jalan sing ada*).

Although enclosed for protection, the outer walls of most compounds have regular apertures to ensure an even flow of wind and water, among other things. Here the terminology often parallels that of the human body, with architectural guidelines directed to ensuring regular causeways are kept clear so as not to become "constipated" or "congested" (B. *embet*)—for which reason the central courtyard is also swept twice daily.[13] When one of our neighbors in Batan Nangka complained of night sweats and chronic lower back pain, a priestly adviser instructed him to knock a hole in a wall that he had recently constructed along the western edge of his compound. He was told that the newly erected wall obstructed the daily movements of an intangible resident of a nearby ravine, who was in the habit of passing through their houseyard on his way to bathe in the river.

A well-maintained houseyard is also ordered both horizontally and vertically with respect to the overlapping registers of hierarchy and purity. In principle, this entails orienting that which is purer and higher ranking toward the island's central volcanic mountain, Gunung Agung, and the lower, less refined counterparts "downriver," toward the sea. With an eye to matters both tangible and otherwise, this orientation serves to facilitate the unencumbered pursuit of various forms of life-sustaining activity—from cooking, sleeping, and preparing offerings to processing agricultural products (e.g., drying coffee and unhusked rice) and caring for domesticated animals. The compound's various pavilions, and their component parts, must be correctly aligned both with respect to one another and in relation to these points external to the houseyard. But any number of more proximate concentrations of potentiality—woods, ravines, temples, or caves—may also warrant attention in the organization of domestic space—as, for instance, with the construction of the "road piercer" and similar shrines.

As home to an extended family, the houseyard compound—and especially the collection of shrines situated in its mountainward corner—localizes ties both to other branches of the family and to their forebears, as well as to the various corporate bodies on which its inhabitants are dependent for their sustenance and well-being. As we saw with Bli Agem's family, the maintenance of domestic space entails a complex of relationships characterized by reciprocal obligation. The houseyard is tied to the ward through its use of, and contribution to, collective labor in the performance of major architectural and life-cycle rites, culminating in the community effort embodied in rites of cremation. One is further tied to the wider village through one's use of village-owned rice fields, a debt reciprocated during periodic rites for the central village temples. The houseyard is moreover tied to a priestly (and most frequently brahmanical) house through its performance of periodic rites that require specialist advice, instruments, and services. It may also be tied to a local palace and minor aristocratic houses through long-standing relations of fealty, patronage, and protection. And finally, though not least importantly, it is tied to the intangible beings and forces resident in its vicinity through regular relations of exchange and protection—but also battle when necessary.

This would suggest that, when properly maintained, a houseyard is inhabited, enclosed, uncongested, organized, and bound by relations of mutual obligation. But how are these goods related to one another? And in what ways does the CRG contribute to their pursuit? It would appear *caru* rites are—very generally speaking—directed to preventing the disruption of collective life, understood to involve relations between beings and forces both human and otherwise. It is arguably for this reason that *caru* are performed either as a preliminary step within a regularly occurring ceremony or in response to unfavorable events that are taken to indicate a breakdown in these relations. Provisionally assuming this to be an adequate account, what are the virtues cultivated through realizing these goods in the practice of maintaining a houseyard?

Perhaps most readily apparent is the recognition and fulfillment of one's obligations. In the tangible world of social relations, this was where Agem's son got himself and his family into trouble. But recognition also extends to relations with the myriad intangible beings and forces with which one's daily life is entangled. While appropriate generosity is essential to one's safety and prosperity, equally important is the ability to receive graciously. Ward regulations stipulate neighborly assistance during major rites. But, when the work is done, to leave without having eaten is to deprive your neighbors of the opportunity to repay the favor, thereby leaving them overtly indebted and humiliated by the snub.[14] While the performance of such rites may be lavish, both parsimony and foresight are crucial to the ability to carry on consistently with one's obligations. A frequent topic of commentary in improvised theater is the growing tendency to spend beyond one's means in hosting weddings and cremations, thereby leaving the family with inadequate funds for subsequent rites, to say nothing of day-to-day subsistence. While generosity and trust are highly valued, they must be tempered by caution. Balinese folk stories are filled with tales of mistaken identity and unrecognized danger, where one's willingness to help may be repaid with an untimely death (H. Geertz 2016). As a final addition to this working list of virtues, one might include skill in what is best described as the prosaic arts—including such things as cookery, butchery, carpentry, and the preparation of offerings. Those who possess these skills—and are ready with their assistance when required—are generally held in high regard and may count on the beneficence of their neighbors in difficult times.

Fostering a Healthy Home

Generally the aforementioned goods and virtues only gain explicit formulation when a problem arises. This was in part the reason for dwelling on the vignette. When discussing these matters directly with Balinese, the more readily cited ideals for maintaining domestic space are rather different—and, more specifically, they tend to be those of the "healthy home," or *rumah sehat* (I.), as promulgated by the state in earnest from the late 1960s. These are the ideals one is "supposed" to espouse, as they are cultivated formally in school and more diffusely through television and other media. The call to foster a *rumah sehat* may be seen in especially stark form in the annual competitions sponsored by local branches of the Indonesian Family Welfare Organization (PKK, *Pembinaan Kesejahteraan Keluarga*), in which houseyards are judged with reference to a series of criteria—ranging from cleanliness and modern convenience to conformity with an idealized understanding of traditional architecture.

As home to the "small, happy, and prosperous family" (I. *keluarga kecil bahagia sejahtera*), the *rumah sehat* is to be organized in a manner conducive to developing the virtues of patriarchal domesticity and modernization.[15] These include the generalized virtues of personal hygiene, industriousness, and productivity but also religious observation, cultural identity, and national belonging. These virtues are further inflected by the age- and gender-specific ideals (e.g., housewifely frugality, fatherly financial responsibility, teenage enthusiasm and industriousness, childhood dependence) that link bodies and domestic space more directly to the imperatives of wage labor, capital accumulation, and consumption. The space of the family home is to be employed in such a way as to maximize the cultivation of these relatively novel virtues. In recent years, this has been most visibly embodied in the proliferation of new household appliances and furniture—such as sofas, kitchen countertops, laptops, and washing machines—which many Balinese are still learning how to use.[16]

In contrast to older sensibilities, houseyard temple anniversaries have come to figure in the maintenance of the *rumah sehat* as an expression of the personalized spirituality associated with state bureaucratic Hinduism. Here offerings are to be dedicated as an act of pious devotion to God, with the wider ceremony itself construed as something like a religious service.[17] Understood in these terms, *caru* rites like the CRG are seen as "symbolizing" (I. *menyimbulkan*) a spiritual "purification" that prepares the religious adherent to pray (I. *sembahyang*) with sincerity (I. *dengan tulus ikhlas*) and without hope of gaining anything in return (I. *tanpa pamrih akan hasilnya*).[18] In this idiom, the malevolent forces in play are often psychologized, with *bhutakala* figuring as our baser passions and desires—as, again, "symbolized" by the *caru*'s characteristic offerings of meat and liquor.[19] Like the offerings them-selves, the "pure letters" of the rite's inscribed instruments are also primarily seen to be "symbolic"—an idea notably at odds with the use of these *aksara* as means of fortification and defense. The arduous process of preparing offer-ings at home remains preferable. But, when taken as a symbolic expression of piety, there is nothing to prevent one from purchasing offerings as part of a "package" (I. *paket*)—which is becoming ever more important with the growing demands of salaried labor and domestic life within the small, nu-clear family. In one sense, the purchase of offerings may strengthen relations with one's priestly patrons. But, as many in Batan Nangka have noted, it also diminishes ties with the neighbors and others on whom one ordinarily would rely for assistance.

On the Way to Practice

The events recounted from Batan Nangka show how a practice, such as houseyard maintenance, may become the occasion for conflict between rival projects for personal and collective transformation—exemplified here by competing conceptions of ceremonial work and the written instruments em-ployed in its performance. This sort of complexity potentially poses a prob-lem for conventional understandings of history and precedent, as we shall see. But, before proceeding, it is worth reflecting briefly on the line of question-ing for which this argument—and these examples—is a provisional response.

In an effort to specify the nature of *writing* as a topic of critical enquiry, in the previous chapter I began by asking what it would mean to interpret Balinese uses and acts of *aksara* under the description of practice. We have now considered the CRG by way of example, recalling that the critique from ecology (chapter 2) had encouraged attention to the "rootedness," or "em-beddedness," of writing practices within a broader way of life. But this phrase—"a way of life"—ended up raising as many questions as it purported to answer. Not least among our difficulties was the emphasis on coherence. In examining script and writing in Batan Nangka (chapter 3), we found not a unitary way of life but rather a congeries of conflicting articulations of agency, community, and the common good—a degree of complexity simi-lar to what we have now seen in the CRG. What I would like to suggest is that, despite this lack of unity, we might yet approach writing with reference to "ways of life." But this will only be with the proviso that the emphasis fall squarely on *multiplicity* and on the *directionality*, or *movement*, implicit in the term *ways*—that is, as a force driving forward in a particular direction, often in competition with countervailing forces pulling in one or more *other* ways. Developing the metaphor, writing might then be seen not so much as "rooted" or "embedded" in a given way of life but rather as carried along by it and at the same time impelling action along this trajectory still further forward. Thus a single act of writing—such as those associated with the CRG—might concurrently *drive* and *be driven* along multiple "ways," with a sort of teleological overdetermination—that is, with several, often conflicting purposes (e.g., payment, battle, purification) embodied in one and the same act.

Overdetermination presents an interesting problem for our account of practice, all the more so as MacIntyre's later work appears to give increasing importance to a hierarchical ordering of goods. As I read him, practices that are in "good working order" are characterized by the unity and coherence of their teleology. On this approach, the myriad incongruities we noted in Batan Nangka would probably fall rather short of the mark. The question is what to make of this. Can we be sure that the apparent lack of "coherence" points to a problem in what Balinese are doing? Or, alternatively, does it suggest a limitation of MacIntyre's approach? One might argue that Balinese understandings of collective ceremonial work, or *karya*, resemble the confused state of moral enquiry decried in MacIntyre's oft-cited "disquieting suggestion" at the opening of *After Virtue*. Here he described a postapocalyptic dystopia in which the natural sciences had been lost and only partially recovered in piecemeal—leaving "a world in which the language of natural science, or parts of it at least, continues to be used but is in a grave state of disorder." The conceit of this disquieting suggestion was that it described the state of moral enquiry in the modern era, in which the ordering principles and presuppositions that gave meaning to moral concepts had been lost, together with the tradition of the virtues. As he put it, "We continue to use many of the key expressions. But we have—very largely, if not entirely—lost our comprehension, both theoretical and practical, of morality" ([1981] 2010, 2). With the CRG's seemingly incongruous juxtaposition of battle, exchange, transformation, and cleansing, one might be inclined to think that Balinese were similarly adrift when it came to the purposes animating their religious rites. And yet the Balinese notion of *karya*, as ceremonial work, has historically turned on precisely the ability to articulate potentially conflicting forces, in order to bring about a specific transformation in the world.[20] Interestingly enough, this resembles one of MacIntyre's earlier descriptions of *tradition*, as "hold[ing] together conflicting social, political and even metaphysical claims in a creative way" (MacIntyre [1979] 1998, 67; cf. chapter 2)—an idea that may prove important in thinking further about script and writing in Bali.

Chapter 6

Tradition as Argument

The Maha Bajra Sandhi Group was selected [to represent Indonesia at the
2004 Cultural Olympiad in Athens] because of their radical approach to
revitalizing the role of an archaic alphabet in daily life, bringing the symbolic
down to earth, and reviving the rites of music, offering an alternative
understanding of art, family and even life itself in modern society.[1]

—Indonesian National Committee for the Cultural Olympiad, Athens, 2004

The history of any society is thus in key part the history of
an extended conflict or set of conflicts. And as it is with societies,
so too is it with traditions.

A tradition is an argument extended through time in which certain
fundamental agreements are defined and redefined in terms of two kinds of
conflict: those with critics and enemies external to the tradition who reject all
or at least key parts of those fundamental agreements, and those internal,
interpretive debates through which the meaning and rationale of the
fundamental agreements come to be expressed and by whose progress a
tradition is constituted.

—Alasdair MacIntyre, *Whose Justice? Which Rationality?*

In the preceding chapter I suggested that the *Caru Rsi Gana* (CRG) would
not itself qualify as a "practice" in MacIntyre's sense of the term but would
instead be seen to contribute to the wider practice of maintaining a
houseyard—much as bricklaying contributes to architecture or ice skating
to hockey. Yet, in contrast to MacIntyre's ideal, the practice of houseyard
maintenance in Batan Nangka was not directed to realizing a unitary and
determinate system of goods and virtues. Rather, it was performed in pursuit of at least two distinguishable—and often conflicting—visions for
human flourishing. One was directed to ensuring safety, sustenance, and a
localizing form of solidarity; the other was guided by the imperatives of national development. At various points I referred to these ideals as *traditional*
and *modernizing*, respectively. But, beyond their mutually defining opposition,

neither of these terms is particularly informative. How, then, are we to distinguish between the various projects for transformation embodied in the CRG? Can they be differentiated without falling back into the reifying habits of thought criticized in previous chapters? Or is cultural analysis ultimately incapable of escaping the strictures of an objectifying scientism? Part of the problem appears to spring from a set of widespread, yet mostly unreflective, assumptions regarding the nature of history and precedent— that is, a certain commonsensical understanding of the-past-in-the-present that is grounded in essentializing metaphors of *cultural influence* and the *transmission of ideas*. In continuing to think about "practice" as it pertains to Balinese *aksara*, I wish to suggest that a more critical approach to tradition may offer a way forward.[2]

On Tradition

The idea of tradition looms large in the literature on Balinese culture and society, and it has been made to mean many things for as many purposes. In its most general usage, the term figures as a loosely conceptualized historical period ("traditional Bali") and as a cipher for the lost "religion" and "spirituality" mourned in the West. It is deployed in this sense as a badge of authenticity, and it almost as frequently appears as a synecdoche for "text" ("according to tradition"). In the more recent scholarship, the English word *tradition* has been used to translate the Indonesian word *adat*, which is itself borrowed from Arabic. But *tradition* may also be translated back into Indonesian as *tradisi*—which, as a less formal designation, is rarely coterminous with *adat*. For Euro-American cultural historians, Balinese tradition has been exposed as a "discourse" of identity linked to shifting articulations of economy and polity. Meanwhile, for Indonesian government officials, it is a form of cultural "capital" to be managed judiciously for social and economic development. "Balinese tradition" has been all of these things and many others besides. But might it still be of any use as a critical concept?

Given this convoluted jumble of associations, one might be forgiven for wanting to abandon the idea of tradition altogether. Yet what I wish to argue is that we need tradition, or something like it, if we hope to render other people's practices intelligible as reasonable human action. For novel utterances and actions can only be said to "make sense" insofar as they may be interpreted with reference to the precedent set by one or more prior acts.[3] Or, to restate the point negatively, the absolutely new is also absolutely unintelligible. So our ability to interpret an act of writing, let alone a practice—for example, with reference to its presuppositions and the purposes it aims to fulfill—entails a prior knowledge of other acts similarly directed. It seems that, in this respect, interpretability would ride on the recognition of precedent.[4] And what I wish to suggest is that tradition may usefully be understood as embodying a special form of precedent. But, as with actions and utterances, a "traditional practice" cannot simply be a repetition of a prior moment, even—or perhaps especially—if this is its commonsense meaning.[5] So what is tradition, if it is at once necessary for the interpretability of practices and yet something other than a simple repetition of the past? Or, to take the question from another angle, how can we recognize a debt to historical precedent without reifying it in opposition to "the present"?

In an effort to answer these questions, and so continue developing our approach to practice, I would like to explore some of the implications that follow from MacIntyre's account of tradition as a form of "argument." This will be with specific reference to a series of performative events celebrating "the power of Balinese letters" that were organized by the Balinese scholar and public intellectual Ida Wayan Oka Granoka.[6] It is my provisional contention that, despite its innovative and eclectic appearance, Granoka's project embodies a style of *argumentation* that reflects prior responses to crisis, in both Bali and potentially other parts of the archipelago. Put another way, I wish to suggest that these performances exemplified an aspect of how at least some Indonesians have argued during times of cultural and political upheaval. As a critical response to the problems presently facing Balinese, my sense is that Granoka's efforts to "revitalize the tradition of Balinese *aksara*" are unlikely to achieve their aim, but this for reasons that may ultimately prove instructive. By way of introduction, let us begin by examining a little more closely the idea of "Balinese tradition."

The Idea of Tradition in Bali

The use of tradition in Bali has tended to be of three varieties, which I would describe as *positive*, *genealogical*, and *operationalized*, respectively. The *positive* deployment of tradition encompasses those implicitly legitimizing uses in which we are told that a given art form, ceremonial rite, or social institution has its origins in the premodern past. Bridging scholarly, state bureaucratic, and various popular forms, this "positive" use of tradition tends to cut two ways. In the first instance, it may appear as an emblem of folk authenticity, set in opposition to the self-conscious creativity of modern art and artifice. In this case, the traditional is often communal, as opposed to individual. Alternatively, tradition may also imply classical standards of excellence—as in the composition of court poetry (especially *kakawin*), where the ideal is aesthetic, as opposed to instrumental. Such usage is often *positive* in an evaluative sense while at the same time presuming to refer *positively* to something "out there" in the world. To this end, the term *tradition* commonly qualifies, or is qualified by, something else. So we have "local tradition," "oral tradition," "traditional theater, music, and dance"; there is "traditional attire," "traditional agriculture," "the tantric tradition," and "the Hindu-Buddhist tradition," as well as a series of "returns to tradition" that are informed by the expertise of foreign scholars and often underwritten by international aid agencies. Taken together, these contribute to a more generalized notion of "traditional Bali" as a loosely conceptualized historical period—an idea that is arguably implicit in much of our work, even as we endeavor to write against it.[7]

The second way the scholarship has tended to speak of tradition—what I would like to call the *genealogical*—is rather narrower in focus, and it takes a comparatively critical view of the island's history.[8] If the *positive* deployment of tradition has served to set a fixed point in opposition to which we might recognize change on the contemporary scene, this *genealogical* approach reveals change *within* the "discourse" of tradition itself.[9] In this case, the term *tradition* appears most commonly as a translation for Indonesian uses of the Arabic loanword *adat*. But, more recently, it has also been linked to the idea of the *désa pakraman* as the "traditional village."[10] Here the organizing problematic for historical enquiry has been the emergence of "Balinese identity"—and the idea of "Balineseness," or *kebalian*—in relation to notions of religion, culture, and tradition. It is on this basis that we now look askance at unreflective uses of *religion, culture,* and *tradition,* in the knowledge that *agama, budaya,* and *adat* each has a history that is closely tied to changing articulations of economy, politics, and power. This genealogical sensibility is arguably the default position in Balinese studies today; and it owes much to a series of important publications from James Boon (1977),

Henk Schulte Nordholt (1986, 1999), Adrian Vickers (1989), and Michel Picard (e.g., 1990, 1996, 2004, 2011a, 2011b). Here the decisive procedure is one of unmasking—an *ironic* revelation of contingency, complicity, and transformation where we had previously assumed an *earnest* determinacy, authenticity, and stasis.[11]

Third we have what I would call *operationalized* tradition, by which I mean the various ways tradition has been reified and put to work by the state but also by the tourism industry and in local politics. This is, in the first place, tradition understood as "capital" (I. *modal*) that must be guarded and put to work for social and economic development, as well as more immediate commercial gain. This is the tradition of bureaucrats, entrepreneurs, and managers. But it is also the tradition of Balinese schoolchildren. For, in addition to television, it is in the classroom that one first learns to recognize oneself as embodying distinctively Balinese styles of attire and of daily comportment. Speaking very generally, the defining feature of such operationalized tradition is deliberate objectification toward a particular, and commonly mercantile, end.[12]

So what are we to make of these three deployments of tradition—the *positive*, the *genealogical*, and the *operationalized*? How are they related to one another? In what ways have they contributed to the interpretation of Balinese social life? And, more specifically, how might they inform our approach to practice, with reference to issues of script and writing? What I have called operationalized tradition has received a fair bit of attention in the recent literature,[13] so I would like to focus for the moment on the other two.

First, we have the *positive* deployment. The positive uses of tradition have the advantage of rendering intelligible both change and our sense of the modern. Yet this has come at the cost of conceding an essentialized, if not always romanticized, vision of the past as static. This Archimedean point, from which we view and evaluate the present, has been variously embodied in text (e.g., C. Hooykaas 1964), ritual (e.g., Schulte Nordholt 1991), "the village republic" (Korn 1960), "the theatre state" (C. Geertz 1980), or some other exemplar of a prior era. Here what is important about tradition is that it *sit still* so that we might measure Bali's progressive movement away from it.

The *genealogical* deployment, by contrast, recognizes this essentialization for what it is, revealing all such calls to tradition as fundamentally "invented," in a variation on a theme made famous by Eric Hobsbawm and Terence Ranger (1983). Everything from Balinese culture and religion to the arts has been an elaborate ruse, we are told—serving the will to power or perhaps, as we now more commonly say, "the discursive construction of identity."[14]

There is considerable merit to the genealogical argument, not least in the evidentiary nuance and theoretical sophistication it has brought to Balinese historiography. The problem is that our most prominent genealogists have come unstuck on the question of *community*. I take it that genealogy is correct in highlighting the impossibility of representing Bali "as it really is" and that historicizing key terms such as *religion, culture*, and *tradition* helps to highlight changes that would otherwise go unnoticed.[15] Yet, on closer inspection, it would appear genealogy falls foul of its own critique when it finds itself referring to "the Balinese" as a positivity—that is to say, as a reified "populace" that is somehow *mis*represented by the "discourse of Balineseness." On the genealogical approach, it seems we would eschew universals in one breath ("Balinese identity is a discursive construct") and then reassert them in the very next ("This misleading discourse was constructed by/foisted on/misrepresents actual Balinese"). As a result, the Balinese emerge as the ontology that dare not speak its name. Genealogical decorum will not countenance open positivism. So the genealogically inclined are left to sneak their normative vision of Balinese society in through the back door, with phrases that are dropped in passing—such as "ordinary Balinese," "most Balinese," "the Balinese population at large," "typical Balinese," and other similarly covert gestures made in the direction of universality.

What, then, are the alternatives? The *positive* invocation of tradition no longer appears viable, and this is largely thanks to the critique from genealogy. Yet, while genealogy seems to offer a more nuanced account of historical change, it too is not without its own skeletons in the metaphysical closet. Cast in grammatical terms, perhaps the lesson to be taken is that representation is always carried out in the optative. In this respect a "society," be it Indonesian or otherwise, would be best understood as a *desideratum*, as opposed to a *datum*. It is something one endeavors to call into being performatively, something for which one *argues*—as opposed to something that is *given*. Why might this matter? Given the interpretive importance of precedent that was noted earlier, it would suggest, among other things, that our reflections on *writing* as a practice may call for closer attention to the problem of tradition. And here I believe that something like MacIntyre's account of *tradition as argument* may offer a particularly fitting point of departure, most notably for its emphasis on the rivalry between multiple and potentially conflicting styles of reasoning.[16]

Tradition as Argument

We might begin by noting that MacIntyre's account of tradition answers to a line of questioning that has both critical and constructive aspects. It responds in the first instance to the failure of modern ethics to generate judgments that satisfy its practitioners' own standards for universality (MacIntyre 1988, 6). For MacIntyre, this failure was the inevitable outcome of a historical decoupling of rationality from the authority of tradition—and, more particularly, from an Aristotelian conception of moral teleology and the virtues. Following from this observation, his later work has been devoted to a reconstruction of moral enquiry centered on reasoned argumentation and the cultivation of shared goods.[17] Tradition figures positively in this reconstruction as the final step in a three-stage conception of virtue, in which it is preceded by accounts of practice and what he has described as the narrative unity of a single human life.[18]

Setting aside for the moment both practice and narrative unity, we might say of tradition that it describes the temporal condition of moral enquiry.[19] In very general terms, we inherit both a set of questions and resources for addressing those questions, as embodied in our language of judgment and argumentation—including not merely *what* counts as good evidence for a given argument but also the criteria for choosing between rival interpretations of what is taken as given. Together these elements make up the "substantive rationality" that MacIntyre has described as being at once "tradition-constituted" and "tradition-constitutive" (e.g., 1988, 9–10 passim; cf. Lutz 2004, 33–64). Commenting on rival accounts of justice, he explained,

> Where Aristotle's formulations are in terms of *archē, telos, psychē, logos, ergon, praxis, pathos, aretē* and *polis*, Hume's deploy *impression, idea, passions calm and violent, nature, artifice, virtue, society* and *government*. It is not that there are [*sic*] not a range of shared meanings and references in the uses of these two sets of terms; were it not so, we could not recognize them as rival conceptions of one and the same subject-matter. Nonetheless the radical differences between them are such that if the Aristotelian concepts have

application in the way and to the degree that Aristotelians have held, then the Humean concepts are thereby precluded by and large from having application, and vice versa. (1991, 150)

While MacIntyre's historicism draws on the work of R. G. Collingwood, his emphasis on language is more directly indebted to Hans-Georg Gadamer. But, whereas for Gadamer tradition was always construed in the singular (Knight 2007, 98–99), for MacIntyre it is both plural and characterized by conflict—as an "argument extended through time." Yet he emphasized "it is not merely that different participants in a tradition disagree; they also disagree as to how to characterize their disagreements and as to how to resolve them. They disagree as to what constitutes appropriate reasoning, decisive evidence, conclusive proof" (MacIntyre 2006, 11). On MacIntyre's account, it is through the provision and collective evaluation of reasons—that is, through argument—that traditions are seen historically to be capable of progress, as judged by their own standards.[20] But, crucially, these standards may change as a result of critique occasioned either by the objective challenges posed by social and environmental transformation or by conflict with rival traditions of enquiry.

This understanding of progress in the rationality of a moral tradition is patterned on MacIntyre's reading of Imre Lakatos on progress in the natural sciences.[21] Drawing out the parallels with moral enquiry, he suggested, "The criterion of a successful theory is that it enables us to understand its predecessors in a newly intelligible way. It, at one and the same time, enables us to understand precisely why its predecessors have to be rejected or modified and also why, without and before its illumination, past theory could have remained credible. It introduces new standards for evaluating the past. It recasts the narrative which constitutes the continuous reconstruction of the scientific tradition" (MacIntyre 2006, 11). Crucial for our purposes is the emphasis on a decisive victory of one theory, tradition, or research program over another. This is in keeping with an understanding of argument as something like a contest in rationality, a trope with innumerable iterations stretching from the Athenian polis to the present-day seminar room.[22] The point is not so much that MacIntyre saw the forward march of *progress in rationality* as characteristic of ordinary life. Clearly he did not. And yet achieving victory through superior reasoning is explicitly recommended as an ideal. Here conceptual conflict and "contradiction" are taken to be a problematic (and preferably temporary) state of affairs, which is gerundively to be overcome through the *agōn* of rational competition. To be sure, this may be an apt characterization of certain strands in the history of western thought. It may even be a model to which one could aspire. (Though at times the sportiness of it all makes rationality sound rather like something conceived on the playing fields of Eton.) The question is whether this style of argumentation, and so tradition, is so readily exportable elsewhere—in our case, to Bali and the uses and acts of *aksara*. From MacIntyre, especially in his later work, we get an insightful and intellectually productive interpretation of broadly western traditions of enquiry and their attempts to grapple with both themselves and one another in pursuit of truth. But how do these encounters look when viewed from beyond Europe and the Near East? If we discovered other, differing forms of argumentation elsewhere, what implications would follow for our account of tradition as argument? As a way into the problem, I would like to set MacIntyre's approach against a series of performative events organized by the Balinese impresario and scholar, Ida Wayan Oka Granoka.

Letters in Motion

> It's hard to say what just took place. It was a parade of sorts, culminating in a performance. Or was it a procession culminating in a ritual? Or something else? It was meant to commemorate the *Puputan Badung* of 1906. But it was also a statement about the future. There were large script-bearing canvasses that looked like *rarajahan*. But there were also boys and girls dressed in nationalist red-and-white. There was holy water and incense. And there were plenty of priests, and prayers, and weapons. But there was poetry, too. The event was several things at once—parade and procession, ritual and commemoration—and yet, in some sense, it was none of these things.
>
> —Field notes, September 20, 2012

For reasons that hopefully will become clear enough, the process of enquiring about these events—and the way others responded—was as important as anything else that I learned along the way. It began with a visit to the workshop of Pak Saru, an architect I knew by reputation as something of a recluse who, though generous in his support for local projects, was often circumspect in his dealings with the community. I had recently expressed an interest in the use of Balinese *aksara* in rites of establishment performed for

Photo 6.1. The crowd assembled around the *baris* dancers at the conclusion
of the Grebeg Aksara.

new buildings and shrines. And he was recommended to me as someone who might be able to help with questions that others had been unable to answer. True to his reputation, Saru's remarks were vague and often seemingly beside the point.[23] But he suggested that, if I were interested in contemporary uses of Balinese letters, I could do worse than to attend something called the Grebeg Aksara, which would take place in the provincial capital of Denpasar later that week.[24] He then abruptly ended our meeting, leaving for another engagement.

Later that day I was informed that Saru had arranged for someone to take me to Denpasar for the event. It turned out the person he asked was Putu Subrata, a friend and collaborator on several previous research projects—whose *lontar*, incidentally, I was still hoping to examine (see chapter 1). Putu did not seem especially pleased at the assignment, and he even went so far as to imply the trip would be a waste of my time. But he agreed to drop me off a little ways from the ward assembly pavilion (B. *balé banjar*) in Tainsiat, where we had been told the event would begin. As I approached the pavilion on foot, the situation seemed anything but unfamiliar. There were men, women, and children bustling about in *pakaian adat* (I. "traditional attire") while police directed traffic and military onlookers stood importantly by (see photo 6.2). A marching gamelan orchestra could be heard playing sporadically in the background as motorbikes sped along the road

Photo 6.2. Police, military, and community officials awaiting the start of the procession.

bearing passengers loaded down with offerings and boxes of refreshments. My first impression was that it appeared very much like any of the many temple festivals and processions performed in this part of the island.

When I arrived at the pavilion itself, the differences became more readily apparent. Most striking were the stacks upon stacks of framed canvases, some well over a meter in height, bearing intricate diagrams and configurations of Balinese script. The framed depictions of *aksara* were painted in black against a white background, and many appeared to incorporate images of the weapons and powerful beings—for example, divinities, serpents, and tigers—found in the *rarajahan* drawings used for sorcery and self-protection. Based on my experience in Batan Nangka, I assumed these drawings were thought to be "alive"—and so inherently powerful and potentially dangerous. I took it that such objects were to be treated with caution and respect. And yet here were a bunch of young men and women joking about, casually handling these "living letters" as if they were of no particular significance. Some were so bold as to step over them—wearing shoes, no less—as they made their way across the pavilion—an act of unthinkable recklessness, if indeed these framed images were anything like the efficacious drawings I took them to resemble (see photo 6.3).

In the hope of finding out what was going on, I struck up a conversation with a middle-aged security guard affiliated with the local ward. Having answered the usual questions (Where are you from? Do you have children? etc.),

Photo 6.3. Students handing out the framed canvases bearing *rarajahan* and related configurations of *aksara* and other designs.

I asked what they were planning to do with all the framed drawings. He said that he had no idea what they were for but that his job was to ensure the students remained at the ward pavilion until they were called to the procession. He went on to explain that the event brought together a range of organizations—including multiple NGOs, dance ensembles, student groups, and local ward associations. When I asked again about the framed diagrams, he directed me to a young woman called Cipta, who he said was the leader of the student group. When I expressed surprise at the handling of the framed images, Cipta explained that these were not *rarajahan*, nor were they actually "alive." Rather, the images were a form of art (I. *seni*) designed by the students and meant to symbolize (I. *menyimbulkan*) the power of Balinese script and literature. As part of the Grebeg Aksara, they would be used to commemorate the Puputan of 1906, at which the royal court of Badung marched willfully into Dutch artillery rather than accept defeat.[25] She then pointed across the ward pavilion to a large statue in the crossroads of a man carrying a *keris* dagger in one hand and a *lontar* manuscript in the other, explaining that he was the last of the great precolonial rulers of Badung and an exemplary scholar of Balinese literature. It was in memory of his bravery, as embodied in the Puputan, that her supervisor at the university, Granoka, had organized the procession.

Photo 6.4. Rows of young men and women dressed in nationalist red and white,
waving Indonesian flags.

I had wanted to ask why one would wish to commemorate these events so elaborately on this particular occasion—106 years after the event. But the marching gamelan orchestra suddenly began to play, and the students scrambled into position on the road. The ensuing procession brought together a disparate array of themes, persons, and objects. Out in front were a group of elegantly costumed dancers and musicians, followed by an elephant-headed *barong*—a powerful and generally benevolent figure—carried along by two men and wearing a large, white sheet covered in Balinese script (see photo 6.5). Behind the *barong* stood a row of four *rangda*, Bali's iconically fearsome and ambivalently powerful sorceresses, each carrying a folding fan inscribed with a *keris* dagger surrounded by Balinese *aksara*. Then came several rows of students dressed in temple attire and carrying the script-bearing canvases, behind which was a line of younger men and women wearing red and white headbands and waving large Indonesian flags—seemingly exemplifying the "revolutionary youth" depicted in popular images recalling the Indonesian War of Independence (see photo 6.4). In and among the ranks of the marching students were small groups of older men and women holding above their heads various objects—including what appeared to be masks, swords, and palm-leaf manuscripts—many of which were wrapped in sheets of gold-embroidered cloth and housed in intricately decorated boxes borne on palanquins—much like those used to carry the statues

Photo 6.5. The procession lined up and about to begin, with the *aksara*-bearing *barong* ahead of the four fan-wielding *rangda*, followed by the contingent of flag-waving youths.

and other objects occupied by the divinities and related forces "called down" during temple anniversaries. Over the sound of the gamelan could also be heard the low, loud—and, at least to my ear, belligerent—pounding of four massive drums, which were pushed insistently forward on a wheeled cart by a contingent of boisterous young men taking turns at beating the drums with large leather mallets. And, as with any major public event in Bali today, photographers darted in and out of the procession, vying for position with casual onlookers who were shooting videos and taking photographs on their phones.

Once underway, the procession moved slowly southward along the main street to the crossroads located just above Puputan Square, where the famous Catur Muka (Four-Faced) statue of Lord Brahma stood towering over the assembled gamelan orchestra. On arriving at the crossroads, each of the groups took up a position around the edges of a stage-like space that had been covered with a giant white tarpaulin marked out with large geometric patterns. Things then rather suddenly went quiet as a man dressed in temple priest's attire marched ceremoniously to the center of the stage and unfurled an enormous scroll from which he read out a series of numbered points in Indonesian. From where I was standing, it was often difficult to make out precisely what he was saying. But it was quite emphatically a call to action—addressing such things as cultural renewal, national pride, and the importance of enthusiastic (I. *semangat*) support for social and economic development (I. *pembangunan*).

The gamelan then started up again, and a group of men took the stage to perform a variation on the *baris*, a militaristic dance that involves moving deftly in line formation (B. *baris*) while handling a lance. The men were soon joined by a larger group of women dancing elegantly with the dagger- and script-bearing cloth fans. Meanwhile, the four *rangda* moved slowly around the edges of the tarpaulin, eventually coming onstage and engaging in battle with the lance-wielding *baris* dancers, who moved to protect the other dancers. But, in the end, as in many popular renditions of the *Calonarang* drama, both the men and women succumbed to the power of *rangda*, finally turning their weapons on themselves—the women stabbing at their chests and torsos with the *aksara*-bearing fans as if they were *keris* daggers. With the performers having collapsed, their limp bodies draped one over another, the gamelan went quiet and the stage was still—no doubt deliberately replicating well-known photographic images of the Puputan in which the members of Badung's fallen court lay in heaps outside the palace gates, having chosen death over defeat (see photo 6.6). But then, as is now characteristic of some popular renditions of the *Calonarang* (perhaps especially those performed for tourists), the elephant-headed *barong* slowly moved in and revived the expired dancers, who came to their feet one by one. The dancers

Photo 6.6. The dancers with their fans, having collapsed under the spell of *rangda*.

then took a bow, the assembled onlookers applauded, and a woman's voice came over the PA system to announce that the event was over—after which the assembled crowd slowly dispersed, wandering off along the side streets.

As I made my way back up the road to meet Putu, I tried to work out what had just taken place. In some twenty years of visiting Bali, I could not recall having ever seen anything quite like this Grebeg Aksara. And yet, taken individually, many of its more prominent elements were readily recognizable—from the gamelan music and *baris* dance to the photographers and the procession of ornately attired men, women, and children bearing empowered objects for assembly at a particular location. Such processions are most commonly associated with the celebration of temple festivals. But on this occasion none of the local temples appeared to be celebrating their anniversaries. So what was the point of all this? How was the procession related to the call for cultural renewal and national pride? And why did Balinese *aksara* figure so prominently in the event?

The Local Critics

When I asked what he had thought of the procession, Putu seemed singularly unimpressed. As a graduate of the Fine Arts Academy and an accomplished professional musician, he has performed in hundreds—if not thousands—of dance dramas, light operas, and comedies. And so he has developed what many of his friends consider a jaded view of artistic innovation. Yet, despite my asking repeatedly, Putu was careful not to specify his criticism—perhaps because he had been asked to accompany me to the event by Pak Saru, whom he saw as a patron and a respected member of the community. It was only on arriving back in Batan Nangka that I got a better sense of his objection.

Pulling up to a local coffee stall, we met by chance with Saru's son, Pénjor, who looked up to Putu as a mentor and was, as it happened, a recent graduate of the literature program from which the Grebeg Aksara drew many of its student volunteers. When he heard we had been in Denpasar for the event, Pénjor groaned and rolled his eyes. I explained that I was confused by what I had seen and wondered whether he might be able to tell me what it was all about. Pénjor replied, with what I took to be a hint of sarcasm, that the Grebeg Aksara was simply "too sophisticated" (B. *bes wayah*) for the likes of "us ordinary folk" (B. *'nak biasa*). He quickly added that the organizer of the event, Pak Granoka, was a "genius" (in English), joking that his ideas were beyond the ken of mere mortals. It was at this point that Putu added in a more serious tone that the event was typical of university-based intellectuals (I. *cendekiawan*), who wanted to help but were out of touch with the realities of day-to-day life beyond the walls of their "academic palace" (I.? *puri akademis*).

The following morning I returned to consult with Ida Rsi and Ratu Padanda, two priests locally recognized for their expert knowledge of ceremonial rites (see chapter 4). I brought with me a set of photographs in the hope of eliciting their thoughts on the event. Ida Rsi listened intently as I described the procession and the casual handling of the *aksara*-bearing canvases. Looking over the photographs, he said the students' actions were both "mistaken" (I. *keliru*) and potentially dangerous (B. *baya*), as even the most apparently mundane objects—to say nothing of such potentially powerful configurations of script—might inadvertently be "brought to life" (B. *idupang*)—implying they could cause great harm.

The brahmin priest, Ratu Padanda, who it seemed had some prior knowledge of the Grebeg Aksara, described the event similarly as an "incorrect" or "improper" (B. *sing patut*) use of Balinese letters. He played on the term *grebeg*, which he said in older Balinese could be used to mean "destroy" (I. *menghancurkan*). He joked that Granoka was acting "like a terrorist" in setting out to "destroy letters" (B. *ngrebeg aksara*), adding, with a chuckle, that the inscribed canvases bore scant relation to anything he would recognize as Balinese "tradition" (I. *tradisi*). So, if Putu and Pénjor criticized the event for being "out of touch" with the lives of ordinary people, it seemed these two priests disapproved of what they took to be a risky and inexpert handling of letters.

Next I went to see Pak Kantor, a retired professor and public intellectual from one of the neighboring wards of Pateluan. As a prominent figure on the Balinese academic scene, he had been invited to participate in a seminar preceding the Grebeg Aksara, though he did not attend the procession itself. When I enquired, he said I was right to be confused, as Granoka's ideas were both abstract (I. *abstrak*) and complex (I. *kompléks*), creating a "synergy of music, semiotics, and mysticism" (I. *sinergi musik, semiotik, dan mistik*) that he himself was unable to grasp. He said the group responsible for organizing the event was Granoka's Sanggar Maha Bajra Sandhi, an organization devoted to the cultivation of "spirituality" (I. *spiritualitas*) through music and dance. He went on to explain that Bali was facing a variety of problems—both environmental and economic but also cultural and religious—and that the Grebeg Aksara was directed to reinvigorating Balinese society (I. *masyarakat Bali*) in the hope of overcoming these problems. However, he quickly added that the means were ill suited to their intended ends. The event was unnecessarily complicated and difficult to understand, and the group itself lacked cohesion. Unlike the efforts undertaken by local ward assemblies (B. *banjar*) and temple congregations (B. *pamaksan*), Granoka's endeavor lacked a foundation in the corporate groups historically constitutive of Balinese social life. The Sanggar was centered, he said, on Granoka's own family. So it lacked grounds for establishing the wider-reaching solidarity required for sustained collective action. It was for this reason, he said, that the event needed "artificial stimulation" (in English) in the form of large monetary donations from the provincial government. Kantor said Granoka and his group had performed the Grebeg Aksara in sequential years at various locations throughout Bali and had received over 1 billion rupiah (approx. US$80,000 at the time) to take the show on the road to Vietnam and later to Europe. I may have looked somewhat incredulous, as Kantor quickly went off to bring me a printout of an article that had been published several years before in *Kompas*, long one of Indonesia's leading quality newspapers.

The article originally appeared in 2006, written by the Balinese poet and public commentator Putu Fajar Arcana and bearing the title "Cultural Mission: A Postcard from Bali" (I. "Misi Kebudayaan: Kartu Pos dari Bali"). As Arcana explained, Granoka's group was sent on tour to perform in a series of cities across Europe in 2006 as part of an effort to repair the island's image as a safe destination for tourists in the wake of the nightclub bombings of 2002 and 2005.[26] He explained that foreign tourist arrivals declined precipitously after the first bombing and had not yet fully recovered. Arcana went on to discuss the economic impact of the downturn, suggesting that the tourism industry had "grown weary of waiting for the government to act" on the problem. Yet, having noted the need for action, the article was sharply critical of Granoka's European tour—both for inadequacy to its stated purpose and, at the same time, for its naive complicity with an orientalist vision of the island and its charms. Arcana argued that the tour was as "cliché," and so meaningless, as a postcard depicting a Balinese dancer—adding wryly, "It's as if there were an implicit 'understanding' between Europeans and Indonesians, and especially Balinese, that their friendly relations must periodically be 'reenergized' with a performance of traditional arts."[27] Having reviewed a lengthy résumé of foreign scholars and artists responsible for creating and perpetuating this exotic and often prurient image of "Balinese culture," he implied, moreover, that the trip abroad was an irresponsible waste of the money—some US$6 million—that Granoka's group is said to have received from local government (Arcana 2006).[28]

Although addressing events that occurred some six years beforehand, Arcana's article provided the first contextualizing information that I had encountered with respect to the Grebeg Aksara. But, beyond its substantive content, his criticism was also interesting for its style of explication. Seeking precursors for contemporary practice in a series of prior moments—embodied in the work of such well-known figures such as Gregor Krause, Walter Spies, Antonin Artaud, and Miguel Covarrubias—Arcana's invocation of history exemplified the genealogical style of critique now prevalent in the European and American scholarship on Balinese arts and culture. Citing both Vickers and Picard, he argued, "We may trace an awareness that culture can work as a magnet for tourism in Bali to the times of the early Dutch colonial government" (Arcana 2006). Having excavated these precedents for Granoka's project, and having tied this history to contemporary economic relations, Arcana was then able to reveal it as, in essence, yet another iteration of Bali as "paradise created"—a phrase made famous by Vickers's (1989) eponymous history of Balinese cultural politics.[29]

Reviewing the criticisms—from Batan Nangka to *Kompas*—it would appear the Grebeg Aksara comes up wanting in respect of each of the three deployments of tradition that were discussed at the outset. First, both the high priests and Pak Kantor gave us reason to question its foundation in "positive" tradition. For the priests, this was on account of its unwarranted innovation and mishandling of letters; meanwhile, according to Kantor, the problem was its lack of grounding in established forms of social organization. Second, we have seen the unmasking of cultural pretense under Arcana's "genealogical" critique, which suggested that Granoka's efforts were not only cliché, but they also replicated themes historically associated with colonial exploitation. Finally, insofar as the event was judged inadequate to the task of repairing Bali's image in the wake of terrorist bombings, it similarly fell short as properly "operationalized" tradition.

Taken on their own terms, it may seem difficult to argue with these evaluations—that is, insofar as Granoka's project is at once innovative, indebted to colonial precedent, and ill suited to the task of economic recovery. Yet the question is whether we might be missing something by limiting ourselves to these three, admittedly influential understandings of Balinese tradition. What I would like to suggest is that we try coming at the problem from a different angle by examining the style of argumentation at play in this celebration of "the power of Balinese letters." For this we must have a closer look at some of the purposes that drove Granoka's organization of the event in the first place.

Konsép Sinkretisme Besar

In the weeks following the Grebeg Aksara, I had the opportunity to speak with Granoka at some length, both about the event itself and about the aims of his work more generally.[30] In the course of our conversations it became clear there was more to Granoka's project than his detractors may have thought. Centered on a sophisticated, if eclectic, vision for producing a "synergy" of artistic creativity, scholarship, and spiritual development, the Grebeg Aksara was meant to further what he called a "holistic transformation toward a new era" (I. *transformasi holistik menuju jaman baru*). On his account, the goal was nothing short of "revolution" (I. *revolusi*)—though it was a revolution directed to the "renewal" (I. *pembaruan*) as opposed to destruction (I. *penghancuran*) of the postcolonial state. Respinning the etymology of *revolution* through a Buddhistic idiom, he cast this as a "turning of the wheel of dharma" (I. *memutar roda dharma*).[31]

Granoka's erudition and intensity were often overwhelming, making it difficult at times to follow his leaps from one idea, thinker, or period of history to another. The links were frequently made through word play, drawing derivations and sequences of equations by homophony. For example, he exemplified what he described as the divinely transformative character of music by running in quick succession from Balinese gamelan orchestra notation (B. *ding, gending*) to an Indonesian epithet for divinity (I. *mahakuasa*) by way of German philosophy (G. *ding an sich*), culminating in the following sequence:

ding . . . gending . . . das ding . . . das ding an sich . . . dalam arti kuasa yang ma-hakuasa.

ding [the musical note] . . . musical phrase . . . the thing . . . the thing in itself . . . meaning the power that is all powerful [i.e., Tuhan, or "God"].

Although we spoke predominantly in Indonesian, with occasional comments in Balinese, his remarks would frequently incorporate words, phrases, and even entire sentences in any number of other languages—from Sanskrit and Kawi to English, German, and Latin. If his terminology was markedly heterogeneous, so too were the ideals he espoused—bringing together the works of the Old Javanese court poets with Vedic hymns and ancient Greek philosophy but also the writings of modern-day anthropologists, philologists, theologians, and authors of pop science.

My initial encounter with this unruly assemblage of languages, ideas, and authors was occasioned by my asking Granoka about his use of Balinese script in the Grebeg Aksara. When he had described his "revolutionary" intentions, I asked whether he meant to use Balinese *aksara* as an "instrument" (B. *prabot*) or "means" (B./I. *sarana*) to this end. He said no, the *aksara* are better understood as a form of what he called *sadana*.[32] Pushing our conversation back into Indonesian, he went on to explain that the idea of an "instrument" (I. *alat*) implied externality, something one used to accomplish an end that was both objective (I. *obyektif*) in character and fully formed from the outset. By contrast, the idea of *sadana* implied transformation of a more imminent nature—it "enters into us" (I. *masuk kedalam kita*) as the energy or capacity (I. *daya*) that "allows us to accomplish our aim." It may, moreover, transform our conception of the ends we envisage for our actions. He then played on the term *daya*, saying that *sadana* goes straight to one's heart (K. *hr-daya*), gradually transforming and developing by stages (I. *bertingkat*) its capacity for change and the realization of one's potential (I. *poténsi*).

So, how might we square this account of spiritual exercise and transformation with the various forms of disapproval I encountered in Batan Nangka? Was it simply that the sophistication of Granoka's project was lost on the villagers? Alternatively, were they right in thinking he was "out of touch"? Could it be both? Or perhaps neither?

Granoka seemed all too aware that his efforts were widely misunderstood and often criticized. Having discussed his work with his former schoolmates and colleagues, my sense was that he had difficulty finding acceptance—first in his home village of Buda Keling, where his ideas were never taken entirely seriously, and later at the university in Denpasar, where he was serially passed over for promotion. A friend from his schooldays in Sideman suggested it was this experience of rejection—and so a desire for recognition—that drove him to strike out on his own.[33] I believe it may also have been in part for this reason that he took such care in answering my questions. In response to my asking when he had first thought of organizing an event like the Grebeg Aksara, he gave me a book entitled *Cultural Reincarnation* (I. *Reinkarnasi Budaya*) that he compiled in 2007 and that he said gave a more comprehensive account of his "vision and mission" (I. *visi dan misi*).[34] During one of our meetings at his home in Denpasar, we looked through the book together, discussing the diagrams and photographs that were juxtaposed with text and other forms of writing in various scripts—Roman (or "Latin") and Balinese for the most part, but also a modified form of Devanāgarī and even a few Chinese characters. Rather like our conversations, the book brought together an almost unbelievably wide range of materials—citing authors, languages, and themes that could in no way be said to constitute a "naturally" cohesive whole. In this regard, there was a notable similarity between Granoka's remarks, his book, and the performance of the Grebeg Aksara. They each appeared to exemplify a style of explication that was directed to accomplishing a particular end; and this end was articulated with reference to an eclectic, yet somehow regular, assemblage of precedents. With an eye to the temporality of tradition, I would like to reflect briefly on each of these aspects in turn—that is, the way in which current circumstance is addressed with reference both to authorized precedent and to a vision for the future.

Of Crisis and Critique

Granoka described contemporary Bali as beset by what he called a "multidimensional crisis" (I. *krisis multisudut*) that was destabilizing everything from the tourism economy and local government to artistic creativity, religion, and morality.[35] He likened the situation to the story of the demon Kala, who swallowed the moon and caused an eclipse—a common metaphor for the benightedness of our times. He explained that it is unclear how one can live virtuously (B. *mayasa*) and effect positive change in an age of darkness

(I. *jaman kala, kegelapan*). Although the eclipse itself may be impermanent, its effects are unforeseeable and often irreversible. By way of example he pointed out that, despite the façade of modern convenience and prosperity in the island's more affluent areas, the institutions that sustain day-to-day life are on the verge of collapse from deep-seated corruption and a lack of substantive purpose and accountability. He explained, for instance, that in Bali today it is likely one will be arrested as a "suspect"—and forced to pay a bribe—if one stops to report an automobile accident by the side of the road; similarly, university students are often expected to present their supervisor with additional (illicit) "fees" before they are allowed to graduate; and the leading local newspaper demands payment for covering significant local events. He explained these are but a few examples of a wider failure to establish the institutions required for a stable and prosperous life. Under the circumstances, it is perhaps unsurprising that efforts to work through established channels to cultivate shared goods ultimately turn out to be counterproductive—that is, insofar as they legitimize and perpetuate the very institutions that are seen to be at the root of the problem. This has been all the more frustrating following the post-Suharto reform movement's inability to deliver on its promises of transparency and good governance. However laudable were the calls for regional autonomy and democratization, for many the most readily apparent consequence of "reform" has been financial uncertainty.

Granoka was clearly, in some sense, arguing for a return to tradition. But he was unimpressed with popular calls to defend Balinese religion and culture under the aegis of Ajeg Bali (see chapter 2), which he saw as a distraction that would lead to "stagnation and mental atrophy" (I. *stagnan atrofi penyusutan otak*). He was equally distraught at the state of the university, which, though notionally the seat of critical enquiry and reflection, had come to epitomize the indulgence and lassitude of a civil service devoted primarily to its own enrichment. It was, as he put it, a mediocracy that rewarded subservience, while much-needed innovation was stifled. A large-scale meltdown was imminent, he said. Yet the people most at risk were too busy trying to make ends meet to do anything about it, while those better positioned to work for reform had become disaffected or complacent. Granoka went on to rail against the irony of musicians shuttled off to play gamelan at the hotels for a pittance while foreign investors reaped millions on the food and alcohol consumed by guests attracted to the restaurants by the musicians'

performance. It would be reassuring, he said, to see this as somehow aber-
rant or unexpected. But these developments were the inevitable—and
foreseeable—coming to fruition (B. *karmapala*) of commodifying Balinese
culture—which, again ironically, was justified in terms of bringing the benefits of economic development to the entire island. He explained it was for
this reason that, although members of his Maha Bajra Sandhi group were
frequently invited to perform for cremation rites and temple ceremonies, he
insisted they refuse payment for their work—which was properly to be understood as a form of service (B. *ayahan*).[36]

Notwithstanding his emphasis on Bali, Granoka described these problems as but symptomatic of a broader predicament facing the nation as a
whole. This was in part the product of what he saw as Indonesia's failure to
become a civilized and prosperous nation (I. *bangsa yang beradab dan sejahtera*) following the defeat of the Dutch and the achievement of independence. Despite the formal sovereignty of the republic, he saw Indonesia as
still very much living "under the shadow of Eurocentrism" (I. *dibawah
bayang-bayang eurosentrisme*)—held back by its "formalism, rationalism and
instrumentalism." In his book Granoka has, moreover, described Indonesians
as "living like slaves" or "servants" (I. *budak*) to a foreign ideology (I. *ideologi
yang asing*), arguing that the upshot is that "we are still a 'colonized' people"
(I. *kita tetap adalah bangsa yang "terjajah"*). In the rush to keep up with modern life, and often simply just to survive, Indonesians have "forgotten their
culture"—which, on a more optimistic note, he said would prove the source
of their renewal. But a slavish return to the past will not suffice. Instead, he
has called for "reducing servitude" (I. *mengurangi perbudakan*) through "peaceful revolution"—which, as he put it, would entail "producing a new configuration by transforming a number of older elements" (I. *transformasi beberapa
elemén lama menjadi konfigurasi baru*). It was to this project of transformation
that the Grebeg Aksara was directed, drawing together familiar elements
in a new way in aid of a particular vision for the future.

Newsystematicsynthesis

As one might expect, Granoka's vision for the future was expressed in language at once deliberately and explicitly eclectic. For example, both in our
conversations and in his book, he frequently repeated the series *verum-*

bonum-pulchram, which he attributed to Plato, but then followed in San-skrit with *satyam-siwam-sundaram*, which he glossed in Indonesian as *benar-baik-indah*—for what is "true, good, and beautiful." Both the tripar-tite combination of terms and the serial juxtaposition of equivalents across languages figured recurrently in his remarks. Having observed Granoka speaking in public forums, it seemed that—as a sort of rhetorical flourish—this style of speech was directed to persuasion by means of erudition and terminological superfluity.[37] But I also believe these juxtapositions may have reflected his desire to exemplify what he called the "unification of all science and knowledge" (I. *penunggalan seluruh ilmu dan pengetahuan*)—for exam-ple, "of east and west, right brain and left brain, dialectic and nondialectic thought." This realization, he said, was a precondition for the prosperity of a nation that aspires to being not merely independent (I. *merdéka*) but also possessed of practical wisdom (I. *mahardika*).

He went on to explain that Indonesians were rightly proud for having achieved independence when they expelled the Dutch following the Second World War. But, as a nation, they were still held back—and "enslaved"—by their unquestioning fealty to the "rationalizing-mechanizing" proclivities of a "Cartesian-Newtonian stream of thought" (I. *aliran Cartesian-Newtonian*). Commenting specifically on the Grebeg Aksara, he said it was the Puputan of 1906 that stood out as an exemplar for Bali's resistance to a crudely ma-terialistic form of domination. The *keris* daggers on which members of the court had impaled themselves were, for Granoka, a symbol (I. *simbul*) of a self-penetrating awareness that would help them to stand steadfast in the face of a physically superior force. Through his efforts with the Maha Bajra Sandhi, he hoped to inculcate a desire to emulate their courage as a means of resisting both intellectual subjugation and the temptation of capitalist exploitation. Playing once again on relations of homophony, he said the aim was to lead Indonesia from independence to practical wisdom (I. *dari merdéka ke mahardika*), from syllabary to indestructability (I. *dari aksara ke a-ksara*),[38] from linguistics to metalinguistics (I. *dari linguistik ke metalin-guistik*), and from physics to metaphysics (I. *dari fisika ke metafisika*).

It was not always clear what he meant by each individual term or phrase. But the language of *movement* was crucial ("from X to Y"). These were not static ideals but rather trajectories. In contrast to the reifying tendencies of our received language of cultural criticism (centered on terms such as *struc-ture, society, culture, meaning, subject, logic, object of study*, etc.), Granoka's aims were articulated in terms of where one was "heading" (I. *menuju*), what one was "bringing to the fore" (I. *mengedepan*), "entering into" (I. *menapaki*), and "going through" or "surpassing" (I. *menembus*). We are, he said, at a "turning point" (I. *titik balik*) that requires the bold vision of a "pilgrim" (I. *peziarah*) who dares to look out onto the future and draw on whatever resources may be necessary—to bring about a newsystematicsynthesis (I.[?] *sintésasistematikbaru*). As his book explains, "This is the form of my refusal regarding the narrowly modernist spatial-formal way of doing things . . . [my approach is by contrast] comprehensive, fulfilling, and heading toward perfection (perfectly holistic). That is the future!" (2007, 102).

The Source of Human Being

The point of departure for Granoka's newsystematicsynthesis was the idea that language (I. *bahasa*) is the source of the human capacity for abstract thought (I. *pikiran abstrak*); it is this capacity that differentiates humans from animals. As he put it, it is language that makes us human from a "cognitive" perspective. But language is also the source of our very being, insofar as DNA is itself a language—what he called "genetish," a term borrowed from the British popular science writer Matt Ridley. More specifically, he saw the lettered proteins that make up DNA as a form of written syllabary not unlike that embodied in the Balinese script employed in rites of empowerment,[39] an idea he summed up with the Old Javanese phrase *wit ning sabda, kamulaning dadi wong*—which might be glossed as something like "the origin of speech, the source of becoming human."[40]

He argued that our mistake has been in limiting the analysis of language to the "semantic level" and our understanding of the cosmos to that of an overly rationalized "material-mechanistic" model—again, following the "Cartesian-Newtonian stream of thought." In so doing, we have overlooked the musical vibrations (I. *vibrasi*) that make up the foundational sound of the universe and so the source of our being—and of our *being human*. He explained in vaguely Pythagorean fashion that we must rediscover the linguistic ground of our *being* in the transformation of musical notes, the primordial sound that is the root of everything. We can return to this "perfect" language (I. *bahasa yang sempurna*; a phrase borrowed from Umberto Eco), which will provide the grounds for moving forward. As we have seen, he feels the world is in a state of crisis and we have reached a "turning point" from which we may begin anew. By taking an unabashedly "eclectic" approach, he argued, we will come to see that musical notes, genetic code, and the ancient letters of the mantric seed syllables are one. Accordingly, the means of transformation—and of redirecting ourselves toward perfection—will be "a synthesis of music, linguistics and mysticism."

Granoka described this transformation as occurring in three stages, which themselves are to take place within the third stage of a larger chronological scheme that links the ancient kingdoms of Sriwijaya and Majapahit with modern Indonesia.[41] Yet, albeit framed in Indonesian nationalist terms, Granoka's efforts toward transformation were made on behalf of "humanity" as a whole. This was enacted most explicitly in Maha Bajra Sandhi's world tours, as exemplified by the *ritus dunia* (world rite) performed at the 2004 Cultural Olympiad in Athens. As a form of spectacle, these events have garnered a degree of attention both within Indonesia and abroad. But what are we to make of Granoka's wider project and of the various criticisms I encountered in Batan Nangka? And how might this contribute to our thinking about argument, and so tradition, in relation to other, ostensibly more conventional uses of script and writing in Bali?

Some Precedents, Implications, and Questions

Drawing on MacIntyre, I suggested that tradition might usefully be understood as the temporal condition of practice, which will vary historically from one set of circumstances to another. Under this description, tradition would embody specifiable styles of orienting desire, and of arguing for a particular kind of future, with reference to an authorized version of the past. Taken in these terms, it probably would not make much sense to ask whether the Grebeg Aksara were authentically "traditional," as opposed to "innovative" or "modern."[42] The question of tradition would instead be directed to discerning its orientation in time. For instance, we have seen that the performance in Denpasar was part of a larger project directed to addressing a contemporary crisis and that it referenced both past and future in distinctive ways. What I wish to suggest is that, despite being distinctive, its mode of argumentation may not be quite so novel as it appears. And, what is more, I would argue that its resonances across other, more familiar aspects of life in

Bali may help us in thinking about the sorts of complexity we encountered in both the uses and acts of *aksara* (chapter 3) and the performance of the CRG (chapters 4 and 5).

We might begin with the way Granoka's project brought together an array of seemingly incongruous elements in an effort to effect a transformation of human agency and collective life. Where MacIntyre's account of tradition stressed victory and displacement, the Grebeg Aksara seemed to exemplify a rather different style of argumentation—one directed neither to vanquishment nor the elimination of inconsistency but rather to a transformative reassemblage. This style of articulation figured in his project, inter alia, thematically, terminologically, textually, orthographically, and soteriologically. But it was perhaps most readily evident in his juxtaposition of languages—with terms and phrases drawn from Indonesian, Kawi, Sanskrit, Balinese, English, Latin, German, and Chinese. These did not each exert equal force; Indonesian stands out clearly as the language of articulation, holding the others together in a seemingly tenuous relation of mutual intensification. And yet the other linguistic registers are not exactly passive, as each brings to bear its own peculiar force—evident, among other places, in the juxtaposition itself.[43] This may be seen (or heard) in compounds such as *sintésasistematikbaru* or in sequences including *spirit-ilmu-taksu* or *verum-bonum-pulchram/satyam-siwam-sundaram/benar-baik-indah*, but also in any of the many phrases and glosses regularly juxtaposed end to end in Granoka's speech and writing.[44] While fairly common in some forms of Kawi composition, where Old Javanese and Sanskrit "synonyms" are combined to form a single semantic unit,[45] this style of juxtaposition contrasts sharply with more standard forms of modern Indonesian syntax.

An analogous series of juxtapositions appears in Granoka's discursive linkage of disparate themes and authorities—from Indic and Javano-Balinese textual sources to Indonesian ideals of nationalism and development, western philosophy, pop science, colonial philology, and neo-Hinduism. Yet no particular effort was made to render explicit a relation of entailment or derivation. Rather, a welter of iconic names, objects, images, and phrases was drawn together and marshaled in exemplification of an overarching "synthesis" that was meant to embody performatively the transformation it describes.[46] Clifford Geertz's (1968, 117) evocative portrayal of an imaginary Indonesian university student, whom he cast as a synecdoche for the country's formative culture, makes for interesting comparison—particularly the student's "extremely complicated, almost cabalistic scheme in which the truths of physics, mathematics, politics, art, and religion are indissolubly, and to my mind indiscriminately, fused." Exemplars of such totalizing amalgamation may be found across many spheres of Indonesian public life—from spiritual movements like Pangestu, which presents itself as encompassing the distilled wisdom of the world's philosophical and religious traditions, to political strategies like Soekarno's Nasakom, which claimed to unify the foundational principles of nationalism (*Nas*), religion (*A*), and communism (*Kom*). In somewhat exaggerated form, the Grebeg Aksara seems to have pursued a similarly totalizing amalgamation through various forms of repetition, word play, and other elements characteristic of older practices of "text-building" in Java and Bali (Becker 1979)—including a propensity for neologism, alliteration, and assonance, as well as a degree of inattention to orthographic convention and consistency.

Here I would argue more broadly that Balinese are comparatively comfortable with—and even value positively—the productive tension that comes with the juxtaposition of opposed forces. This is very clearly evident in masked dance drama (B. *topéng pajegan*), where the action often centers on a ruler's efforts to bring together the disparate and potentially conflicting forces at play in his realm. This diegetic formula draws directly on the dynastic genealogies known as *babad*—which, though relatively recent in composition, embody ideals that appear to be much older.[47] As Vickers said of the sixteenth-century Balinese kingdom of Gélgél, "In the royal palace there was a great collection of all types of humanity, including albino dwarfs and foreigners, whose strangeness represented the forces of diversity and difference . . . which the king symbolically harnessed by including their potentially dangerous presence in the center of his powerful world" (1989, 44–45). One must be careful in extrapolating from ancient examples to the contemporary scene, even when Balinese themselves may be doing just that. But, with this caveat firmly in place, it is worth considering whether such a "harnessing" of difference might be indicative of a more general style of reasoning and argumentation extending beyond the contemporary Balinese scene.

Writing, Rationality, Translation

Taken together, these observations suggest a number of avenues for further thought. First, we might wish to reflect on possible connections to Amin Sweeney's (1987) argument for an "orally" derived style of composition and experience. Very briefly, Sweeney extrapolated from the scholarship on the Greek "literate revolution" (Havelock 1963, 1986; Lord [1960] 1971) to suggest that, while the introduction of literacy has had an important and demonstrable effect on the way Malays think, speak, and write, there is a "residual orality" evident in many aspects of Malay life.[48] This was premised on the idea that the practices associated with "literacy" bring with them new styles of thought and speech—characterized, for example, by analyticity and a separation of the knowing subject from the objects and circumstances in which acts of knowing take place.[49] He argued that this distantiation and analyticity sit in sharp contrast to the sensibilities of non-literate communication, as exemplified by oral composition in shadow theater and related performative styles. Sweeney described the latter as characterized by "distinctive motifemic patterning on the level of plot, character typing, themes, parataxis, repetition, copiousness, parallelisms, formulas, and formulaic expressions" (1987, 84). Several of these features have figured prominently in Granoka's project, much as they do in other aspects of Balinese linguistic practice. The question is how these tendencies are being transformed through collision with more recently emergent ways of thinking, speaking, and acting.

Second, whatever else we may wish to say of this style of argumentation, it is clearly at odds with the hierarchical and broadly Aristotelian ordering of reasons, virtues, and goods espoused by MacIntyre and those who have followed him.[50] But what are the implications of this disjuncture? Here we will need to think carefully about what may be a residual essentialism in MacIntyre's conception of "substantive" rationality. As Christopher S. Lutz succinctly put it, "MacIntyre distinguishes two kinds of rationality: formal and substantive. Formal rationality includes the sorts of bare logical rules on which philosophers generally agree. Within logic, there is really little matter for disagreement. Substantive rationality, however, includes all those determinations and judgments about good reasons and acceptable evidence that arise through tradition and convention, and here we do experience disagreement" (2004, 9). While MacIntyre has devoted at least three book-length monographs ([1981] 2010, 1988, 1990), and any number of articles, to demonstrating the plurality of these tradition-constituted/tradition-constitutive rationalities and how they are related historically to one another, the competition both within and between them is still said to be governed in principle by a "formal rationality" that minimally consists of the law of noncontradiction. Citing Aristotle in the opening sections of *Whose Justice? Which Rationality?*, he suggested that "anyone who denies that basic law of logic, the law of noncontradiction, and who is prepared to defend his or her position by entering into argumentative debate, will in fact be unable to avoid relying upon the very law which he or she purports to reject" (1988, 4). In effect he seems to be saying that granting contradiction entails a forfeiture of grounds for rational judgment. My point is that, while falling foul of noncontradiction may be fatal for a "contest of rationality" modeled on the Greek *agōn*, it is potentially less important for other kinds of argumentation, such as we have seen with both Granoka's project and at least some of the sources on which it has drawn. Without wishing to generalize unduly, Euro-American thought has often cast conflict—and "contradiction"—as a temporary state of affairs on the way to something else (e.g., reaching "consensus");[51] while, for Balinese, the push and pull of rival beings and forces has been seen as an ineliminable aspect of the world—something to be survived, accommodated, and potentially directed to a productive end, as opposed to being definitively overcome. This disjuncture might be taken to suggest that the distinction MacIntyre has drawn between substantive rationality and a more universal set of basic logical principles may need some rethinking. An interesting place to start would be comparison with his own characterization of Descartes's presumption to radical doubt, where a historically particular set of presuppositions was mistaken for the universal characteristics of Mind.[52]

Last there is the question of translation, an issue already raised in passing on several occasions. Discussion has proceeded to this point on the basis of a series of linkages between linguistic registers, implicitly equating one set of terms and phrases in English with another in Sanskrit, Kawi, Balinese, or Indonesian. At various points these linkages were explicitly problematized—as, for example, with "life" and *urip* in chapter 3; or the ideas of "religion," "culture," and "tradition" as they pertain to *agama, kebudayaan,* and *adat* in the present chapter. Yet, such instances aside, these linkages have more frequently been taken for granted than justified, often marked by little more than a parenthetical indication of the original language. Why might this matter? It must be borne in mind that any higher-order conclusions we wish to draw will rest squarely on the interpretation of specific utterances and actions, which will in turn presuppose a set of equivalences that we are in habit of calling "translations." So what exactly are we doing when we translate? Or when we presuppose such an equivalence? What does this aim to accomplish? And on what grounds are we proceeding? The following chapter takes these questions as its point of departure.

Chapter 7

Translational Indeterminacy

This affects all of us, man.
—Walter Sobchak

Much of what we take to be the subject matter of anthropology presupposes an act of translation. This includes most proximately our own translations from ethnographic encounters, literature, and other media. But, as emphasized in the recent scholarship on Southeast Asia, even our so-called primary materials often themselves already engender one or more acts of translation. This has included Islamic translations from Arabic to Malay or Javanese; Buddhists working between Pāli and Thai; Brahmins and others recasting Sanskrit in Old Javanese. The list could no doubt be extended indefinitely. And yet, setting regional specifics aside, one of the more general points to be taken is that translation—of one kind or another—has been a crucial factor in our ability to engage critically with the complexity of other people's lives. Reflecting back on the argument so far, the question is whether our increasingly nuanced attention to this complexity is matched by our theoretical grasp of translation as an aspect of critical enquiry.

In many ways, the book has been building to this point all along. Consider, for example, what we would have overlooked had we been content to follow the dictionary in equating Balinese *urip* with English "life" or Dutch "leven" (chapter 3); or had we taken *bhutakala* simply to be "demons" or "chthonic spirits" (chapter 4); or, again, the idea of *adat* as "tradition" (chapter 6). In each case my aim was to transform a facile assumption of linguistic "equivalence" into a more adequate account of language-in-use. But in what does this claim to "adequacy" consist? And on what foundations does it rest?

The Problem

The stakes may be higher than they appear. To state the problem briefly, insofar as our higher-level theorizing wishes to claim an empirical foundation, it must draw its evidence from the interpretation of specific utterances and actions. And this, in turn, brings into play various forms of contextualization, which themselves are commonly premised on a set of procedures we conventionally call translation. This would suggest that, if the idea of translation were to fail, so too would the intellectual edifice it supports. And yet it has proven exceedingly difficult to specify just what is meant by translation and how one knows when it has happened. This combination of procedural importance and theoretical imprecision has often occasioned a rather fuzzily justificatory logic, even among some of our more astute observers. Consider, for example, Edmund Leach: "The linguists have shown us that all translation is difficult, and that perfect translation is usually impossible. And yet we know that for practical purposes a tolerably satisfactory translation is always possible even when the original 'text' is highly abstruse" (1973, 772). Or, more recently: "It is ironic that exact translation is virtually impossible, but varieties of practically serviceable translation are everywhere" (Hanks 2014, 35). Similar remarks can be found throughout the anthropological literature on translation (cf. Crapanzano 2000, 133; Herzfeld 2003, 130). And, yet, forgoing translational "perfection" in favor of "serviceability" does not really solve the problem. Indeed, it begs a question of potentially wide-reaching import—namely, the critical intelligibility of one of our foundational concepts. So what are anthropologists and other ethnographers actually doing when they translate? How does one know when this has taken place? On what grounds can one judge its success? And with what consequences, both intended and otherwise?

In approaching the problem, it must be borne in mind that the very idea of translation is fundamentally *catachretic*—constituted by a metaphor irreducible to a more "literal" means of expression.[1] So, in designating a "movement between languages," there was never a moment when the term itself—to *translate*, or "to bear across"—was nonmetaphorical.[2] And I would argue that the importance of this point cannot be stressed enough. It may be the case that all societies "translate differently," as Ronit Ricci (2011) has rightly emphasized in her study of Islamic conversion across the Indian Ocean. But from what "perspective"—to use another nonneutral metaphor—do we take stock of this translational difference? If the idea itself is irreducibly metaphorical, there can be no "degree zero" of translation, no way of stating clearly and distinctly what translation *is* apart from stating what it is *like*—that is, without importing a set of comparisons—that are themselves *not* translation—in order to help us point "metaphorically" to what we are unable to state "literally." Setting aside for now the wider applicability of this point, it makes our choice of metaphor extremely important—which is to say, *consequential* for how we imagine the world and the conditions under which it may be represented and transformed. So, having begun by suggesting that our understanding of translation may be beholden to metaphor, what sort of metaphor are we dealing with? And why might it matter?

Etymologically, the idea of translation as a "carrying" or "bearing across"—quite literally a *transfer*—is an example of what Michael J. Reddy (1979) called "the conduit metaphor" for communication—the notion that communicating entails the movement of a subtle substance through space as it travels from one mind to another. This, he argued, is the master trope in our language about language—and a woefully misleading trope at that. Yet we find iterations of this metaphor in everything from popular understandings of globalization to philological conceptions of textual transmission and even cultural studies' theories of mass media. In each case, a substantialized message—be it culture, text, or the dominant ideology—is seen to travel from one place, space, or time to another, undergoing transformation as a consequence of its mediated journey. So, to what extent are prevailing understandings of translation determined by this metaphor of a *carrying across*? Are we still captivated—that is to say, critically *captured*—by this catachresis?

In drawing attention to the metaphorical character of translation as a critical concept, one of the central presuppositions that I wish to query is that of *totality*—in our case, the totality notionally embodied in the "languages" or "cultures" out of which and into which we presume to "translate," or to *move between*. Inspired by the tradition of the German Romantics, as often mediated by the writings of Friedrich Schleiermacher, translation theorists tend to stress the importance of recognizing the relationship between language and the broader cultural milieu of which it is taken to be part. And yet, while anthropological theories of culture are increasingly dynamic and keyed to conflict,[3] a review of the recent scholarship would suggest that our understanding of culture as it pertains to translation remains comparatively static and keyed to consensus.

We might look, for example, to a series of recent publications in *Hau*, the online journal of ethnographic theory. A sequence of essays by William F. Hanks and Carlo Severi (2014), G.E.R. Lloyd (2014), and Amiria J. M. Salmond (2013, 2014), among others, have engaged arguments from a wide range of disciplines to reflect on the importance of translation for our understanding of ethnographic encounter. Here the focus has been on the commensurability of languages and the conditions under which translation may be seen to take place—and, as importantly, to what effect. For good reason, special attention has been given to Willard van Orman Quine's notion of translational indeterminacy—the possibility, as he put it, that "manuals for translating one language into another can be set up in divergent ways, all compatible with the *totality* of speech dispositions, yet incompatible with one another" (1960, 27; emphasis mine).[4] The argument from "radical translation," as Quine called it, is widely recognized for the doubt that it casts on ethnographic common sense—and, more specifically, for the way it has problematized the grounds on which we might adjudicate between conflicting interpretations—and so translations—of the utterances and actions that we encounter "in the field." While anthropological responses to Quine's argument have varied greatly,[5] commentators tend to concur in seeing his position as marking a skeptical vanishing point for interpretive certainty in the commensuration between languages. This has, in effect, served as the "strong" argument against taking translatability for granted.[6] And yet the interesting thing to note here is that, albeit radical in one sense, even Quine's notion of "radical translation" appears to presuppose the unity, determinacy, and systematicity of the languages or "conceptual schemes" (or "theories") between which translation is said to take place.

Looking beyond the anthropological engagement with Quine to social theorists in other fields, we find similarly totalizing presuppositions underpinning remarks on translation from Alasdair MacIntyre (1988) in *Whose Justice? Which Rationality?*[7] and even Judith Butler (2009) in her contribution to the symposium on the question, "Is critique secular?" Where MacIntyre relied on "shared cultural schema" for translating between moral traditions (1988, 22), Butler invoked the notion of "competing moral frameworks" in theorizing, as she called it, "the semantic operation of 'blasphemy' as a term" (2009, 103–4).[8] The point in citing these examples is that, across a range of disciplines, we seem to have a degree of regularity in the way deliberate theorization vis-à-vis language and culture tends to emphasize transformation, conflict, and contingency, whereas less guarded remarks on translation appear by contrast to presuppose stasis, coherence, and determinacy. So, for instance, both Butler's (1999) performative critique of gender identity and MacIntyre's account of moral tradition as "an argument extended through time" (cf. chapter 6) were directed explicitly to unsettling foundationalist assumptions in their respective fields. But, when it came to interpreting specific actions and utterances, the demands of contextualization required a more stable foundation. And so procedural necessity trumped theoretical aspiration. Given the extent to which even some of our most radically detotalizing theorists appear to fall back on a conservative account of totality when it comes to translation, I would like to ask what it might mean to translate on the basis of a more dynamic and open-ended conception of language and culture.

In approaching the problem, I shall focus in particular on a pair of closely related terms of Sanskritic derivation that are in common use both in conversational Balinese and in the national language of Indonesian. These terms are *agama* and *atma*. And they are often simply glossed in English as "religion" and "soul," respectively. But I would like to suggest that closer attention to actual usage, and the specific circumstances under which this usage has changed, may help to highlight some of what we are missing when we translate on the basis of such a reified conception of language—that is, language as a "system," as a "framework," or as the manifestation of a "shared cultural scheme." So, while my emphasis will be on these two terms, the real target is the wider circumstances in which they are being used—and, more particularly, what understanding of *translation*—as a critical procedure—those circumstances may rightfully be said to warrant.

Agama: The Transformation of Religion and Polity

Let us begin with *agama*, the term that is most commonly translated into English as "religion."[9] The use of this term has undergone an important transformation over the past fifty years as a result of the institutionalized cultivation of new forms of agency and community through state-sponsored programs for modernization and national development. As Michel Picard (2011b) has noted recently, this is but one of the many transformations in *agama*'s long history of usage—from early Śaivait and Buddhist associations in Sanskrit and Old Javanese to various Islamic and Christian uses of the term, often in dialogue with colonial and postcolonial programs for religious reform. These latest developments have emerged out of a wider-reaching set of processes described by Robert Hefner as *religionization*—"the reconstruction of a local or regional spiritual tradition with reference to religious ideals and practices seen as standardized, textualized and universally incumbent on believers" (2011, 73). The nature of this transformation has varied greatly from one place and time to another. And my first example comes from recent debates over the redrafting of constitutional regulations (B. *awig-awig*) for the ward of Batan Nangka.

Giving and Receiving

In 2010 it was decided that Batan Nangka needed a new constitution—properly typed up in Microsoft Word and brought into alignment with the regulations for the wider administrative village in which the ward is located. A local man known for his facility with language—and his knowledge of computers—was chosen to prepare the new document, which he then submitted to the ward assembly for approval.

From a procedural perspective, the new document was largely consistent with its predecessor, a handwritten notebook detailing the obligations and privileges associated with membership in the ward. As with the handwritten version, the new document specified those occasions on which one must contribute—in both labor and kind—to collective endeavors, such as temple ceremonies, weddings, and cremations. So, for example, on the death of a neighbor, one is required to contribute a meter of white cotton cloth, a kilo of uncooked rice, and 5,000 rupiah for use in the funeral. Then, at set times, a man and woman from each household in the ward is obligated to report to the home of the deceased in order to help prepare food, offerings, and ritual equipment for the cremation. This can be an onerous responsibility, not least for the growing number of Balinese whose livelihood is tied to salaried labor and regular work hours—an issue to which I shall return in just a moment.

Reading through the earlier version of the regulations closely, one sees that membership in the ward was defined primarily by participation in these ongoing relations of but loosely calculated giving and receiving. To be sure, many of the rites and ceremonies that make up the collective work of the ward are now associated with the state bureaucratic conception of Hindu religiosity, or *Agama Hindu*. But there was nothing in the original regulations to suggest that a Muslim, Buddhist, or Christian could not become a full member of the ward. And, in fact, at least one Muslim man—a masseur from Central Java—had married into the community some ten years before. Despite remaining Muslim—at least on his state identity card (KTP, or I. *kartu tanda penduduk*)—he and his wife participated fully in the ostensibly "religious" activities of the community.

The Idea of Agama

If the new regulations were largely consistent with their handwritten precursors, that is not to say there were not some important differences. Perhaps the most sharply contrasting point came in the opening section, where the new document offered a clear statement of its jurisdiction. Whereas the handwritten constitution—from previous years—had begun with a list of penalties for failing to fulfill one's obligations, the very first line in the new regulations defined ward membership in positive terms of religious affiliation. Now, in order to be a member of the ward community, one must *maagama Hindu*—which is to say, one must have Hinduism as one's *agama*. Clearly I am not the first to point out that, like "religion" itself, contemporary uses of the term *agama* have a long and complex genealogy; and that our use of "religion" to translate *agama*—as if there were a one-to-one correspondence between these two terms—conceals at least as much as it reveals.[10] But, if "religion" does not provide an adequate gloss, what then is this thing called *agama*? And, with an eye to how we might translate the term—or even set about understanding its use—of what consequence were the new regulations in Batan Nangka?

It turns out the language employed in the new ward regulations was borrowed from other, similar documents currently in circulation on the island. So this was not simply one man's innovation. Yet, looking to other published ward regulations,[11] it is also clear that the constitutional specification of membership in terms of religious affiliation is both new and at odds with other aspects of the document. And this is my central reason for focusing on this example. What I wish to suggest is that, with the introduction of these new elements, the regulations for Batan Nangka have given expression to a more widely felt tension between two rival models of polity,[12] each of which understands *agama*—in its relation to the common good—in a fundamentally different way.

Until relatively recently, to say one was *ma-agama* in Bali was to say that one had undergone the life-cycle rites that render their subject fully human—what in Balinese we might call *manusa*. And, at least in this regard, to be human is to engage in relations of reciprocal obligation with others, through precisely the forms of debt and repayment that we find described in the ward regulations. Here religion—as *agama*—is part of the wider articulation and pursuit of shared goods.[13] It is moreover a collective endeavor that is simultaneously constitutive both of its subject and of its community of practice. Crucially, under this description, *agama* is not simply *linked* to polity contingently. Rather, the rites that make up *agama* are at once the precondition and expression of the ward's well-being as a complex agent. To be an operative member of the ward, then, is, by definition, to *maagama*. And so, in the original document—that is, in the handwritten version—there was no need to state explicitly to whom the regulations applied. To engage in these practices was to be a member of the ward; and to be a member of the ward was to engage in these practices.[14]

Another Other

The problem is that such a pragmatic understanding of polity is ill equipped to deal with the realities of life in modern-day Batan Nangka—which, like similar communities throughout the Global South, has undergone substantial transformation through the work of national development and relations with transnational capital. I have already mentioned in passing the challenges posed by salaried labor and regular work hours. As often as not, those with gainful employment choose to pay the nominal fine—usually no more than a few thousand rupiah, around twenty-five cents—for their abstention from collective efforts, such as road maintenance but also assistance with temple anniversaries and life-cycle rites. Here, the ongoing relationship of reciprocal obligation has been replaced by a one-off payment into the coffers of the ward, which—at least in this regard—has come to function more as an administrative unit than as a community of practice.

However, beyond the challenges posed by wage labor, there is also the related question of "outsiders" and "newcomers" to the community—those *penduduk pendatang*, as they are called, for whom the new regulations now stipulate special land taxes and other pecuniary obligations, in place of the collective labor and material contributions traditionally extracted from members of the ward. It is at least in part in trying to address such "strangers in their midst" that *agama*-as-religion has emerged as a means of defining the limits of community.

It must be emphasized that, from a legal perspective, it has long been possible for nonlocals—and even non-Balinese—to buy, or to lease, local land and to build new homes and other structures in among the houseyards of a given ward community. In recognition of this possibility, a formal distinction was drawn—at the provincial level—between full, or what is called "customary" (I. *adat*), membership in the ward, on the one hand, and administrative membership (I. *dinas*), on the other. To join as an "administrative" member requires little beyond paperwork and fees. One simply fills out the forms and pays up. And then one is free to go about one's business, with little or no subsequent contact with the surrounding community, if one is so inclined. By contrast, in joining as a "customary," or *adat*, member of the ward, one commits—at least in principle—to participating fully in the relations of reciprocal obligation that have traditionally constituted the ward as a community of practice. This legal distinction between *adat* and *dinas* membership has helped to address the conceptual problem of "newcomers" and their position vis-à-vis the ward community. But it does nothing to address the fact that the demands of wage labor and regular work hours have made it more expedient to pay fines than to honor one's "customary" obligations. So a new principle of inclusion—and so exclusion—was required.

And, with this, we come full circle, back to the opening section of the new regulations, where it is stated that one must have Hinduism as one's *agama* in order to become a member of the ward community.

What I wish to suggest is that the introduction of religious difference into the new ward regulations—as a defining principle of membership—was an attempt to replace an outdated model of polity with something more attuned to prevailing socioeconomic circumstances. When the new ward regulations for Batan Nangka were drawn up, the idea of *Agama Hindu* was deployed as a means of addressing the displacement of traditional practice wrought by an economy increasingly beholden to capital. But how might we describe these transformations critically? And, with specific reference to the idea of *agama*, what implications will follow for our conventional understanding of translation, grounded, as it is, in a relatively static conception of language and culture?

Religious Differences

We might begin by reviewing briefly what has taken place. I have suggested that, as a complex of practices, *agama* was traditionally constitutive of both its subject and its community. And, in an important sense, this is still the case. But, in the new regulations, the nature of *agama* has changed and, as a consequence, so too have the kinds of agency, polity, and practice that are associated with it. In the past, one had to *maagama* in order to be a member of the ward, and the opposite of *maagama* was to be unintelligible as a social being. To be without *agama* was in a sense to be less than human. Now, by contrast, one must not simply *maagama*. Rather, one must *maagama Hindu* in order to be a member of the ward; and the opposite of *maagama Hindu* is not to be subhuman but rather to be from another *agama*—most conspicuously *Agama Islam*. For, without wishing to put too fine a point on it, one of the crucial aspects of being Hindu in contemporary Bali is being non-Muslim. But positively speaking, then, what does it mean to *maagama Hindu*?

Here the ward relies on the regulations for the wider administrative village, which define Hinduism in terms of what are called the *Panca-sraddha*—the five pillars of belief originally formulated as part of an attempt to garner state recognition for *Agama Hindu* in the late 1950s.[15] These articles of confession include a belief in one god; the immortal soul, or *atma*,[16] to which we will return in a moment; the law of karma; rebirth; and final release, or *mokṣa*. On this account, *agama* is cast as fundamentally a matter of individual conscience and adherence to the teachings associated with one of the five, or now six, communities of faith—or *umat agama*—that, taken together, are seen to compose the organically integrated nation. This is the ideal of *Bhinneka Tunggal Ika*, or "Unity in Diversity," the Indonesian state motto. In contrast to the unremitting particularism of the earlier version of the ward regulations, one's *agamic* obligations—on this state bureaucratic account—are primarily to abstract principles such as monotheism, social solidarity, and intergroup tolerance. This is, in a word, a distinctly Indonesian—one might even say New Order—model of religiosity.

Returning to the original question, what does all this mean for our understanding of translation? With respect to *agama* in particular, to argue that the idea of "religion" might be contested hardly seems controversial.[17] Postcolonial anthropology has been anything but inattentive to issues of antagonism and power. And both cultural and critical media studies have, for their part, long stressed the idea of culture as a "site of struggle." Yet, for all this attention to conflict, when it comes to translation, our theorizing tends to fall back onto a set of presuppositions that are rather closer in spirit to an older and markedly more conservative understanding of culture as *collective representation*. The terminology has been updated. Where we once had static cultures, codes, and *Weltanschauungen*, we now have Michael Silverstein's "linguistic ideologies" (1979), MacIntyre's (1988) and Sherry B. Ortner's (1990) "cultural schemas," Eduardo Viveiros de Castro's "ontologies" (2004), and Butler's "moral frameworks" (2009)—all as "embodied and expressed" in language. This may appear to be generalizing unfairly, for the latter terms were coined in service to a wide range of projects, often entailing quite different theoretical commitments. But, crucially, they have all embodied—in one way or another—a more generally totalizing desire for contextualization as a form of interpretative grounding. Their differences aside, it is this shared commitment to totality that I wish to question.

Of course, many have remained attentive to the possibility of "gaps" or "silences between languages" and the idea that translation is always at once "deficient" and "exuberant"—simultaneously saying "more" and "less" than the original.[18] Variations on these themes from José Ortega y Gasset and Walter Benjamin are anything but uncommon in the literature on translation. And yet, even when the malleability of the so-called target language is acknowledged—say, for example, in the coining of neologisms (Hanks 2014) or Asad's oft-cited notion of "strong and weak languages" (1986a)[19]—there seems to be comparatively little attention to the implications that might follow from ongoing transformation within the "source language" itself—that is, the language undergoing translation, such as we have seen in the example of *agama* in Bali.

As the Russian critic V. N. Vološinov argued, language is always on the run—it is not a thing but rather a happening. Indeed, our very notion of language as a system is, as he noted, "obtained by way of abstraction . . . from the real units that make up the stream of speech—from utterances."[20] He went on to explain that this abstraction was the answer to a practical problem—as he put it, "European linguistic thought formed and matured over concern with the cadavers of written languages; almost all its basic categories, its basic approaches and techniques were worked out in the process of reviving these cadavers" (1973, 71). And our received understanding of translation, I would argue, is no exception. But, leaving aside the "cadavers," what if we wish to attend to the *life* of language? How does one translate—or even more generally interpret—a term like *agama* that is always already on the hoof, bouncing between rival projects for the transformation of collective life?

Returning to our example, what we seem to have are two iterations of *agama*, each of which is articulated in terms of a different conception of polity. And these conceptions of polity are, in turn, defined by contrasting ideals of both personal and shared goods—and the means best suited to their cultivation. On the face of it, the disjuncture seems clear enough. Yet, despite the account that I have just given, it must be emphasized that Batan Nangka has not simply—or unproblematically—shifted from a "traditional" to a state bureaucratic understanding of religion. Rather, the contrasting models of *agama* that I have described are perhaps better understood as *two opposed forces* in an ongoing tug-of-war that is at once *about* and *constitutive of* the ward as a small-scale polity. The conflict is carried out to a certain extent through public debate in the ward assembly itself, over such things as the new regulations.[21] But I hasten to add that this conflict should not be seen as taking place between prediscursive individuals—as "agents" or "stakeholders"—struggling to assert their rights or to maximize their interests. Rather, what I wish to suggest is that the conflict is playing out at a more fundamental level, over the constitution of agency and community through which projects of personal and collective transformation become possible in the first place. In other words, it is the very nature of human *being in the world*—and the capacity to *transform the world*—that is in flux and up for grabs.

Atma: Part-Time Anthropology

To develop this idea a little further, I would now like to turn to our second term, *atma*. Derived from the Sanskrit *ātman*, the term *atma* has a range of uses in contemporary Indonesian and Balinese, as well as textual precedents in both Old Javanese and various forms of literary Balinese. It tends to be glossed in the Anglophone scholarship as "soul," "spirit," or "self," often without further qualification.[22] One of the more insightful comments on the term comes from Linda Connor in one of her early studies of Balinese healers. In this account, *atma* figured as one of several "elements" that together make up what she called "the Balinese view of personality" (1982a, 262). The passage itself stands out from the rest of the text, almost as if it were a glossary entry:

> **The Soul**
> The soul (*atma*) which most closely corresponds to concepts of "soul" in Western European Christian traditions is yet another, more ethereal component of the human. This microcosmic manifestation of the highest divinity . . . is the focus of elaborate mortuary rites rather than meticulous attention in everyday ritual contexts. Cremation ceremonies release and purify the *atma* to the point where it may fuse again with the godhead. (1982a, 262)

Connor's ethnography is undoubtedly among the more nuanced studies of social life on the island. Yet what I wish to suggest is that, both in her account and more generally, the common translation of *atma*—as "soul," "spirit," or "self"—and the way that it has been attributed to Balinese as part of a "cultural schema" or "religious worldview," obscure both the complexity and potential for ambiguity that are characteristic of day-to-day life on the island. And this, I would argue, is because Balinese understandings of personal agency are caught between conflicting anthropologies—a point perhaps best exemplified by way of a brief vignette, which I will call "The Girl with Two Souls."[23]

The Girl with Two Souls

It began one evening when I found myself typing up the official paperwork to legitimate a marriage by capture (B. *malegandang*). In actuality it was more of a mock capture (B. *ngambis*) or partial elopement. But, so far as the bride's family were concerned, the wedding was being performed against their will. The village headman, who was also my landlord, said he needed the paperwork as soon as possible. And, as it happened, I was the only one around with a working laptop and printer. As if assisting in a contentious elopement were not already interesting enough, the bride in this case was a man. For, in Bali, inheritance, both material and otherwise, generally runs down the male line. But, when a family has not been blessed with a son, a daughter may become a jural male and marry a man, who in turn is brought into the family as a woman—much in the way any other woman joins the family of her husband upon marriage. Their male offspring are then recognized as potential heirs to the family's houseyard, rice land, and other material possessions—and the male line carries on by way of the daughter, who is now formally recognized as a son.

In this particular case the couple decided to elope because the young man's family—I shall call him Gdé—strongly objected to his moving away, and this apparently for several reasons. As a conscientious and hardworking mechanic, he had been an important source of income for his family, often covering, I was told, for his father's gambling debts. And Gdé's father, for his part, claimed their descent group did not permit men to marry out to other clans. This, he said, would humiliate the family. And, indeed, the father even threatened suicide.

Now, here it is pertinent to note that the young woman in question—we will call her Dani—was one of four daughters. And so, in principle, any of her three sisters could have taken her place as the heir to her father's line by marrying a man who was willing to join the family as a woman. Moreover, Dani herself had been romantically involved for some seven years with another young man, whom many in the ward had expected her to marry—but with whom she had precipitously broken off relations in order to secure the marriage with Gdé. And this was because, unlike her prior boyfriend, Gdé was willing to join the family as a woman.[24]

So, given that Dani was already involved in a long-standing relationship and moreover had three unmarried sisters, any of whom might equally well have taken on the responsibility, why was such a contentious marriage contracted with Gdé? And what could all this possibly have to do with our understanding of *atma* and the problem of translation?

As I later learned, the family had decided that, of the four sisters, Dani was the one who would have to remain at home and become a jural male. And this was for a rather unusual reason. A couple of years beforehand, her father had experienced a series of illnesses, including a persistent back problem for which he was unable to find a cure. As one often does, the family consulted a spirit medium, through which they learned that the previous owner of the houseyard had not been given the requisite postcremation rites. And this oversight—that is, an oversight on the part of the houseyard's *previous* inhabitants—was seen to be the cause of her father's perduring illness. Although some members of the family remained skeptical, they had received further support for the diagnosis from a second spirit medium.[25] And so, on the advice of yet a third adviser—this time a brahmin priest—they installed a special shrine in the family temple where they might honor the former inhabitant of the houseyard and *his* ancestors alongside their own.

This was in keeping with a detailed request for specific offerings, as relayed by the spirit medium. But, perhaps more to the point, the deceased had also asked that Dani herself remain in the houseyard, rather than marrying out. And this was because, the deceased claimed—again through the medium—that, in addition to carrying on the line of her father, Dani was also the only remaining heir to his *own* line—which, in the absence of proper funerary rites, had remained tied to the houseyard in which Dani's family was now living. So, as the descendant of two separate male lines, Dani was in effect a girl with two souls. Or at least that was how I understood it when Dani first recounted to me the circumstances of her marriage and the need for her to remain at home. But, when I asked for confirmation, neither she nor her father was comfortable with the idea of multiple, or even split, *atma*—which, it may be recalled, are supposed to be the focus of funerary rites. Indeed, there was no readily available Balinese or Indonesian term for what it was that she embodied doubly. The Sanskrit-derived word *purusa* is a Balinese technical term for the male principle embodied in one's descendants.[26] But, used as a substantive, it is not an easy fit for this particular case. Dani embodied (B. *maraga*) the *purusa* both of her father and of the previous inhabitant of the houseyard. But she did not "have" (B. *ngelah/ maduwé*) two *purusa*, any more than she had two *atma*.

So here it seemed that the Sanskritic spiritual anthropology simply did not apply.[27] Yet, as subsequent conversation made clear, there were other Balinese terms associated with something akin to "rebirth," or perhaps "reincarnation," that were a better fit. Among the terms I encountered, *numitis* is perhaps the most telling. Though fairly common in contemporary Balinese, the word is originally an Old Javanese construction derived from the base word *titis*, which is usually associated with the movement of water. In this idiom, one's descendants might be said to flow or even to "sprinkle" from one generation to the next. This is in keeping with the more general notion of a genetic relationship through "water" (B. *yéh*)—red for women (B. *kama bang*), white for men (B. *kama putih*)—which flows through the generations like water running down an irrigation canal. If the Sanskritic term *atma* seems to denote a unitary, bounded, and personal "soul thing," then the language of water—and of sprinkling or flowing—lines up rather more neatly with the idea of a fluid and amorphous "soul stuff" (Wolters 1999, 93–95), which may be more amenable to quantification than simple absence or presence. So how might this affect our understanding of *atma*?

If the general lesson to be taken is that linguistic usage—and so the effort toward translation—is inextricable from circumstance, then the more specific ethnographic point would be that Dani's predicament presupposed a process of ancestral return to embodiment, and to life, that was not unproblematically commensurate with the unique and bounded soul presupposed in both scholarly and state bureaucratic understandings of *atma*—that is to say, in the commentary of scholars such as Connor and in doctrinal formulations such as the *Panca-sraddha*, or "five pillars of belief," already discussed in relation to the state bureaucratic articulation of *agama*.

Yet, all that having been said, at least *sometimes* the notion of a personal *atma* is crucial for Balinese self-understandings of personhood and agency. It just did not happen to be pertinent on this particular occasion. Extrapolating from this point, I would argue more broadly that Balinese persons are situationally constituted and reconstituted according to multiple and not-always-commensurate anthropologies.[28] However, unlike the situation with *agama*, "the girl with two souls" does not simply exemplify a disjuncture between ideals old and new. For *atma* itself is not without premodern precedent, as I noted in passing with reference to Old Javanese and Balinese literary usage. Rather, when it comes to personhood, my best guess is that Balinese tradition probably never had the sort of "coherence" that is presupposed in prevailing accounts of translation—though I would be quick to add that I doubt if any other tradition ever did either. But how then are we to know when one or another "conception" of agency, and of human being, is in play? Is it even safe to assume that Balinese themselves would be certain at any given time? And, if not, what does this say for the nature of action, and of utterance, as something to be "translated"? What sort of "conceptual scheme" or "moral framework" could account for such seeming indeterminacy?

When Totality Fails

These are difficult questions, for which definitive answers may remain elusive. But I would like to end by reflecting briefly on a series of observations pertaining to the ethnography and the broader implications that follow from the critique of translation. The first is that Balinese themselves seem to be aware of, and even to exploit, something similar to what Quine described in terms of multiple translation manuals.[29] In addition to *agama* and *atma*, there are any number of other terms and phrases that are caught between conflicting projects for the transformation of both individual and collective life. To cite but a single example, there is a wide range of rites performed in Bali today that are directed to generating a condition that is described as *suci*, both in conversational Balinese and in Indonesian. We saw earlier that, as the aim of ritual action, *suci* is usually glossed in the scholarly literature as a "state of purity."[30] And this is largely in keeping with its Sanskritic etymology. In casual conversation one is likely to have such a philologically grounded understanding of *suci* confirmed by one's Balinese interlocutors. And this is in no small part because that is what they were taught in school—namely, that ceremonial rites are directed to the production of spiritual purity under the rubric of *suci*. This is *suci* as *murni* (I.): pure, clean, and genuine; and *suci* as *tidak tercemar* (I.): uncontaminated or unpolluted.

However, if one listens a little more carefully and pays attention to the broader aims of the rites in question, and the circumstances under which they are actually performed, one begins to see that *suci*—as often as not—also points beyond ideals of purity to a range of other goals that are different from, and even antagonistic to, the model of purity-through-ritual-action that is taught as a principle of state Hinduism. In actual usage, *suci* often appears to be equated with something closer to what Balinese call *sakti*, another

Sanskrit loanword that, in Bali, has come to be associated with various forms of empowerment, invulnerability, and efficacy.[31] So in casting ceremonial rites as an act of *menyucikan,* or *nyuciang* in Balinese—that is, as a *making suci*—one can, in effect, avoid being a good Hindu by being a good Hindu. One can be seen to do one thing while doing another at the same time. That is, one can be a docile subject of state religiosity while simultaneously fortifying oneself against attack and perhaps even procuring power for an assault on one's adversaries. To put it another way, the possibility of multiple translation manuals has become part of a wider Balinese "art of not being governed" (Scott 2009). My suspicion is that a similar play between linguistic and cultural registers may be the rule, as opposed to the exception, through much of Southeast Asia.

But, if the first observation was that Balinese exploit an almost Quinean indeterminacy in the movement between languages, my second point is that, from a critical ethnographic perspective, Quine did not go far enough. I began by suggesting that even our most radically detotalizing social theorists tend to fall back on a totalizing conception of language and of culture when they are forced to think about translation. This totality has taken many forms—from the idea of language "itself" as a system of signification to more subtle invocations of moral frameworks, conceptual schemes, and shared worldviews. At issue in these seemingly innocuous little turns of phrase is nothing less than our ability to "contextualize"—and so to interpret and eventually translate—foreign actions and utterances into an idiom that we think we understand.

Quine famously argued for the "indeterminacy" of such acts of translation—a notion that has been at the center of debate both within and between a range of disciplines. Whether in assent or dissent, to use a Quinean phrase, the argument has generally *taken as given* the unity and determinacy of the languages or theories between which one presumes to translate at any given moment. And I would argue that the spatial metaphor with which we began—that is, the idea of translation as a "carrying across"—has probably played a rather large part in naturalizing this understanding of language as a stable and bounded whole. Yet, as the examples of *agama, atma,* and *suci* were meant to suggest, assuming this understanding of language may have been to assume too much. While *agama* pointed to the ongoing transformation of language-in-use, *atma* and "the girl with two souls" seemed to point to a plurality of conflicting anthropologies within what is ostensibly a single cultural milieu. And, as for *suci*, this would appear to be a case of Balinese playing on the resulting ambiguity, presumably with varying degrees of awareness. Taken together, these count as three points against the stability and systematicity of the "cultural schemes" that are presupposed in prevailing accounts of translation. Significantly, the latter ride on what Vološinov described as a philological conception of language as a fixed and systematic totality, which was born of the need to revive the "cadavers" of long-dead languages. As he noted with no little flare, "Philological need gave birth to linguistics, rocked its cradle, and left its philological flute wrapped in its swaddling clothes. The flute was supposed to be able to awaken the dead. But it lacked the range necessary for mastering living speech as actually and continuously generated" (1973, 71). So, what would it mean to engage critically with "living speech as actually and continuously generated"? Assuming this to reflect something other than a residual desire for self-presence (Derrida 1974), Vološinov's remark suggests a number of pressing problems—not least that of generalizability. It may be recalled that we came to the problem of translation by way of enquiry into Balinese uses of script and writing. But we might have arrived by any number of alternative routes. As Sobchak put it, "This affects all of us." From kinship studies and the anthropology of ethics to practice theory and the so-called ontological turn, anthropological theorizing has depended for its evidence on the interpretation of specific utterances and actions. And this, as I suggested at the outset, has presupposed various forms of contextualization—which are themselves premised on a set of procedures we are in the habit of calling translation.[32] Yet accounts of translation tend to rely on an assumption of *totality* that anthropologists would be loath to embrace in their more general discussion of language and culture. The examples from Bali were meant to show how such totalizing assumptions fail to do justice to their ostensible object—namely, for reasons of ongoing transformation through time (cf. *agama*) and a lack of cultural uniformity at any given moment (cf. *atma*). The problem is that, if our working understanding of translation proves untenable, this potentially calls into question everything that has been built upon it. The point is not so much that higher-level theorizing must be jettisoned *tout court*. It is rather to highlight the need for a more critically nuanced account of what ethnographers and other anthropologists are actually doing when they presume to "translate"—an account that is radically attuned to both the ambiguities and ineluctably performative character of language-in-use. If it turns

out that language is not a stable and bounded totality, nor translation a "carrying across," what exactly have we been doing all this time? What was the
nature of the linguistic operations underpinning our analysis of the uses and
acts of *aksara*? The CRG? Or the Grebeg Aksara? And how might this affect our theorization of things such as *practice* and *tradition*? At issue, I
would argue, are not simply the foundations of ethnographic enquiry and so
any theoretical conclusions we might wish to derive therefrom. Instead, I believe this speaks directly to the purposes these activities are meant to serve—
on which I would like to offer a few brief thoughts by way of conclusion.

Chapter 8

Wagging the Dog

I set out to do three things in this book. The first was to make a modest contribution to the scholarship on Balinese uses of script and writing, with an eye to the wider study of religion in Southeast Asia. This was, in turn, directed to problematizing our received understandings of textual practice and the notions of history and precedent that inform them. And, finally, the purpose driving this critique was to open up new avenues for thinking differently—here and now—about our relationship to writing both as a *practice* and as a *medium* for actualizing ideals of human flourishing and collective life.

Recapitulation

We began with I Gusti Ngurah Bagus's inaugural lecture as Bali's first professor of anthropology. Rather than address issues current in his field, or those that might be of interest to his local audience, Bagus chose instead to discuss the letters of the Balinese alphabet. These *aksara Bali*, he argued, were more than simply an instrument for the representation of language. In contrast to oil lamps that might be replaced with electric lights, Balinese letters could not "so easily be erased or rubbed out" in favor of romanization. And this was because they bore a special relationship to what he described as the island's traditional "religion" and "culture." Bagus's use of this terminology allied his remarks with the state bureaucratic imperatives associated with national Unity in Diversity. But, at the same time, his discussion of Balinese *aksara* in rites of healing and self-fortification intimated a rather different understanding of Balinese tradition—one for which written characters might be seen to possess a potency of their own. An appreciation for this potency seemed to figure both in my frustrated efforts to view one set of *lontar* and in the perceived consequences of a local man's mistreatment of another. The question was how to understand the relationship between these rival conceptions of Balinese tradition.

In chapter 2 I pursued this line of enquiry with specific reference to the idea of cultural heritage, as embodied in recent debates over the place of Balinese language instruction in the national curriculum. As with Bagus's inaugural address, the public discussion was characterized by a juxtaposition of contrasting sensibilities regarding the nature of Balinese script and the uses to which it might be put. A series of examples were used to show how each of these *styles of writing*, as I called them, was allied to a different *style of reasoning*. With *aksara* caught between competing articulations of agency, matter, and what it means to be "alive," the question became one of specifying "writing" as an object of study. Extrapolating from the scholarship on language ecology, we considered the argument for approaching writing as a "practice" grounded, or "embedded," in a broader "way of life." But it was unclear how this would play out in a Balinese context, given the apparent multiplicity of ideals. Could one simultaneously inhabit two or more "ways of life"? And, if so, what would it mean to say that a practice was "embedded" therein? It seemed there was, moreover, a misleading tendency toward reification in our received critical terminology (e.g., *object* of study, cultural *formation*, social *structure*, subject *position*). So I provisionally suggested we approach acts of writing in terms of the purposes toward which they are directed, remaining open to the possibility of overdetermination.

Taking up this approach, the third chapter developed the contrast between our two contrasting styles of writing by reflecting on the rather curious notion that Balinese *aksara* are "alive." Starting from the pragmatic assumption that "life" is what living things do, we examined the uses and acts of *aksara* in Batan Nangka. Here we discovered that life—at least in Balinese—was less a *state* than it was a set of *relations*. As with villages, granaries, and human bodies, the written characters of the Balinese alphabet are forged and perdure through their ongoing participation in a complex of relationships—both internal to themselves and with others. This may begin with the linkage of their constituent elements and subsequent affixation to other *aksara* (e.g., in palm-leaf manuscripts or copper amulets). But it seems the life of letters, as with other living objects, is ultimately contingent on a form of solidarity grounded in reciprocal obligation. Reflecting back on "the madness of Mbok Tut" (chapter 1), we began to see why Balinese might be reticent to handle letters haphazardly. With script potentially possessed of both independent will and the ability to participate in relations of debt and repayment, we were faced with an articulation of agency, life, and matter that differed sharply from the reductive notion of *aksara* as a symbol of cultural heritage or as a medium for representing the sounds of the Balinese language.

The critique from language ecology had recommended a focus on practices of writing. So, in chapter 4, I asked what it would mean to approach the uses and acts of *aksara* under the description of practice. To this point I had used the term *practice* rather loosely to mean something like "what people do." And my primary aim in so doing had been to shift our attention away from scholarly abstractions onto historically situated uses of script and writing. But now I wanted to see whether we might give a more precise account of this seemingly crucial term. Having earlier proposed an approach centered on the purposes of writing, we began by exploring the use of script-bearing instruments in the performance of a rite called *Caru Rsi Gana* (CRG). I was particularly interested in how the use of these instruments related to the wider purposes of the rite. Previous chapters had emphasized the disjuncture between two contrasting styles of writing and their corresponding styles of reasoning. But conversations surrounding the CRG suggested an even wider array of purposes, many of which appeared contradictory. The question was whether we might find an account of practice that could accommodate this degree of complexity.

The fifth chapter took this question as its point of departure. Stepping back from the ethnography to consider some of the broader issues at stake, we noted that so-called practice theory seemed to cover a diverse range of approaches with equally disparate understandings of what constitutes a practice and the conditions under which enquiry might proceed. It became apparent that recourse to "the facts" would not offer viable grounds for adjudicating between conflicting accounts. And so an alternative route was proposed, by way of comparing the central questions, presuppositions, and projects of transformation embodied in the work of two prominent social theorists: Alasdair MacIntyre and Pierre Bourdieu. We found Bourdieu's theory of practice to engender a number of difficulties, arising in large part from his commitment to a precritical social ontology and scientistic epistemology. By contrast, MacIntyre's approach seemed comparatively well attuned to the philosophical challenges of enquiry into cultural traditions other than one's own. And his teleological account of practice, centered on the cultivation of goods and virtues, appeared to offer a fruitful line of questioning. But, on closer inspection, it was not altogether clear that the CRG itself would qualify as a practice under MacIntyre's description. So, instead, we approached the rite as one of the procedures constitutive of the wider practice of maintaining a houseyard. Through events surrounding the death of a local businessman, we saw how the practice of houseyard maintenance brought together conflicting projects for human flourishing and collective life. Given its emphasis on teleological coherence and the hierarchical ordering of goods, there remained some question as to whether such a restrictive account of practice was suitable for export to Bali. But it was also noted that in MacIntyre's earlier work he had suggested that a "viable tradition is one which holds together conflicting social, political and even metaphysical claims in a creative way" ([1979] 1988, 67). Whatever relationship this bore to his later thoughts on practice, it was strikingly similar to Balinese understandings of polity as the product of collective ceremonial work.

Chapter 6 carried forward with the idea of *tradition* as the temporal condition of practice. It was argued that we presuppose tradition, or something like it, when we set out to interpret other people's practices as reasonable human action. For novel utterances and actions can only be said to "make sense" insofar as they may be referred to some form of precedent—or, as I put it there, the absolutely *new* is also absolutely *unintelligible*. The question was how best to construe tradition—that is, if it were at once necessary and, at the same time, something other than a simple repetition of the past. We reviewed what I called the "positive," "genealogical," and "operationalized" models of tradition, as applied to Balinese culture and society. But each came up wanting. So, as an alternative, I suggested we examine MacIntyre's approach to tradition as an "argument extended through time." And, with this, we turned to Ida Wayan Oka Granoka's Grebeg Aksara. Here we saw how Granoka's "celebration of the power of Balinese script" reworked elements of the past to address present concerns, with the aim of bringing about a particular kind of future. His project was fraught from the start, but no less interesting for that. Local priests and other commentators were critical of his pretensions. Yet Granoka's style of argumentation seemed to reflect a certain "additive" sensibility evident in prior responses to crisis, in both Bali and other parts of the archipelago—but also potentially in the wider Southeast Asian region. As we saw with his account of practice, the ethnography seemed to suggest certain limitations in MacIntyre's approach. More specifically, there appeared to be a residual essentialism in his retention of a "formal rationality" as the grounds for adjudicating between the "substantive rationalities" of rival traditions. This was not to dismiss MacIntyre's account but rather to point up a set of issues that may require further thought.

The argument to this point appeared to beg the question of translation. We had considered a range of materials from Bali in our reflections on writing and its theorization. Yet at no point had we taken account of the "movement between languages" on which this line of enquiry depended. The aim of chapter 7 was to face the problem squarely, in order to specify what we were doing when we presumed to "translate." I noted that even our most radically detotalizing theorists tended to fall back on a totalizing theory of language and culture when it came to accounting for translation. So we turned to a pair of ethnographic vignettes in which key terms were caught between rival understandings of human agency and collective life. This gave us the opportunity to think more carefully about the many examples of cultural complexity encountered to this point—from Professor Bagus's inaugural lecture to the CRG and the Grebeg Aksara. It had earlier been noted that our analytical terminology has a "built-in" tendency toward reification. And we could now see how this predisposed us to naturalize a model of language and culture as unitary, determinate, and bounded. But the examples of *agama, atma,* and *suci* forced us to confront the implications of overdetermination—and so a degree of indeterminacy in the interpretation of utterances and actions. This suggested the possibility that even those directly involved in a given activity or practice might not be able to specify which of two or more anthropologies, and conceptions of polity, were "presupposed" at a particular moment.

The lack of closure may be disappointing for some. But, for those who aspire to a world other than the one we have, indeterminacy ought to come as a relief. It is not simply that there are more things in heaven and earth than are dreamt of in our philosophy. It is also that the world tends to be more open ended than we imagine. As I see it, Balinese uses and acts of *aksara* exemplify (among other things) a creative engagement with this open-endedness—and its myriad opportunities and dangers.

A Few Unresolved Issues

In pursuing this line of thought, a number of issues were left unaddressed. Before ending I would like to mention a few that I take to be among the more important. The first centers on the idea of *practice* and what we might ultimately hope to accomplish in using the term. Initially I had referred to practice as a prospective "object of study." This was partially inspired by the critique from ecology but also by a longer-standing admiration for both the American pragmatist tradition and the Marxian theorists of praxis. To the extent that a given line of enquiry presupposes a foundational divide between the knowing subject and its intended object, asking after the "object of study" can be an effective way of teasing out unacknowledged assumptions. But, having reflected at some length on the difficulties inherent in such a dualistic mode of knowing, I stopped calling practice an object of study and began referring to it instead as a "frame of reference." Under this description, *practice* was meant to point in more general terms to an emerging critical orientation—or, better still, a way of asking questions. The idea was to hold ethnographic encounter in dialectical tension with theoretical reflection, allowing each to affect the other recursively. So the questions from which I began afforded a certain kind of experience, which in turn helped to transform my line of questioning, giving rise to a marginally different kind of experience, and so on.

Yet, albeit an improvement, I was never entirely comfortable with the idea of *framing*—if for no other reason than its metaphorical grounding in a spatialized and distantiated conception of knowing (which, again, was a problem we had considered in some detail). In this respect, taking practice as a frame of reference appeared to be little more than a kinder, gentler means of objectification. And it was with this in mind that I began talking of our "approach" to practice, or how we might "account" for practice. Does swapping terms solve the problem? Probably not. At least not so long as these *approaches* and *accounts* are simply strapped onto an otherwise unreconstructed scientism. So, what do we mean by *practice*? Could it be that taking practice seriously would undermine the grounds on which it was originally invoked? Realizing that this could be a problem, I asked whether the idea of practice might be at its best when deployed in aid of critique—that is, when demonstrating the limitations of more conventional theorizing, without necessarily offering an alternative. This was in the fifth chapter, and the question was left hanging; I was not yet in a position to propose an answer. But I would now tentatively suggest that, while apophatic approaches to divinity may be appealing, the *via negativa* would be misleading when it comes to theorizing anthropology. This is not because we are on the verge of finally achieving an objective knowledge of what it means to be human—in terms of practice or otherwise. It is rather because ethnographic dialogue always already presupposes an effort to engage constructively with Others, based on a positive (if ever-provisional) articulation of personal agency and community—but also, at least potentially, with an eye to formulating and pursuing common goods. An anthropological orientation to practice, then, might helpfully be understood as signaling the conditions under which such dialogic encounters take place.

The second issue is closely related and derives from a potential slippage between *analytic procedure* and what might best be described as the *prologue to action*.[1] With the latter phrase I am pointing to the moment of "purpose," which figured in my account as the force that motivates a given action. What concerns me is the way this *prologue*—namely, the act's motivating *purpose*—also stands as the focus of our interpretation after the act itself has been performed. On the face of it, this seems perfectly sensible—that the purpose impelling an act would also be central to how we interpret it after the fact. Such is the very essence of a teleological approach to human action. And it appeared the ethnography was well served by this approach, even when the analysis of purpose was not entirely straightforward. In examining acts of writing in the CRG, for example, I argued that multiple and conflicting purposes might be driving one and the same act. But could this already have been to assume too much? Toward the middle of the chapter on translation,

I mentioned V. N. Vološinov's historical remarks on the rise of philology.[2] He said that language-as-system began life as a heuristic tool for interpreting culturally distant utterances but that the idea of *system* was then projected out onto the world as the ground that gave rise to those utterances in the first place.[3] As a consequence of this erroneous projection, he argued, the figure of language was transformed from an interpretive instrument into a generative principle—from a convenient fiction into an ontological foundation. The question is whether a teleological approach to action may inadvertently involve a similar sleight of hand—unduly domesticating ways of life that differ in a manner we are as yet incapable of recognizing. Put another way, how and to what extent has the process of analysis transformed Balinese actions by articulating their *prologue* as one of "purpose" and "presupposition"? Is it really safe to assume that the movement of teleology is universal? If not, what consequences might follow for the idea of interpretability? I cannot possibly hope to resolve the issue here. It is a difficult problem that arguably cuts to the very core of the human sciences. And my suspicion is that, like many of the issues I have tried to address in this book, the difficulties are not merely technical but rather derive from the more fundamental assumptions that inform scholarly self-understanding. One prospective avenue for addressing the problem might start from rethinking interpretation with reference to a Wittgensteinian approach to *understanding* as knowing "how to go on from here." How might this affect the dialectic of ethnographic encounter and theoretical reflection? The focus on futurity—asking where scholarship, and its practitioners, might *go on from here*—would help to shift attention onto the ineluctably constructive character of empirical enquiry, highlighting the oft-unacknowledged *ought* that prefigures our analysis of what *is*. But, again, this would take a great deal more thought and a quite separate study.

The third issue pertains more narrowly to Southeast Asian cultural history and Sheldon Pollock's influential notion of "the Sanskrit cosmopolis." In brief, this is the idea that over a period of some one thousand years, between 300 and 1300 CE, a geographical expanse encompassing what we now call South and Southeast Asia was "characterized by a transregionally shared set of assumptions about the basics of power, or at least about the ways in which power is reproduced at the level of representation in language, and Sanskrit's unique suitability for this task" (1996, 199). It was noted earlier that Pollock's analysis has provided new possibilities for exploring the historical interplay of "cosmopolitan" and "vernacular" sensibilities at work in pre-modern South Asia. But I would argue that, in naturalizing a philological orientation to writing—by privileging the figure of "the text" as a sense-bearing object—his approach potentially obscures a range of equally important uses of writing on the subcontinent and beyond. For instance, despite widespread scholarly familiarity with the popular use of amulets, apotropaic tattoos, and other forms of "script magic" throughout Southeast Asia, both Pollock and those who have followed him have often glossed over philologically noncompliant uses of script and writing—to say nothing of the problems of interpretation to which they give rise. In fairness, these "other" uses of writing may not be self-evidently pertinent to Pollock's primary interest in the historical transformation of literature and polity. And, what is more, the universal character of "making sense" may itself have seemed a reasonable assumption, given the happy congruence between modern philology and many of the South Asian commentarial practices that it has taken as its object. Yet, even setting aside difficult theoretical questions around the conception of textual "sense," Pollock's account of philology begs the question as to whether these "texts" were always meant to be read—that is, whether it was their textuality, so construed, that mattered most in the assemblage and use of these inscribed objects.[4] Invoking one of his own formulations, one might be inclined to suggest that a philologically extractable *sense* originally governed the historical production of a given text, whatever else tradition may have done with it subsequently. But the ethnographic and historical record indicates this has not always been the case. Pollock's account of philology is presented as both reflexively aware of its disciplinary history and attentive to the dangers of ethnocentrism. But it seems to have comparatively little concern for writing practices irreducible to the norms of philological analysis. My point is not so much to query the specific claims Pollock has made in relation to the broader contours of a so-called Sanskrit cosmopolis but rather to point up some of its limitations—where other projects and processes may elude the grasp of a philology restricted to "making sense of texts."

So where does this leave us? At the very least we may want to reconsider the assumption that our received understandings of script and writing are universally applicable. From healing and architecture to sorcery and self-fortification, we have seen numerous "uses and acts of *aksara*" that exceed

what a philologically inclined observer might expect from the written characters of the Balinese alphabet. And yet, while it is one thing to acknowledge
that Balinese have "different" ideas about *aksara*, it would be quite another
to take them "at their word," let alone to follow through on what recognizing this difference might entail. An instrumentalized conception of writing,
as a technology of communication, is not an isolated or free-standing idea.
Entrenched assumptions regarding the nature of language and text—and
so, by extension, our approach to historical evidence and precedent—all
presuppose this underlying theory of script as a neutral medium for the formulation, expression, and transmission of meaning. If our theory of the
medium fails, so too does much else that we have taken for granted.

Indeed it is only by virtue of an unexamined presumption to superior
comprehension that these analytical procedures may continue to be "applied"
transitively to other people's practices, as if from a place apart. If, for example, the conceptual underpinnings of textual study are as contingent as they
appear, it may be worth reflecting on what there is to learn by inverting the
model. We might ask, for instance, what sorts of relations sustain the "life"
of scholarly writing? And what forms of solidarity are cultivated through its
networks of loosely calculated debt and repayment? Taking a different tack,
we could similarly ask after the self-fortification achieved through peer-
reviewed publication or, again, the dangers inherent in the untutored
handling of writings for which one is ill prepared. It takes little imagination
to extrapolate from Balinese sorcery to the harm often deliberately effected
by means of published review, or the apotropaic purposes served by preemp-
tory self-criticism. As with *aksara*, scholarly writing is *more than words*. It
embodies a multitude of projects for human flourishing and collective life—
some clearly more attractive than others. We are usually inclined to think of
these illocutionary aspects of our writing as supplemental to the "real" work
we claim to be doing. But, as with so many appendices, perhaps it is the tail
that has been wagging the dog all along.

Notes

1. Manuscripts, Madness

1. The title of the address was "Aksara in Balinese Culture: An Anthropological Study" ("Aksara dalam Kebudayaan Bali: Suatu Kajian Anthropologi"; Bagus 1980). For a discussion of Bagus's promotion to professor, see Nyoman Wijaya's (2012) detailed intellectual biography. For a more general overview of Bagus's scholarly publications, see H. Geertz 1998.

2. Like the Indic scripts from which it was derived, the *aksara Bali* comprise an *abugida*, or alphasyllabary, in which each consonantal character carries with it an implicit vowel that may be modified or removed through the addition of diacritical marks Balinese commonly call "clothing" (B. *panganggon*). So, for example, by adding specific marks to the basic /na/ syllable, it can be transformed into /ni/, /né/, /nĕ/, /nu/, or /no/, or reduced to /n/; see figure 1.2.

3. The Indonesian text reads as follows: "Penghapusan atau penggeseran itu tidak semudah mengganti sembe (lampu Bali) dengan listrik" (Bagus 1980, 23). See Hornbacher 2016b on the history of the broadly western conception of letters as arbitrary signs, and how this contrasts with Balinese understandings of the "presence" of the written *aksara*.

4. *Agama:* To follow the dictionary in glossing the term *agama* as "religion" conceals as much as it reveals; chapter 7 addresses the problem in some detail. *Dunia gaib*: The

term *gaib* is an Arabic loanword often simply translated into English as "mystical," "spiritual," or "supernatural." But each of these terms carries connotations that *gaib* generally does not. I have often heard Balinese use the term *nis* as a gloss on *gaib*, where *nis* is an abbreviation of *niskala*—a Sanskrit loanword that in colloquial Balinese means something like "beyond what can be known by way of the senses." This is my reason for rendering Bagus's reference to *dunia gaib* as "the supersensory world."

5. In an earlier study (Fox 2011, 55–132), I examined the language employed in state bureaucratic articulations of Hindu religiosity. Of particular importance here would be Bagus's invocation of "scripture" (I. *pustaka*) and "religious teachings" (I. *ajaran agama*; cf. Fox 2011, 95–97).

6. For an early set of essays historicizing the idea of Hindu religiosity in Bali, see contributions to Ramstedt 2004. Through a series of more recent publications, Michel Picard (e.g., 2008, 2011a, 2011b) has developed a genealogy for the idea of "Balineseness" (I. *kebalian*) as an articulation of "religion" (I. *agama*), "culture" (I. *kebudayaan*), and "traditional custom" (I. *adat*). See his jointly edited volume with Rémy Madinier (2011) for a series of studies that take a similar approach to the idea of religion in other parts of Indonesia.

7. Among items I will not be discussing are the myriad photocopied booklets produced and distributed through informal networks and roadside bookshops. These would make an interesting, if challenging, area for further study. Nor will I be looking in any detail at the contemplative treatises addressed by Rubinstein (2000). Current uses of script and writing clearly bear a marked affinity with the latter. But the nature of their relationship remains anything but self-evident. The idea that day-to-day practices are simply an instantiation of an underlying philosophy (e.g., as explicated in one or another *tutur* manuscript; see note 9 below) is one of the central assumptions this book aims to question. Another important area that goes beyond the scope of this book is the increasing importance of the internet for contemporary understandings of Balinese tradition. This includes not only the availability of texts through various online databases but also a wider-reaching and more profound transformation in how Balinese orient themselves to script and writing.

8. Comments on Balinese uses of script and writing may also be found in earlier studies of theological speculation (Goris 1926), funerary rites (Wirz 1928), medicinal practice (Weck 1937), and sorcery (C. Hooykaas 1980).

9. In colloquial Balinese, the word *tutur* is generally used in reference to advice or instruction. But it is also a term associated with a style of literary exposition, or textual genre, that explicates the nature of the universe and the condition of those residing within it—often with an emphasis on spiritual exercises directed to developing special powers, attaining enlightenment, or achieving release from the phenomenal world. This has been a topic of particular focus in recent work from Andrea Acri (see, e.g., 2006, 2011, 2013, 2016).

10. Here the idea of "magic" probably tells us more about European concerns than it does those of Balinese (see Wiener 2007).

11. As part of our work for the collaborative research initiative on material text cultures at the University of Heidelberg, Hornbacher and I have also jointly edited a volume that brings together anthropological and philological perspectives on the materiality and efficacy of Balinese letters (Fox and Hornbacher 2016).

12. Particularly illustrative examples may be seen in Bizot 1981; Tannenbaum 1987; Swearer 2004, 69–71; Tsumura 2009; McDaniel 2011, 89; Patton 2012; and Terwiel 2012, 165–69.

13. For examples of this critique and its practical implications, see, e.g., Hayashi 2003; McDaniel 2011; Kitiarsa 2012; Patton 2012.

14. With a few notable exceptions (e.g., Skeat 1900; Woods 2007; Yahya 2015), such uses of script are usually mentioned but in passing (e.g., C. Geertz 1960, 103; Koentjaraningrat 1985, 417; Ricklefs 2006, 87; Sweeney 1987, 110–11).

15. See, e.g., Hunter 2007; Acri 2010; Romain 2011.

16. See, e.g., Ricci 2011; Tschacher 2009.

17. On philology as "the discipline of making sense of texts," see, e.g., Pollock 2009, 934; 2015, 34. In addition to its seeming inapplicability to nonliterary uses of writing, there are other issues worth noting. For instance, Pollock's account of text is grounded in a threefold theory of "meaning" (2009, 950–58; 2014)—historicist, traditionalist, presentist—that presupposes both the "non-traditional" character of philological historicism and a fourth (unnamed and unexplicated) perspective from which the other three may be objectified. I shall return to consider some of the implications in chapter 8.

18. A comprehensive survey of the literature would require a separate monograph, covering an extensive array of approaches, locations, and historical periods. A selective overview is provided by Frank Salomon and Mercedes Niño-Murcia (2011, 11–18), which is itself one of several recent studies of writing practices in South America that focuses particularly on Peru (see Burns 2010; Rappaport and Cummins 2012; cf. Rama 1996). Exemplary studies from other regions would include analyses of writing in Japan (Rubinger 2007), ancient Greece and Rome (Johnson and Parker 2009), the Democratic Republic of the Congo (Blommaert 2008), and Nepal (Ahearn 2001), but also earlier work in the Philippines (Raphael 1988), Yemen (Messick 1993), and Polynesia (Besnier 1995).

19. See, e.g., Street 2003; Collins and Blot 2003; Cole and Cole 2006; Barton 2007; Olson 2009; Barton and Papen 2010.

20. See, e.g., Havelock 1963, 1986; Ong 1967, 1982; Goody 1968, 1986; Olson 1994, 1996. On Ong in particular, see chapter 6, note 49.

21. See, e.g., Larson 1996; Bloch 1998; Postill 2003.

22. See, e.g., Finnegan 1973; Frake 1983. Debate over "the great divide" (or, alternatively, "the cognitive divide") replays key aspects of earlier arguments on "primitive thought" (see, e.g., Lévy-Bruhl 1926; Malinowski 1948; Evans-Pritchard 1934) and what has often been called "the rationality debate" (see Winch 1964; contributions to Wilson 1970, Hollis and Lukes 1982, and Overing 1985; see Hobart 1992 for a critical assessment of the key issues).

23. See, e.g., Street 1984; Halverson 1992a.

24. For an oft-cited example, see John Halverson's (1991, 1992a, 1992b) successive attacks on Olson, Havelock, and Goody. Summing up his argument against Goody, he concluded, "The *medium* of communication—which is the issue here—has no *intrinsic* significance in the communication of ideas or the development of logical thought processes" (1992a, 314; emphases in original). But, as we shall see in the following chapter, separating "the medium"—in our case, *writing*—from such things as "ideas" and "thought processes" may be more easily said than done.

25. For characteristic overstatements of argument, see, e.g., Ong 1986, 35, 42–43; cf. Michael Cole and Jennifer Cole (2006) on Goody. The appearance of a similar determinism may be seen in the subtitle for one of Olson's essays ("What Writing Does to Language and Mind"; 1996), if not necessarily its content. By contrast, Havelock and Ivan Illich and Barry Sanders seem to have been more circumspect.

26. Crucially, criticism was often premised on mistaking an argument from social practice for one made at the level of individual consciousness. It has also tended to presuppose an instrumentalized conception of "media," to which those criticized bore an ambivalent relationship (see, e.g., Havelock's [1986, 34] remarks on the circularity of studying literacy from within a literate tradition; cf. Ong 1986, 28; Illich and Sanders 1988).

27. I think John Postill (2003) was right to look to an anthropology of media for the study of "literacy"; but we differ in our understanding of both media and practice (see chapter 5).

28. I use *ward* to render the Balinese term *banjar*, instead of the more common *hamlet*, as the *banjar* designates (jurally, at least) a corporate group of households, as opposed to a specific location or territory (see Hobart 1979).

29. Primary fieldwork for the book was conducted over a period of six months in 2012 and 2013, with a follow-up visit in 2015. This period of study built on eighteen months' prior fieldwork in Batan Nangka and the wider Pateluan area, and an additional twenty-four months' research in other parts of the island.

30. In Batan Nangka and its environs, traditional healers are most commonly addressed as "Jero Mangku" and referred to elliptically as *orang pintar* ("clever person," or "one in the know"). Although this phrase is also used in other parts of Indonesia, the term *pintar* is commonly linked with the Balinese terms *wikan* and *duweg*—which in this usage would likely imply familiarity with intangible beings and forces that can be employed to ends benevolent or otherwise. Although frequently used in the scholarly literature, the term *balian* is locally considered derogatory, perhaps on par with using the English term *quack* in reference to a doctor.

31. The residents of Batan Nangka go to a wide range of experts for architectural consultation—including, e.g., *padanda, rsi bhujangga, mangku masceti, mangku mayun*, and various types of what they tend simply to call *orang pintar* (see previous note). On the elusive character of "the traditional Balinese architect," or *undagi*, see MacRae and Parker 2002.

32. Both the scholarly literature and the Balinese press generally refer to these palm-leaf manuscripts as *lontar*; for readability I shall do the same. But in Batan Nangka people tend to use the word *'ntal*, a shortened form of *rontal*, meaning leaf (B. *ron*) of the *tal* tree (L. *Borassus flabelliformis*). The word *lontar* itself is a variation on this term (see Hinzler 1993, 450).

33. Contemporary usage links the term *saraswati* to an anthropomorphic deity (Déwi Saraswati) patterned on Indian iconography. But for Balinese this may be a relatively recent association. Despite the ubiquity of broadly Hindu and Buddhist figures exemplified in statuary and related media, Christiaan Hooykaas (1964) noted the apparent absence of Déwi Saraswati in the premodern archaeological and art historical record. Based in part on the aims and sensibilities discussed in chapter 3, I suspect the term

saraswati is more closely tied to an impersonal *potency*—or perhaps *potentiality*—that is embodied in script and actualized through the act of writing.

34. The technical term *cakepan* may be used in referring to palm-leaf manuscripts of this kind, which are bound between boards (see photo 1.1). But in Batan Nangka and the surrounding region, they tend simply to be called *lontar*—or more commonly still, *(e)ntal* (see note 32).

35. When illness is seen to be caused by an attack from a sorcerer, the "cure" is likely to entail a counterattack, or protective measures of a similarly combative nature. Practically speaking, this often renders healing and sorcery indistinguishable—employing, as they do, many of the same procedures and instruments. Here the scholarly tendency to distinguish categorically between "black" and "white" magic would be deeply misleading. Balinese may differentiate between the "left-" and "right-handed" manipulation of intangible forces. But, like so much in Bali, the designation is highly contingent.

36. See especially Hunter 2007, 2016; Hauser-Schäublin 2012; Hornbacher 2016a; Wiener 2016; but also Zurbuchen 1987; Rubinstein 2000; for Java, cf. Zoetmulder 2007 and Florida 1995.

37. Using a metal or wooden sheet to block the front door at night is not uncommon. But to do so during the daytime looks more than a little unfriendly when it is clear there are people at home—especially in a small, semirural community like Batan Nangka.

38. Dédé and his wife had moved into the houseyard some years before, when his recently deceased uncle had become too old to care for the family temple and its accompanying rice land.

39. As with the *lontar* containing tiny script (see the earlier discussion in the main text), many such stories circulate in the form of rumor and speculation.

40. On rites of preparation, see chapter 3.

41. When I enquired, Mén Dana used the term *nyem* in reference to Mbok Tut's illness, although she did so with some reticence. This term can be used in a number of more general senses, including "cool," "insipid," and "flat" (e.g., of food or drink). But I am still a little uncertain as to what exactly it meant here. She was quite emphatic that it was not simply a matter of being "crazy" or under "stress."

42. It is important to bear in mind that such "western-style" scholarship is not the sole preserve of western-born scholars (see, e.g., Poerbatjaraka 1926; Soebadio 1971; Santoso 1975; Supomo 2000).

43. By *common sense* I mean something like Antonio Gramsci's (1971, 323–43) notion of a largely unquestioned body of assumptions that may be distinguished both from "philosophical" insight and practical "good sense."

2. Writing and the Idea of Ecology

1. See C. Hooykaas 1963 for an early comment on local publishing in Bali.

2. *Bhinéka Tunggal Ika*, the official motto of the Indonesian Republic.

3. While not without its critics, the state-sponsored initiative to "Indonesianize" the romanization of Balinese was unlikely to meet with much open resistance—coming, as it did, but a mere seven years after the anticommunist pogroms in which some one hundred

thousand Balinese were murdered under the direction of the military (Robinson 1995; Dwyer and Santikarma 2003).

4. Becoming a language teacher is a common career path pursued by those studying Balinese language and literature at university.

5. The 1999 legislation included laws 1999/22 (on regional governance) and 1999/25 (on fiscal relations between the national and regional administrations); these were replaced in 2004 with laws 2004/32 and 2004/33, respectively.

6. As George Aditjondro (1995) remarked in the mid-1990s, a similar pattern was evident in the flow of tourism revenues from Bali—or, as he called it, "Jakarta's colony."

7. In the past, schoolbooks were often passed along to younger children, either within the extended family or in nearby houseyards. Now similar networks are employed to gather money for books required by the ever-changing curriculum.

8. The two languages were Javanese and Sundanese.

9. As Helen Creese has noted, "In the 1990s, specific legislative measures were introduced [at the regional level] to support the maintenance and development of Balinese language, most notably the establishment of the Language, Script and Literature Development Board (*Badan Pembina Bahasa, Aksara dan Sastra Bali*) in 1995 and the subsequent campaign to include Balinese names for all public signs on the island" (2009, 221).

10. An important precedent for this argument was laid out in a series of articles published in the *Bali Post* in 1986 under the name Nirta, most likely a pseudonym (see Sumarta 2001). The language here parallels in many ways that of the broadly western scholarship on Balinese tradition; see Fox 2003 and 2005 for discussion of the central metaphors.

11. The Constitution of 1945 (§ XV.36) established Bahasa Indonesia as the national language of the republic; this was followed by additional legislation requiring the use of the Indonesian language in all communication of an official nature (see Articles 26 to 40 of Law No. 24 of 2009 [*Undang-Undang 24/2009*]). The latter included such things as legal contracts, state documents, and presidential speeches but also scientific correspondence, the naming of buildings, and workplace communication.

12. Here it is not simply a question of speaking formally and employing the appropriate speech register, which are requirements widely recognized as both difficult and anxiety inducing. The point is that even the seemingly "fluent" use of Balinese in day-to-day conversation incorporates both terminological and syntactic elements of the national language for which there is no easy Balinese equivalent (see Zurbuchen 1984).

13. Elsewhere (Fox 2010) I examined uses of *media* and *history* in the scholarship on Ajeg Bali. There my central contention was that foreign observers writing about Bali have tended to naturalize an account of the island's recent history that is organized around an urban intellectual elite and its changing relations to capital and the state apparatus. The problem is not merely that this marginalizes other experiences of Balinese history but also that it unwittingly abets the hegemonic aspirations of those elites who have worked as informants for prominent western scholars.

14. It must be remembered, however, that large parts of Indonesia do not have Muslim-majority populations—such as West Papua and areas in Sulawesi, Maluku, and Sumatra (to name just a few).

15. See Becker 1995b for reflections on the importance of script for language learning in a Burmese context. Drawing a directly pertinent comparison, he said of lessons

with his Burmese teacher, "At first it seemed to me a small price to pay, to phonemicize his language. But over the years—particularly twenty years later, in Java and Bali—I learned how that kind of written figure (a centre and marks above, below, before, and after it; the figure of the Burmese and Javanese and Balinese syllable) was for many Southeast Asians a mnemonic frame: everything in the encyclopedic repertoire of terms was ordered that way: directions (the compass rose), diseases, gods, colors, social roles, foods—everything (Zurbuchen 1981, 75f). It was the natural shape of remembered knowledge, a basic icon" (Becker 1995b, 195).

16. As part of a separate project I have asked several people in Batan Nangka to record their conversations on selected topics. Producing and interpreting transcripts of these informal chats have been informative and at times exceedingly difficult. Among the more challenging aspects has been disentangling the various threads of what people take for granted when not speaking before—let alone solely for the benefit of—a foreign researcher. (NB: All parties to the conversations have given permission for these recordings.) Reference to commonly known people, places, and events aside, the grounds for agreement and persuasion often require extended commentary before they become intelligible to someone without the requisite preunderstanding (Fox 2017).

17. Various moments (e.g., Hale et al. 1992) have been cited by different authors as sounding the "wake-up call" (compare, e.g., Himmelmann 2008 with Austin and Sallabank 2011).

18. "Language shift" is now seen to be an even greater accelerant of endangerment than a diminishing population (see, e.g., Grenoble 2011, 27).

19. Among the spurs to reflection has been the recognition of such phenomena as "areal diffusion" (Enfield 2005), in which an otherwise unrelated language has taken on the defining traits (e.g., a tonal system) of a language spoken by a geographically proximate community through "contact" over long periods of time. With this decoupling of essence and filiation, the idea of the "language family" seems to lose at least some of its explanatory power. On the importance of linguistic borrowing, also see Mühlhäusler 1992, 174.

20. Here it is worth noting that, while the terminology may often be Wittgensteinian in tenor, the broader approach does not always follow suit.

21. It would require a separate study to explore the implications of a more radical reading—one that called into question, for instance, the unity of language itself as an object of study, or of preservation. Chapter 7 presents a discussion of the underlying theoretical problems from the vantage of translation theory.

22. The words *matur* and *ngaturang* are both derived from the base word *atur*, while both *mapaica* and *ngicén* are derived from *ica*. The former base (B. *atur*) is generally associated with upward giving, the latter (B. *ica*) with downward bestowal. See note 48 later in this chapter.

23. As with spoken language, the idea of ecology has also been used to highlight the embeddedness of written language and literacy in both their "natural" surroundings and other forms of activity (e.g., Cooper 1986; Barton 2007).

24. Though it was less common in the past, the use of a high priest to complete marriage ceremonies is now de rigueur—arguably a product of what Leopold E. A. Howe (2005, 132) has described in terms of "ritual inflation."

25. There are no doubt good reasons for this reticence, not least of which would likely have included a desire to avoid speaking of things—especially powerful things—of which one does not have direct, and so certain, knowledge (see the discussion later in this chapter).

26. There is a fine line between attributions of *use* (B. *guna*) and *purpose* (B. *tetujon*) in Balinese, on which see Hobart 2015.

27. The title Bali Orti was taken by many of those with whom I was working as probably playing off the phrase "Napi Orti?" ("What's the news?" or perhaps "How are you?").

28. My thanks to Rebecca Wollenberg for the comparison.

29. The articles cited (*Bali Post*, Bali Orti 2013a, 2013b, 2013c) were published on April 21, 2013.

30. It is worth highlighting once again the use of Indonesian terminology in discussing the preservation of Balinese language, even when the article is otherwise written in Balinese. The text of the article runs as follows, with Indonesian terms underlined (italics in original): "Kruna lontar mawit saking kruna *ron* lan *tal* sané maartos daun ental. Daun puniki mawit saking taru siwulan sané katuhang tur kawigunayang pinaka serana nyurat aksara. *Naskah-naskah* utawi cakepan sané ketah kasambat *manuskrip* puniki kakaryanin antuk daun lontar puniki kadadosan sinalih tunggil <u>*sumber informasi sejarah*</u> sané kasimpen ring *museum* utawi *perpustakaan*. Sedih pisan rasané yéning *tatacara* nyurat lontar puniki *mesti* ical santukan kagerus antuk panglimbak *masa* tur panglimbak *teknologi* sané sayan *modern*. Tios punika, akedik arsa para krama sané kayun ngwacén lontar. Pinaka krama Bali, nelebin daging *budaya* sané kaduénang sakadi nyurat aksara ring daun lontar utawi ngwacén lontar ri kala akéh krama utawi yowana sané sampun lali ring *budaya* sané kaduénang punika becik pisan. Kahanan sakadi punika patut kalimbakang pinaka utsaha nglestariang kawéntenan lontar inucap."

31. Whatever its other merits, it is important to note the extent to which the article's mode of address ("Come Let's Preserve . . .") and vision of collective life appear to replicate ideals promulgated under the New Order (see Fox 2011, chap. 5).

32. It may be noted in passing that *culture* (I. *budaya*) is being reified in a way that would be difficult to express without the aid of Indonesian-language terminology. *Lestariang* is here obviously a Balinese transposition of the Indonesian *lestarikan*, with all that it implies (see Santikarma 2003).

33. I found considerable variation in the use of *ulap-ulap* in Batan Nangka. Many used these little cloth amulets for all buildings (I. *bangunan*) and shrines (B. *palinggih*); several others used them only for shrines; while there were also a few who did not use them at all. To date I have not been able to find a clear explanation for the differences from one houseyard to another (e.g., that one sort of arrangement would correspond to where a given household went for advice on such matters).

34. As with such terminology in Bali more generally, the term *ulap-ulap* is probably best understood as indicating a use or function, as opposed to being a proper name. For a similar pattern of "naming," see Christiaan Hooykaas's (1980) collection of the drawings commonly called *rarajahan*.

35. There is no little uncertainty when it comes to specifying what is "beckoned" or "called in" (B. *kaulapin*). One's vital energy, or *bayu*, is one of the possibilities entertained in more reflective discussion (see the discussion that follows in the text; cf. note 39),

though people will often say instead that it is their spirit or soul (*jiwa, atma*) that is recalled. Here it is important to note the potential for there to be multiple and conflicting anthropologies in play—both in this case and more generally (see chapter 7).

36. Here one is reminded of the *kidung warga sari*, which is often sung at a crucial stage in the performance of temple ceremonies (B. *odalan*). The reference to power coming down from "on high" invokes an ambiguous and potentially ambivalent source of power—*leluhur*, which is often facilely rendered into English as "ancestors."

37. One might compare the use of similar cloth amulets in architectural rites elsewhere in Southeast Asia (e.g., for a suggestive account of Thai house-building rites, see Terwiel 2012, 165–70).

38. *Nm. v. e. levend makende mantra* (van der Tuuk, cited by C. Hooykaas 1978, 63, with slightly modified translation); cf. Goris 1926, 61–62; Weck 1937, 74–76; Boeles 1947, 56; Lovric 1987, 68, 187–88; also see Nala 2006, 206, for instructions on making a *dasabayu*-bearing instrument employed to increase a baby's strength and endurance.

39. In the published notes to her sequence of films on the Balinese healer Jero Tapakan, Linda Connor observed, "Ordinary people, and even [healers] who are not literate in the [*lontar* manuscripts], think about *bayu* as undifferentiated energy that is an essential element of bodily well-being. Those who are feeling ill and listless may explain it by statements like *wus bayun tiangé* ('my vital energy has escaped') and will point to the top fontanel as the place where *bayu* can escape from the body. Mothers often apply a thick herbal paste to the fontanels of their young babies to prevent escape of *bayu*. Of lively, strong babies, especially boys, people will often admiringly say *gedé bayuné* ('his life-force is strong,' or 'great')" (1986, 189–90).

40. Recent articles by Thomas M. Hunter (2016) and Andrea Acri (2016) address this practice in greater detail—the former with specific reference to the Balinese notion of *miyasa*, the latter offering a survey of the Sanskrit and Old Javanese texts that provide lists of the syllables and their locations on the body.

41. This raises the important question as to why one would require such additional "energy" when newly married. I would provisionally suggest that the reference to newlyweds as "living corpses" (see earlier discussion) is highly suggestive in this connection, and that the etymology of terms such as *leteh* and *sebel*—as potentially implying a dissipation of vitality (despite their more common gloss as "impurity")—may have much to teach us about the transformation of Balinese ideas concerning the aims of ceremonial work (B. *gaé, karya*). But this is a complex topic requiring further research and a quite separate study. For some initial steps in this direction, see Fox 2015, 46–50.

42. Traditional healers (B. *balian*) are also important manipulators of *aksara*, making one's relationship to such a person potentially risky. Whereas the *padanda*'s assistance is required as a matter of course (e.g., for marriages, death rites, new courses of study, the making of holy water), a *balian*'s help is only requested in response to an unanticipated problem, most commonly relating to illness, death, or sorcery.

43. These days *ulap-ulap* are commonly silkscreened, an innovation on which there is a wide range of opinion. But most of the more senior priests and healers with whom I spoke said they must be handwritten to be effective.

44. The question of numbers, and who counts as a Hindu, is anything but straightforward. See Fox 2013a for a discussion of some of the political considerations.

45. See Picard 2011a on the issues and events surrounding the emergence of *Agama Hindu*.

46. The terms *shared ideals* and *the common good* are meant to imply not faits accomplis but rather works in progress—as embodied in the aims, or *teloi*, that direct both individual action and collective activity. Chapter 5 explores the problem in greater detail.

47. I take this point from a recent performance on the Balinese stage, where one of the comic *bondrés* characters explained, "We are indeed the heirs [to tradition]. . . . [But] you should carry on only with those [parts of tradition that are] fit to be carried on! And get rid of what needs to be gotten rid of! Don't [try to keep] all of it!" (B. "Nak mula ragaé dadi sentana, ané patut tulad, tulad! Ané patut kutang, kutang! 'De jek makejang!'")

48. The *sor/singgih* register marks the hierarchical directionality of an utterance. To speak "down" to an inferior is to *ngesor*, a term also meaning to "defeat" someone in battle. By contrast, to honor the one spoken to, or about, is to *nyinggihang* (the transitive verbal form derived from the base word *singgih*). These distinctions are marked by intonation and bodily posture but also by diction. So to "give" to a superior is to *ngaturang* (see earlier discussion); for giving to an inferior, the term is *mapaica* (to bestow); and giving on the level (more or less) is simply to *maang* (to give).

49. See Picard (2004) on debates over similar issues in the 1930s, centering on polemics between Surya Kanta and Bali Adnyana.

50. This is more or less comparable to the English saying "Out of the frying pan and into the fire."

51. Anthony C. Woodbury qualified this statement, concluding that the proposition he ultimately wished to defend was as follows: "Interrupted transmission of an integrated lexical and grammatical heritage spells the direct end of some cultural traditions and is part of the unraveling, restructuring, and reevaluation of others" (1993, 116).

52. The distinction between figurative and literal forms of language may ultimately mark what is more a difference of degree than of kind. For a discussion of the closely related contrast between "semantic" and "poetic" meaning, see Burke 1973.

53. See Descombes 1987 on the American reception of Foucault.

54. Recalling the previous chapter, this terminology reflects a visualist epistemology that Eric A. Havelock (1963) and Walter J. Ong (1958a) among others, have associated with the use of a phonetic alphabet and the objectifying style of knowledge that it enabled.

3. The Meaning of Life, or How to Do Things with Letters

1. Pertinent scholarly examples would include Zurbuchen 1987, 56; Rubinstein 2000, 194; and Hunter 2007, 283–84.

2. I have had no little difficulty in trying to find a phrase in colloquial Balinese that approximates the broadly western notion of "dead matter." To my amusement, and that of my Balinese consultants, a mechanical rendering of the phrase "dead matter"—as *lakar mati*—is more readily understood to mean "will die." (*Lakar* is the common term used for the stuff of which something is made. But it is also used to indicate a simple future tense, as in "Tyang lakar madaar," or "I am going to eat.") It is perhaps telling

that the national language of Indonesian, the linguistic register associated with economic development and modernization, has a more readily available equivalent to "dead matter" in the phrase *barang mati*, an "inanimate object."

3. The idea of the "living house" is by no means unique to Bali. Of Indonesia more generally, Roxana Waterson noted that "houses are regarded in many societies of the archipelago as having a vitality of their own, interdependent with the vitality of their occupants" (2009, 116).

4. Given the chapter title's allusion to J. L. Austin, it is worth highlighting the difference between the figure of agency in his formulation of speech act theory (where one "does things with words") and the sorts of agency we see at work in the uses and acts of *aksara* (where the inscribed letters are often attributed with the capacity to transform the world in their own right). One might see in the latter a certain parallel to the Latourian notion of "actants"; on Latour more generally, see note 42 in this chapter.

5. See Santikarma 2003; Picard 2008; Fox 2010; also cf. chapter 2.

6. The *jilbab* is the head covering worn by many Indonesian Muslim women; the *kopiah* is a fez-shaped hat worn by many Indonesian Muslim men, often associated with nationalism.

7. This form of reading involves singing, or "sounding," short excerpts of a metrical text—in Old or "Middle" Javanese, or literary Balinese—which is then followed by a stylized gloss in vernacular Balinese. This reading practice, often called *mabasan* or *pepaosan*, is practiced in poetry clubs (B. *pasantian*) and during temple festivals and other large ceremonial rites. There is a growing scholarly literature on *mabasan* reading (see, e.g., Bhadra 1937; Robson 1972; Hunter 1988; Zurbuchen 1987, 1989; Rubinstein 1993, 2000; Jendra 1996; specifically on its rise to popularity on television and radio, see Creese 2009, 2014, 2016; Darma Putra and Creese 2012; Fox 2011, 120–30).

8. Sugi Lanus (2014) has traced the history of the *Tri Sandhya* mantra and its formulation as both a thrice-daily "prayer" and as a Hindu answer to the Islamic *shalat*.

9. On uses of the phrase *Om Swastyastu*, see Fox 2011, 63.

10. Many of these books are photocopied locally, with their original Kawi text on the left page and a gloss in (comparatively) vernacular Balinese facing on the right. When they are brought out for reading, these books are stacked on a low table alongside microphones, the requisite offerings, and a bookstand to support the text being sung.

11. The act of reading publicly—singing and then glossing in the vernacular—is also taken to be a "traditional" activity and so an expression of Balinese Hindu identity (as discussed earlier). This is clearly evident on *Dharma Gita* and related programs on both radio and television (see note 7 in this chapter).

12. See the example from the wedding in chapter 2. Literary precedents for such writing on the tongue include the tale of Anak Ubuh (*Anak Oeboeh*, K 1759; on which, see J. Hooykaas 1959, 178–79; cf. Hooykaas-van Leeuwen Boomkamp 1963, no. 38; also see Alton L. Becker's [1995a] oft-cited discussion of a Balinese drawing associated with the story of Ari Dharma).

13. I say *ostensibly* polluted on account of my growing sense that the language of "pollution and purity" (e.g., *sebel* and *suci*) overwrites a quite different set of sensibilities that, despite having been displaced, is still very much at work in shaping Balinese practices (see chapter 2, note 41)

14. There appears to be a blurring of categories here. On the one hand, the knife must remain "pure" (B. *sukla*), in the sense that it is not used to cut anything other than the materials encasing a corpse—this can be its only use (B./I. *guna*). On the other, it is considered a "pure" (B./I. *suci*) knife in a broader sense that is something like "sacred" (I. *sakral*). I suspect the latter association is at least in part derived from the state bureaucratic conception of Hinduism that is taught in schools and disseminated on television.

15. I have placed the term *offering* in quotes because, despite its being the most common English gloss for the Balinese term *banten*, not all *banten* are meant to be "offered" (see Fox 2015).

16. A more elaborate account of these rites is given in Howe's (1983) previously cited essay; although the general pattern he describes is familiar, things today are done somewhat differently in Batan Nangka.

17. In my experience Balinese do not take for granted that such rites of animation always work, as evidenced by the rites of "testing" (B. *ngeréh*) performed for newly constructed, or recently repaired, *rangda* and *barong* figures—themselves the material embodiment of beings said to rule (interestingly, also B. *ngeréh*) over a particular locale.

18. The term *embet*—"bunged up" or "constipated"—is used in the case of both bodies and architecture. Additional terms of interest in this connection include *bengke, seret, ngambet,* and *seket.*

19. When specifically configured as a ritual instrument (B. *upakara*), they may also be called *rarajahan*—as, for instance, on an inscribed sash (B. *sabuk*) worn for invigoration and protection (see the discussion later in this chapter). Though recognized as technical terms (I. *istilah*), these words tend to be used interchangeably by many in Batan Nangka.

20. Professor I Gusti Ngurah Bagus (1980, 13–14) offered examples of *modré* and their pronunciation in the inaugural lecture discussed in chapter 1.

21. The text itself is written in ink on evenly cut pieces of wood that approximate the shape of *lontar* leaves and are roughly three-quarters of a centimeter thick.

22. This use of the term *atma* is neither entirely idiosyncratic nor as common as its more conventional use as a technical term associated with state Hinduism. Rather, it points to the fluid and highly situational use of such terminology in day-to-day practice.

23. The term *bekel* was decidedly ambiguous here. In very general terms it can mean something given, as a reserve, for use in the future—such as a little food or money taken on one's travels. But it is also a "reserve" of power or protection. This may take the form of a small amulet or spoken formula; but it can also be an object buried and periodically presented with offerings (see chapter 4).

24. As with so many of these practices, the use of a second cloth *kajang* is contested. One particularly prominent *padanda* stated emphatically that this was a novel development reflecting the desire among some descent groups to charge large fees for their production.

25. It is not altogether clear whether the use of the name in this context—whether written or otherwise—is taken to affirm a determinate relationship or to fix one that is as yet unestablished.

26. The irreducibly embodied character of self is evident, among other places, in the use of language. Two of the more common terms for the body—*awak* and *raga*—are used in standard forms of both the first- and second-person Balinese pronouns.

27. The name itself, *kanda mpat*, clearly suggests they are four (*mpat*) in number. However, at least in the Pateluan area, I have on more than one occasion heard reference to six siblings—often still retaining the phrase *kanda mpat*, as if it were a technical term that implied something other than their number. It should be noted that this idea of "spiritual siblings" is found elsewhere in Southeast Asia and sometimes in other numbers (e.g., on the seven among the Ara in South Sulawesi, see T. Gibson [1994, 191]; compare Retsikas [2010, S152] on the four siblings in Java).

28. As in other broadly Indic traditions of South and Southeast Asia, Balinese link various colors, directions, deities, syllables, weapons, days, and numbers—among other things (see chapter 4, figure 4.1). So, for example, we have the series red, south, Brahma, *bam* (syllable), club (weapon), Saturday, and nine. Although the scholarly literature reproduces any number of these lists, and their variations, it has offered comparatively little insight into the rationale for elaborating such complex systems of association. My approach has been to look at the procedures in which these series are employed and the purposes they are meant to serve.

29. In my view the healer's notion of "opening *cakras*" owes at least as much to recent, and broadly western (e.g., New Age), precedents as it does to anything originating more directly from the South Asian or Javano-Balinese textual tradition. Although other of his techniques are clearly grounded in ideals associated with the latter, he also meets frequently with foreign yoga practitioners and those he refers to as "paranormals." He may also be drawing on what he has learned from reading the newspaper, watching television, or speaking with members of new religious movements inspired by a growing—and transnational—network of "emerging spiritualities."

30. On the *uat*, or "connecting channels," see Connor 1986, 187–91.

31. Given both the use of such powerful sashes in Bali and the importance of guarding the navel and midsection of the body—as the locus of vital energy—in other parts of Indonesia (see, e.g., Errington 1983), it may be worth querying the popular association of temple sashes (I. *selendang*) with ideals of purity (B. *suci*).

32. See Margaret J. Wiener's (1995) discussion of I Seliksik as a similarly self-mobile weapon, and the description of Panji Sakti's *keris* in the *Babad Buleleng* (Worsley 1972), which is possessed of its own will and capacity to act independently.

33. A sort of fake *lontar* (B. *lontar-lontaran*) prepared from young palm leaves is usually employed in performance.

34. This obviously has implications for what one might conclude from the houseyard survey discussed in chapter 1.

35. In the Pateluan area, for example, there are at least four priests or healers—two *padanda*, one *rsi bhujangga*, and a *balian*—known for precisely these character traits. In my conversations with their clients, these traits were consistently thought to be connected in some substantive fashion to their high level of accomplishment as ritual officiants, healers, and sorcerers—three categories that quite commonly overlap.

36. Instructive comparisons may be drawn with Buddhist Southeast Asia. As Thomas N. Patton remarked on the use of *yantra* in Burma, for instance, "Although there are numerous *yantra* to be found in published books and magazines, palm-leaf manuscripts, *weizzā gaing* (congregation) manuals, and personal practitioners' journals and notebooks, a *yantra* used from one of these sources without the knowledge

and guidance of a teacher is not only believed to be useless but also harmful to the practitioner, for not every *yantra* is suitable to be used by just any person. Moreover, there is the fear among publishers of *weizzā* manuals and *weizzā* path practitioners that if such sources provided detailed instructions for how to use such *yantra*, then anyone could potentially use the *yantra* for his/her own malevolent purposes" (2012, 214). The sources and nature of danger may differ, but the more general orientation to the potency of writing seems remarkably similar.

37. In Pateluan and the surrounding area, it is not unusual for the term *panjak* (subject) to be used in reference to the clients of a *padanda*.

38. In this case a complex of offerings, including the *banten pajati*, is dedicated at the foot of the tree before the cutting of its branches.

39. Examples include, for instance, the rites of lustration (B. *malukat*) and preparation (B. *mawinten*), through which one requests the beneficence of the divine embodiment of letters and learning (as, e.g., B. *nunas panugrahan saking Ida Sang Hyang Saraswati*). But also see chapter 1, note 33.

40. See the section "The Madness of Mbok Tut" in chapter 1.

41. This conception of "life" shares obvious affinities with other Southeast Asian traditions that have been described under the rubric of a "new animism" (Århem and Sprenger 2016; cf. Bird-David 1999). The latter is linked to a range of recent developments in anthropological theory, including inter alia the study of hunter-gatherer societies (e.g., Willerslev 2007), new approaches to ecology and the environment (e.g., Ingold 2000), and the so-called ontological turn (e.g., Descola 2013; Viveiros de Castro 2015). For now I must leave as an open question the link between these accounts of "animism" and Balinese conceptions of "life." To address the pertinent issues—and requisite translations between traditions (see chapter 7)—in anything other than a superficial manner would require a quite separate study.

42. These "Latourian litanies" are meant as a nod in the direction of work inspired by Bruno Latour (e.g., 2005), more recently carried out under the rubric of "object-oriented ontology" (see, e.g., Meillassoux 2008). I am a little uncertain as to the coherence of its *relationism* (see Harman 2009) and, more specifically, its seeming disregard for problems of language and representation (which, I believe, it claims to have transcended). But I find the broadening of agency an important corrective to the sometimes naive valorization of intentional, or "expressive," agency in the human sciences.

43. It is interesting to note that the same terminology is often employed by women, in casual conversation, to refer to the "affixing" (B. *masang*) of birth control devices, such as the IUD.

44. It is in part on these grounds that I believe we may wish to question the simple equivalence of terms like *leteh* and *sebel* with impurity.

45. *Bayu* is often glossed in English as "action," which is not exactly incorrect. But it is somewhat imprecise. As I have tried to indicate, *bayu* in this context is linked at once to ideas of self-driven *movement* and *the exertion of force* on other objects.

46. Less commonly, the series may be referred to as *tri-jñāna* or *tri-tattwa*.

47. It is instructive to note that the term *jotan* is also used in reference to the food parcel one gives to relatives, friends, and neighbors when performing a major ceremony.

48. In an earlier essay (Fox 2015), I have considered this problem with reference to Balinese offerings.

4. Practice and the Problem of Complexity

1. The phrase is teeming with ethnocentric presuppositions smuggled in under cover of common sense—e.g., naturalizing "people" as agents, specifying "practice" in opposition to "theory" and, elsewhere, "essence." If nothing else, the uses and acts of *aksara* examined in the previous chapter should give ample reason to question the universality of these assumptions.

2. See, e.g., Jacoba Hooykaas-van Leeuwen Boomkamp's (1961) study of the *lis* water sprinkler.

3. To speak of "the" *Caru Rsi Gana*—as if there were an ideal form of the rite (e.g., as found in one or another ritual manual) with reference to which specific performances might be judged—would be to impose a misplaced conception of orthopraxy. This is not to say Balinese are averse to the idea of there being a correct way of doing things. Quite the contrary. But the "correct" way is in part determined, as Balinese have come to say, by "place, time, and circumstance" (B. *désa, kala, patra*).

4. Dong Tawang's husband had married into his wife's family as a jural female. This allowed them to inherit the houseyard in Batan Nangka previously held by a cousin who had recently died. On marriage and becoming a jural female (or male), see the section "The Girl with Two Souls," chapter 7.

5. Anecdotal evidence would suggest that, as recently as the early 1990s, this rite was rarely if ever performed in ordinary houseyards.

6. That the rite is to be performed at regular intervals appears to be an idea of recent origin, often attributed to one of Bali's televised priest-celebrities.

7. Dong Tawang's houseyard temple in Batan Nangka was established as a branch, or offshoot (B. *carang*), of her family's "great houseyard temple" (B. *sanggah gdé*) located in an easterly ward of Pateluan. Ordinarily one would expect such a major *caru* to be performed first in the more senior of the two houseyard temples. But events at Mbok Tawang's required immediate attention, and the family could not afford to perform the rite in both places at once.

8. Recent years have seen the creation of new cooperatives designed to ameliorate the impact this expense, sharing it out among a group of participants over a longer period of time.

9. This included several local *pamangku* priests, the officiating high priest, and a consecrated shadow puppeteer, or *dalang*, who performed a daytime puppet show (B. *wayang lemah*) as a requisite component of the rite.

10. See, e.g., Wikarman 2006, 5; Swastika 2008, 13–14; Arwati 2008, 4. As David J. Stuart-Fox has noted, "Caru is originally a Sanskrit word meaning 'oblation,' or in Old Javanese 'offering,' while in Bali it came to be used only for the animal sacrifice" (2002, 155; cf. Creese 2004, 272; also see Gonda 1987 on Vedic usage; for an example of *caru* in tantric Buddhist rites, see Bentor 1996, 285–87).

11. This fivefold classification is taught as one of the official tenets of Indonesian state Hinduism, and it is frequently reported by western scholars as a fact of Balinese religiosity. Here two points should be mentioned. The first is that, outside elite circles, these categories rarely figure as more than a tertiary elaboration on what people are doing (e.g., in speeches and on banners publicizing major rites or when Balinese act as informants to foreign researchers). Second, there is often a great deal of overlap between the rites and procedures that would fall under these five categories respectively. See C. Hooykaas 1975 for a comparison of Indic and Balinese uses of the phrase *pañca-yajñya/ panca-yajnya* (or *-yadnya*).

12. It is also sometimes described as a *carun palemahan* (*caru* of place), as opposed to a *carun sasih* (*caru* of occasion; Wikarman 2006). Yet there are also those who insist the CRG is not in fact a *caru* rite at all but rather a form of devotion to the elephant-headed deity Ganapati, or Gaṇeśa. My sense is that this is driven by a desire to align local practice with the devotional style of spirituality associated with a reform Hinduism oriented to India.

13. The representation of ceremonial rites as *upacara* situates them within the tripartite division of "Hindu religion" as wisdom, ethics, and ritual (I. *tattwa, susila,* and *yadnya;* see PHDKT 1979).

14. Despite the proliferation of taxonomy in formal representations of the island's religious and cultural traditions, in my experience Balinese habits of thought and action do not favor this style of classification (see, e.g., Picard 1990 on the difficulties that arose from the bureaucratic effort to distinguish between "sacred" and "profane" dances).

15. See, e.g., Warren 1993; Barth 1993; Stephen 2005. It is worth noting that this designation implies a specificity that Balinese will often go to some lengths to avoid. Fine distinctions may be drawn in the gradual refinement and purification of the souls of the deceased, for which terms such as *pirata, pitara,* and *déwata* or *déwa-pitara* are used. Yet, in nonexpert commentary, one of the most commonly employed Balinese terms is *leluhur,* which is an abstract noun indicating something like "who or what is up there."

16. Stuart-Fox (2002, 159–79) has described this process in terms of a five-stage "idiom of ritual" that includes purification, invitation, prestation, counterprestation, and dispersion. Despite similarities in terminology, I have taken a somewhat different approach to how these rites are understood by those involved in their performance— and, as importantly, what this means for their status as events (see later in this chapter).

17. The ward regulations current at the time of my fieldwork stipulated that each of the neighboring houseyards send both a man and a woman to contribute a single day's labor. In the past, they were to receive in return a package containing a fixed portion of rice, meat, vegetables, and spices. In an effort to reduce the expense of major ceremonies, a new provision had recently been added to the regulations banning this provision of food. But the ban was commonly ignored, even by those responsible for writing it— raising some question as to the purposes impelling the enactment of new legislation.

18. The situation has been greatly improved with the ready availability of private automobiles and, more recently, cellular phones. However, one is often still left waiting for priests, a fact perhaps not unrelated to the deference embodied in the act of waiting.

19. Each direction is associated with a chicken of a different color plumage (see Stuart-Fox 2002, 98). And every chicken is to be accompanied by, e.g., the directional

number of Chinese coins, satay sticks, rice cones, and portions of the various spiced meat mixtures and related offerings. Several of the rice offerings incorporate the colors associated with their directional orientations, as do their flags, which may also be marked with the appropriate weapons (see, e.g., Arwati 2008; Wikarman 2006; cf. Stuart-Fox 2002, 153–58).

20. On *nyāsa*, see C. Hooykaas 1964, 36–38, as well as both Hunter 2016 and Acri 2016.

21. As with the five chickens laid out on the ground, the white duck is also to be splayed out "as if alive," its insides having been removed to make small piles of red- and white-colored mixtures of meat, vegetables, and spices (B. *urab*). These are to be laid out in accordance with the *urip* (life[?]) numbers associated with the compass directions. But, in contrast to the chickens, the duck is not accompanied by sticks of satay (B./K. *jatah*).

22. This includes the four cardinal directions plus the center. There is a fair degree of variation in actual usage (e.g., on *ulap-ulap*).

23. The ordered sequence (B. *éédan*) for activating the preparatory instruments was described by the *rsi* as follows: *pabiakaonan, tebasan durmanggala, prayascita, pangulapan, panglukatan, pabersihan, sasarik tepung tawar,* and the *lis*. See Arwati 2003 for descriptions of the *pabiakaonan, tebasan durmanggala,* and *prayascita*; on the *lis*, see Hooykaas-van Leeuwen Boomkamp 1961.

24. I have heard this piece of music called *dug dag pur*, imitating its main sequence of tones or "notes." But it may also simply be called *baléganjur*, referring to the arrangement of instruments. Interestingly, when I enquired about the latter with one of Batan Nangka's leading musicians, he replied, "Here it's often called *galé ganjur*. But in my opinion this may actually come from the term *kala*, as in *kalé ganjur*, because the word *Balaganjur* means 'motivator of the *bala*,' the forces of battle. Who knows . . . maybe it's also a motivator for *bhutakala*."

25. The counterclockwise direction is commonly linked to processes of undoing or destruction (B. *pralina*). In subsequent conversation, a brahmin high priest explained this in terms of shutting down the pathway by which the recently transformed *bhutakala* might regain their malevolent character. As evidence, he pointed to the way the small temporary shrines are torn down at this stage in the rite.

26. Shortly thereafter a *segehan agung* offering was dedicated to the *rsi bhujangga*'s signature bell, the *bajra uter*. This included decapitating a black baby chick.

27. See, e.g., Belo 1953; C. Hooykaas 1977; Lovric 1987, 138–40; Stephen 2005, 16; cf. Howe 2005, 80, for a vaguely structuralist recasting of the apotropaic argument in terms of *caru* as a "re-ordering" of the world.

28. The Balinese phrase *bhuta ya, déwa ya* (meaning something like "they're *bhuta*, they're *déwa*") is frequently used in improvised drama as indicative of this transformation. Although I am unaware of a specific textual precedent, my guess is that this is a Balinized reworking of the Sanskrit datives *bhūtāya* and *devāya*, as one finds in exhortations of praise (e.g., *oṃ namaḥ śivāya*, "homage to Śiva!").

29. Note that, as with so many of the forces addressed through ceremonial work in Bali, the agent of this phrase was left unspecified.

30. As a younger man, Ida Rsi had been both a schoolteacher and an accomplished actor; but his family was also known to specialize in a martial art that entailed the cultivation of invulnerability.

31. B./I. "Yan makna caru 'nika nggih . . . membersihkan secara niskala."

32. Another commonly encountered term is *netralisir*, "to neutralize."

33. In contrast to some of Bali's other high-profile religious commentators, his call to simplify the preparation of offerings is generally tempered by respect for local variation.

34. There are several possible reasons for the *padanda*'s decision to speak Indonesian. The most obvious is my inexpert handling of the formal register employed in addressing someone of such exalted status. In speaking Indonesian, he may also have been trying to avoid the use of pronouns and related terminology that would betray an exaggerated investment in his position. Hierarchy is clearly important to Ratu Padanda, in terms of both caste and office. But he would often affect a certain casualness that I took to be directed to putting his clients at ease and to establishing rapport built on the mutual recognition of "religion" as but one of the many competing demands of modern life. In my experience, this modernizing sensibility seems to be one of the ways in which he tries to distinguish himself from others of his station. Like Ida Rsi, he often speaks Indonesian with his younger petitioners.

35. In my experience Balinese tend not to deal in absolutes, which would suggest that the change might be limited to the comportment of these beings toward a particular person or group—namely, those who had provided the offerings and entertainment.

36. The Indonesian/Balinese transcript reads as follows:

Self: Kalau upakara itu yang ditanam dan di-anu . . . karajah 'nika . . . sané marajah aksara 'nika . . . kalau yang itu . . . seperti ulap-ulap . . . apakah itu bisa dipakai juga untuk memangg . . .

Padanda: Mamanggil? Nggak. Memanggil, nggak.

Self: Tidak?

Padanda: Nggak. Béda. Ulap-ulap hanya yang . . . ini yang disebut dengan ulap-ulap.

Self: Ya.

Padanda: Kalau itu, nggak. Yang marajah namanya itu. Béda.

Self: Oh, tan tan. Maksud saya . . . Napi gunan ipun . . . pateh ring sané kaanggén . . .

Padanda: Nggak, nggak. Béda.

Self: Béda?

Padanda: Kalau umpamanya . . . yang marajah nawasanga itu . . . di tepung itu . . . memohon kepada déwata nawasanga agar lingkungnya itu dijaga ketat.

Self: Jaga ketat?

Padanda: Ya, jaga ketat . . . supaya jangan ada unsur negatif lagi masuk, 'gitu.

Self: Sakadi bénténg?

Padanda: Bénténg itu. Itu memang bénténg. Istilah Balinya tumbal itu.

Self: Tumbal?

Padanda: Tumbal ya. Istilah Balinya itu tumbal. Pangijeng, ya. Yang lebih kasar pangijeng. Kalau Bahasa Indonesianya penjaga.

37. As Hildred Geertz (1994, 2) has noted, in Bali the line between "sorcery" and "religion" is not so easily drawn.

38. For instance, there may be more to sweeping than meets the eye. My older consultants in Batan Nangka recalled brooms (B. *sampat*) envisaged as a sort of weapon. When a small child went to sleep, for example, one would place a palm-rib broom (B. *sampat lidi*) down beside the child as a *penolak* ("refuser" or "repeller") to ward off potentially dangerous beings and forces. The simile often used was *sampat dadi sungga*, where the *sungga* was a sharpened set of bamboo shafts placed with one end in the ground and the other facing in (or out) of one's garden (B. *kebun*) to prevent people from going in to steal fruit—if they run in or out, they will impale their shins on the *sungga*. Similarly, if one must sleep outside and is afraid of what might attack, one may also erect a *sampat dadi sungga*—with the sweeping ends of the palm-rib broom sticking up into the air.

39. When I enquired, the *rsi* said that he had learned what he knew of these rites from his preceptor and not from reading texts.

40. The Hooykaas-Ketut Sangka Collection is the product of the Balinese Manuscript Project, which was started by Christiaan Hooykaas in 1970 in collaboration with with Ngurah Ketut Sangka from Puri Gede in Kerambitan, Tabanan. The project picked up from the colonial-era collection of manuscripts housed at the Gedong Kirtya in Singaraja and has been continued by Hedi Hinzler and Déwa Gedé Catra in Karangasem (see Hinzler 1983).

41. As several of my more thoughtful interlocutors pointed out, it is difficult to know quite how to interpret the term *kaputusan* in this connection. Most would initially take it as "the final word" on the CRG, in analogy to Indonesian *keputusan*. But, on further reflection, several pointed to other associations of the Kawi term, leaning more to the idea of "perfection" or "the completed form." Variations on the instructions themselves are replicated in any number of *lontar* dealing with the maintenance of a houseyard, usually figuring in a sequence of similar sections dealing with other *caru* rites (e.g., *caru nangluk merana*). Some examples would include *Babacakan Caru* (HKS 7045), *Caru Pambalik Sumpah mwang Resigana* (HKS 7377), *Dharma ning Astakosali* (HKS 6958), and *Tutur Lebur Gangsa* (K 3660, HKS 2491, Or. 15.635).

42. Compare Shelley Errington's (1979, 240) remark on Malay *hikayat*.

43. As already suggested, the term *suci* may not always mean "pure" but rather a sort of intensified or empowered condition (see concluding section of chapter 7).

44. The Kawi-Balinese text reads as follows: "salwiring panes, yan mati salah pati, kalebon amuk, snambering gelap, makrana sang adruwé umah kabaya-baya."

45. The phrasing is interesting, if not unusual. One might wish to see in *kojarana* (K. "is/will/would be said") reference to a tradition of effective apotropaic measures—i.e., as the thing gerundively "to be done" under such conditions. But it is also consonant with a more general tendency in colloquial Balinese to hedge uncertainty, where "it is said" (B. *koné*) may be added to any statement for which one is lacking directly substantiating evidence.

46. This is not to suggest that multiple readings are not possible. It is simply to specify the "translation manual" (Quine 1960, 27; see chapter 7) required to get from the Kawi-Balinese terminology of the *BKh* to the specific reading presented as its Indonesian "translation" (I. *terjemahan*).

47. There are also *lontar* manuscripts that bear the descriptor *tatulak agung* (e.g., HKS 6826) and closely related terms (e.g., HKS 1111; HKS 3394; HKS 6464).

5. Maintaining a Houseyard as a Practice

1. There is potentially a slippage here between the ideals teleologically impelling an act and those invoked subsequently in accounting for its performance—a problem to which I shall return in the final chapter.

2. A case in point is the incommensurate lines of enquiry brought together in the Hobart-Couldry exchange on "media practices" (see Couldry 2010; Hobart 2010; Couldry and Hobart 2010).

3. See Laidlaw 2014 for a critique of the anthropology of ethics as reduced to what Zygmund Baumann characterized in terms of "the science of unfreedom."

4. By *common sense* I mean to suggest something like Gramsci's (1971, 323–43) use of the phrase (see chapter 1, note 43).

5. As Kelvin Knight explained, "What the concept of a virtue is secondary to on his account is not a metaphysical biology but a 'logical development' of three stages in which 'each later stage presupposes the earlier, but not *vice versa*' " (1998, 10).

6. It must be emphasized that this is not progress in any absolute sense but rather as judged with reference to criteria that belong to the practice itself. As Christopher S. Lutz noted in his commentary on *After Virtue*, "American football is conventional, but its development is real, and if Walter Camp or Knute Rockne were to attend a contemporary college football game, they would probably be surprised at the size, strength, speed, skill and achievements of today's players" (2012, 120).

7. As James Laidlaw has pointed out, with Bourdieu "a great deal of ingenuity goes into demonstrating that everything that might be thought to lie outside the economic logic of competition and struggle can really be reduced analytically to another modality of the movement of capital. . . . Disinterestedness indeed is an ideological illusion" (2014, 6).

8. This was precisely the issue at stake in suggesting we emulate David Halperin's approach to taking the ancient Greeks "at their word" on sex (see chapter 1).

9. His body was whisked out the front gates and into a parked vehicle so that he would not be seen to die in the houseyard itself, which would have necessitated a series of costly purification rites. In turn this would likely have entailed a deferral of the wedding, which would have been both risky and potentially embarrassing for the prospective bride's family, as she was already visibly pregnant.

10. At the center of most Balinese wards is a large wooden slit-gong (B. *kulkul*) suspended from an elevated pavilion. It is beaten in specified rhythms to alert the community to various events, from the start of communal labor to deaths, fires, and incidents of violence or danger. To answer the call of the slit-gong is one of the exemplary acts of ward membership.

11. See, e.g., C. Geertz 1973, 446; Vickers 1991, 94–103. The liveliness of a temple festival obviously differs from that of day-to-day life in one's houseyard. But, in both cases, the term *ramé* may be used to designate the desired condition—particularly when it is lacking, as in a houseyard with no children.

12. A room that has long been out of use is often said to have a similar feeling, which can be dispelled by sleeping in the room for one or more nights. A member of the family may perform this duty before a disused room is offered to a houseguest, to ensure it gives

off a welcoming, "lived in" feeling. It may be noted that, although less tangible beings and forces—"spirits of the place"—may often seem an unwelcome intrusion, they can also potentially be called on as protectors. Those who "dare" (B. *bani*) may even deliberately choose to live in locations frequented by such beings—e.g., beside streams, woods, or ravines—in the hope of gaining their favor.

13. Note that sweeping is generally done at the same interstitial moments—dawn and dusk—when the small offerings are made at regular points throughout the houseyard and its surrounding environs. The importance of fluid movement and the avoidance of congestion seems somehow important for both.

14. For example, one of Pateluan's leading comic actors would make but perfunctory visits to family events, leaving before the food had been presented. As he had built a new compound for himself on purchased land, he avoided helping in the preparations for the rite; but, as he had not erected a proper family temple in his new houseyard, neither was he obliged to perform a ceremony of his own. By abstaining from preparations and refusing to accept a gift of food, his denial of responsibility was double. Though the family was not seen to complain publicly, the arrogance and humiliation was not lost on the wider community.

15. The "small, happy, and prosperous family" norm was fostered through programs for family planning and village-level education (see, e.g., Newland 2001; Niehof and Lubis 2003).

16. It is in part through learning to "use" these items that Balinese are coming to embody the virtues of this relatively novel style of domesticity.

17. In the case of larger temples, the anniversary ceremony will often include a sermon, or religious talk (I. *dharma wacana*), from a well-known priest. This is indicative of a broader transformation of priests from learned (and so potentially dangerous) technicians into spiritual advisers.

18. Note the transformation engendered in the shift from Balinese *maraga* and *pinaka* to Indonesian *menyimbulkan*. While the former terms suggest a relation of imminence ("embodying" and "being used as," respectively), the latter implies the transcendence of an object that is but secondarily and contingently represented by its "symbol" (I. *simbul*).

19. The psychologization of destructive forces is a regular feature of articles run in the *Bali Post* on feast days and holidays, such as Pagerwesi, Siwalatri, and Galungan. Here a long-standing emphasis on the efficacy of ceremonial rites and collective labor is clawed back to the personal spirituality and "introspection" (I. *mawas dari*) of state bureaucratic Hinduism.

20. Elsewhere (Fox 2011, chaps. 8 and 9), I have examined theatrical representations of this ideal, with an emphasis on the figure of the ruler as an agent that articulates, and so ensures the well-being of, the realm.

6. Tradition as Argument

1. The original Indonesian text reads, "Dipilihnya Sanggar Maha Bajra Sandhi karena pemikirannya yang radikal dalam usaha merevitalisasi peranan aksara yang

arkhais dalam kehidupan sehari-hari, membumikan yang simbolis dan menghidupkan kembali ritus musik, memberikan alternatif tentang pengertian seni, keluarga dan hidup itu sendiri dalam masyarakat modern" (quoted on the cover of Granoka 2007).

2. For an alternative approach to the idea of tradition in Southeast Asia, see Carbine 2011; cf. contributions to Engler and Grieve 2005.

3. By starting from the interpretability of practices, and emphasizing its reliance on tradition, I am reversing the order of priority in MacIntyre's early account (see [1981] 2010, 186–87; cf. "Differing in Practice" section in chapter 5).

4. Consider, for instance, the cross-referencing employed in scholarly translations of ancient or otherwise arcane texts, where precedent is cited as evidence in support of the interpretation of a given word or phrase.

5. Ironically, both tradition's most vehement champions (self-designated "conservatives") and its detractors (those "progressive" critics of the "invention of tradition") share this common, yet problematic, understanding of tradition.

6. All names of Balinese people and places are pseudonymous, apart from Ida Wayan Oka Granoka and locations within the provincial capital of Denpasar and Buda Keling.

7. In her study of *kakawin* composition, Rachelle Rubinstein has offered an explicit statement on tradition as periodization, writing, "Traditional Bali is, for me, dominated by a set of nineteenth century or earlier cultural values, including values pertaining to literacy. It cannot be delimited by dates, for strong pockets of traditional Bali exist alongside 'modern Bali,' and resist the influence of 'modern Bali,' the period that commenced when the Dutch succeeded in colonizing Bali—North Bali in 1849, and South Bali from 1906 to 1908" (2000, 3). Something similar to this understanding of the traditional is implicit in much of the scholarship on religion and culture in Southeast Asia, though it usually goes without the benefit of such careful qualification.

8. In using the term *genealogical*, I do not wish to link this usage too closely with either Friedrich Nietzsche or the later work of Michel Foucault. But I do want to indicate more generally both a nuanced attention to shifting uses of terminology and a desire to problematize the language of enquiry.

9. It is worth emphasizing that the *positive* and *genealogical* uses of tradition are often found together within one and the same publication.

10. Michel Picard has described the oppositional circumstances surrounding the emergence of the *désa pakraman*: "In order to give the newly restored customary village a more specific Balinese flavour, its name was changed from *desa adat* to *desa pakraman*. Unlike the word *adat*, which has both a colonial and an Islamic connotation, the term *pakraman* claims its authority from old Balinese inscriptions and is derived from the Sanskrit root *krama*, meaning 'rule sanctioned by tradition'" (2008, 106).

11. This reflects very neatly the ironic emplotment of modern historiography (White 1973).

12. My point is not so much that operationalized forms of Balinese tradition are all alike. I simply wish to note a certain commonality—namely, purposeful reification. As the engine of cultural tourism, tradition has been appropriated as a source of revenue. As an instrument of the state, it has been used to foster national unity through the regularization and management of religious, ethnic, and linguistic difference. And more recently, with Ajeg Bali, the idea of Balinese tradition has been made to serve the interests

of those who wish to marginalize non-Balinese residents of the island while at the same time controlling access to the revenue generated through the tourism industry.

13. See, e.g., Noszlopy 2002; Schulte Nordholt 2007; Picard 2008; Vickers 2011.

14. My aim is not to collapse arguments from *identity* into those made in terms of a purportedly universal *will to power* but rather to point up both a common hermeneutic of suspicion and shared battery of critical procedures.

15. See the section on *agama* in chapter 7 for a discussion of the difficulties inherent in critical uses of the term *religion*.

16. "So rationality itself, whether theoretical or practical, is a concept with a history: indeed, since there are [*sic*] a diversity of traditions of enquiry, with histories, there are, so it will turn out, rationalities rather than rationality, just as it will also turn out that there are justices rather than justice" (MacIntyre 1988, 9).

17. Here I can provide but a thumbnail sketch of his project's primary contours. For, beyond MacIntyre's own writings, which are extensive, a complex and at times highly technical commentarial literature has grown up around his work. See Knight 2007 for a detailed assessment of MacIntyre's relation to the wider Aristotelian tradition and Lutz 2004 on the idea of "tradition" in particular.

18. See chapter 5 on the three-stage reconstruction of virtue, with specific reference to practice. With regard to the narrative unity of a single human life, my understanding is that this is directed at once to a critique of the broadly modern liberal proclivity for a compartmentalization of life, whereby "no overall ordering of goods is possible" (MacIntyre 1988, 337), and at the same time to the problem of rendering intelligible—as a form of rational progress—those forms of transformation that entail a change in one's commitments—whether in the pursuit of scientific, religious, or moral forms of enquiry (MacIntyre 2006, 19).

19. Citing MacIntyre, Talal Asad (1986b) developed this temporal aspect in an early essay on Islamic "discursive traditions," which he proposed as the object of study proper to the anthropology of Islam. On my reading, Asad's aim was to raise new and more constructive questions by shifting critical attention away from the abstractions of "social structure" and "shared cultural meanings" onto the history of embodied practices—such as those of pedagogical discipline, ethical exhortation, and public piety (see, e.g., Mahmood 2005; Hirschkind 2006).

20. The pursuit of progress in rationality is itself envisaged constructively (i.e., "normatively") as a practice and so as dependent on the virtues of justice, courage, and truthfulness (MacIntyre [1981] 2010, 194).

21. For MacIntyre's extrapolation from Lakatos against Thomas S. Kuhn and Paul Feyerabend, see MacIntyre 2006; cf. Lutz 2012, 7.

22. As George A. Kennedy wrote in his oft-cited study of classical rhetoric, "The Greek male orator, like the Greek male athlete, seeks to win and gain honor from defeating an opponent" (1999, 6; cf. MacIntyre 1988, 27–29); on metaphorical iterations of "argument as war," see Lakoff and Johnson 1980, 4–5.

23. Such indirection is widely recognized as a sign of wisdom and sophistication, while my inability to discern his meaning would be seen as reflecting my naïveté.

24. The term *grebeg* is also used in reference to other events at which powerful objects and forces are called together. In Pateluan, for example, all the *rangda* and *barong*

assemble annually at the Pura Puseh to be venerated and, at least on some accounts, to assess the state of their realm and subjects. In Balinese usage, the term *grebeg* may suggest a procession, especially pertaining to royalty. It is possible this draws on the term's more general sense in Kawi, as "the thunderous tramping of many feet" (Zoetmulder 1982, vol.1, 543). It is also worth noting there is a series of well-known rites performed in Yogyakarta known as the *garebeg mulud*, *garebeg sawal*, and *garebeg besar*. These associations may all have factored in Granoka's conception of the event as a "Grebeg Aksara."

25. See Schulte Nordholt 1996, 213–14.

26. As I later learned, the group was also sent to Athens in 2004 as part of the Indonesian delegation to the Cultural Olympiad (see quotation at the beginning of this chapter).

27. The Indonesian text reads, "Seperti ada 'kesepahaman' antara orang-orang Eropa dan Indonesia, terutama Bali, bahwa jalinan persahabatan itu mesti diberi 'energi' ulang dengan pementasan kesenian tradisi."

28. It is difficult to know how one could reliably confirm these sums.

29. It must be noted that Arcana is not alone in having taken this genealogical approach to the cultural politics of contemporary Bali. Other Balinese commentators—including, e.g., Degung Santikarma, Ngurah Suryawan, Nyoman Darma Putra, Nyoman Wijaya, and Wayan Juniartha—have made similarly sophisticated use of the recent historical scholarship in their writings and other contributions to public debate. These Balinese scholar-commentators are actively involved in a range of projects directed to improving collective life on the island. In contrast to the work of their broadly western counterparts, the political import of their scholarship is usually quite explicit. As I have tried to show elsewhere (Fox 2010), the current Euro-American scholarship on Balinese history owes much to these very figures—Darma Putra, Santikarma, et al.—as they were originally some of its key informants. The resulting circularity of citation warrants closer attention.

30. The title for this section is borrowed from a phrase Granoka himself has often used, which I would provisionally translate as "The Big Syncretism Concept." In addition to leading the Sanggar Maha Bajra Sandhi, Granoka lectured in the Faculty of Letters at the island's flagship university and has published scholarly works on various aspects of Balinese language and literature. He is also an as yet unconsecrated member of a priestly lineage from the community of Buda Kling, home to the island's famed "Bauddha Brahmins" (C. Hooykaas 1963), which he proudly cites as the source of Bali's true spiritual legacy and hope for the future.

31. This is presumably an Indonesian play on the well-known Pāli/Sanskrit term *dhammacakkappavattana/dharmacakrapravartana*, associated with the *sūtra* of that name.

32. The Sanskrit term *sādhana* suggests very generally the idea of bringing something about, of "accomplishing" or "effecting" (Apte [1890] 2014, 1115; cf. Monier-Williams 1899, 1201). In Buddhist discourse, and particularly in the *tantras*, it comes to refer more specifically to rites of self-transformation and empowerment (see Bentor 1996, 1–8). The corpus entries in P. J. Zoetmulder's *Old Javanese-English Dictionary* (1982, 1586) suggest that a similar sense is not uncommon in Kawi. Although Granoka was not forthcoming with respect to his sources, it would not be surprising if he were familiar with these usages.

33. This is not to say that Granoka's elaborations on *aksara* were entirely of his own invention—a point some feel he has not adequately acknowledged. As a former university colleague put it, "In my opinion Granoka was greatly inspired by Ngurah Bagus' inaugural lecture [on which see chapter 1]. Just ask him directly! If he doesn't admit it, he's being less than honest [I. *kurang jujur*]." As if by way of evidence, he later sent me a heavily annotated photocopy of Bagus's lecture with Granoka's name handwritten on the cover (i.e., seemingly indicating that the original had been Granoka's own copy). Yet, in the acknowledgments section of *Reinkarnasi Budaya*, Granoka cited Bagus not so much as an inspiration but rather as "the former teacher of mine who best understood what I've desired and have been doing all this time" (2007, xxvi–xxvii).

34. The phrase *visi dan misi* is standard Indonesian bureaucratese, encountered in everything from nongovernmental organizations and government projects to local school initiatives and banking cooperatives.

35. The language of "crisis" (I. *krisis*) came into popular usage in Indonesian following the financial crisis of 1997, with such turns of phrase as, e.g., "Monetary Crisis" (*Krismon*), "Economic Crisis" (*Kriskon*), and even "Total Crisis" (*Kristal*).

36. This is standard practice for those invited to perform on such occasions, where a careful balance must be struck between refusing "payment" and accepting a monetary token of "sincerity" or "appreciation" for services rendered.

37. Pénjor (see earlier discussion) had suggested this was an important part of Granoka's "strategy"—to "dazzle" with rapid-fire lateral associations, then "strike" while his interlocutor is bewildered and defenseless.

38. This particular play on words—viz. the movement from "letters" (*aksara*) to "indestructibility" (*a-ksara*; I. *tidak termusnahkan*)—may have been drawn from the Dutch scholarship on Balinese literature (see C. Hooykaas 1978, 76).

39. As Granoka noted, the letters *A*, *C*, *T*, and *G* are used to represent DNA sequences in scientific practice.

40. The paratactic juxtaposition of nominal phrases is not uncommon in Kawi composition, an issue to which I shall return in just a moment.

41. This form of periodization has precedents in precolonial Javanese historiography. Commenting on a well-known genre of Javanese prophetic texts called *Jangka Jayabaya*, Nancy Florida has written, "The schema for the periodization of Javanese history presented by these texts divides historical time into three major eras (*kala*), each consisting of 700 years" (1995, 273). Florida's description of these texts offers several interesting points of comparison with Granoka's project.

42. The notion of an "invented tradition" would then, it seems, be either tautologous or incoherent.

43. Very briefly, the associations forged by Granoka's linguistic panoply include the following: alongside its work as the language of articulation, Indonesian signals the ideals of national unity and the hopes of modernity; Balinese bears the stamp of cultural authenticity and pertinence to "everyday village life"; Sanskrit forges the link between the former two and an Indic high tradition of ancient wisdom and spirituality; Old Javanese exemplifies a more localized strain of esoteric power and knowledge, as well as continuity with the glory of Majapahit, providing the charter for a better Indonesia;

English further demonstrates the modernizing sensibilities of science and cosmopolitanism; German is predominately talismanic, channeling high literary and academic culture; Latin similarly points to an idealized and broadly Eurocentric vision of academic culture; and, finally, Chinese serves as an inoculation (Barthes 1972) of high Asian civilization directed to countering the appearance of western hegemony implicit in the preponderance of English, German, and Latin terminology.

44. Here one might also compare the way in which Granoka's *Reinkarnasi Budaya* rearranges syllables to form new words and phrases as a sort of contemplative instrument, or *yantra*—e.g., DE-SA MA-PRA-YO-GA, SA-MA PRA-YO-GA DE, MA-PRA-YO-GA DE-SA, PRA-YO-GA DE SA-MA (2007, 160).

45. See Gonda [1973] 1998, 472–73.

46. There is potentially an interesting comparison to be made with the broadly Thai Buddhist ideal that Justin T. McDaniel (2011, 67–68) has described in terms of "abundance" *(udom sombun)*.

47. The dating of *babad* is an uncertain endeavor at best. With the exception of the *Kidung Pamancangah*, it is difficult to date any *babad* to a point before the Dutch takeover of Buleleng (Adrian Vickers and Jarrah Sastrawan, personal communication, June 16, 2017; cf. Hobart 2007, 113n13).

48. There is a problematic tendency toward essentialization ("the literate mind," etc.) in both Sweeney's writing and the scholarship on which he was drawing. However, the more general point regarding "media" and the articulation of human agency and collective life is highly suggestive.

49. See Ong 1958a on the historical transformation of knowledge and pedagogy associated with the sixteenth-century scholastic Peter Ramus. There is an unfortunate tendency to dismiss Walter J. Ong's work on the grounds of his later, more popular writings (especially 1982)—and as often on the basis of secondary or tertiary commentary. In my view, anthropologists would have much to gain from a more careful and sustained engagement with his work (see the section entitled "Toward an Ethnography of Script," chapter 1).

50. For now I would prefer to leave as an open question the connection between Sweeney's argument for an "oral" style of composition, on the one hand, and the fundamentally "literate" character of Aristotelian thought, on the other.

51. Obviously there are many exceptions; an interesting example may be found in accounts of radical (or "agonistic") democracy, which developed insights from the political philosophy of Carl Schmitt (see, e.g., Laclau and Mouffe 1985 [2001]; Mouffe 2000). Notably, these too are organized around a combative metaphor for rationality.

52. "Descartes's failure is complex. First of all he does not recognize that among the features of the universe which he is not putting in doubt is his own capacity not only to use the French and the Latin languages, but even to express the same thought in both languages; and as a consequence he does not put in doubt what he has inherited in and with these languages, namely, a way of ordering both thought and the world expressed in a set of meanings. These meanings have a history; seventeenth-century Latin bears the marks of having been the language of scholasticism, just as scholasticism was itself marked by the influence of twelfth and thirteenth- century Latin. It was perhaps because

the presence of his languages was invisible to the Descartes of the *Discours* and the *Meditationes* that he did not notice either what Gilson pointed out in detail, how much of what he took to be the spontaneous reflections of his own mind was in fact a repetition of sentences and phrases from his school textbooks. Even the Cogito is to be found in Saint Augustine" (MacIntyre 2006, 9).

7. Translational Indeterminacy

1. For an oft-cited definition of *catachresis* as a rhetorical figure, see Lausberg 1963, 65. By way of example, Roland Barthes observed in *S/Z*, "There is no other possible word to denote the 'wings' of a house, or the 'arms' of a chair, and yet 'wings' and 'arms' are *instantly, already* metaphorical" (Barthes 1974, 34; on the more general importance of catachresis for the historical constitution of the human sciences, see Foucault [1966] 2002, 122–25).

2. As David Bellos observed, "A translator only 'carries [something] across [some obstacle]' because the word that is used to describe what he does meant 'bear across' in an ancient language" (2012, 26).

3. See, e.g., Hobart 2000; Hodgson 2011; Abu-Lughod 2013.

4. Mary Douglas recognized early on the implications for anthropology, noting that Quine's "arguments are directed against many of our time-honoured and favourite fallacies, from pre-logical mentality to the idea that meaning is an independent, free floating entity, which words try to capture more or less completely" (1972, 28).

5. See, e.g., Douglas 1972; Evens 1983; Salmond 1989; Hobart 1991a; Hanks 2014.

6. According to Hanks and Severi, for instance, "Quine presses this dilemma [viz. of "radical translation"], and the critique of empiricism it implies, from the limits on intelligibility of an unknown foreign language all the way to limits on understanding our own language, at which point reference truly goes 'inscrutable'" (2014, 4).

7. MacIntyre specified this assumption with exemplary clarity: "Central to every culture is a shared schema of greater or lesser complexity by means of which each agent is able to render the actions of others intelligible so that he or she knows how to respond to them. This schema is not necessarily ever explicitly articulated by agents themselves, and even when it is so articulated, they may make mistakes and misunderstand what it is that they do in understanding others. But an external observer, particularly one coming from an alien culture, cannot hope to understand action and transaction except in terms of such an interpretive schema" (1988, 22).

8. Butler (2004) has written a separate essay that specifically addresses the problem of translation. And yet, while more detailed than her passing remarks in the 2009 symposium, her concerns remain focused on the relationship *between* languages, as if the very notion of a language were itself unproblematic.

9. As Michel Picard pointed out in response to an earlier draft of this chapter, the Indonesian Board of Education's Balinese-Indonesian dictionary (Warna 1990, 7) offers three Indonesian terms under the entry for *agama*. These are (1) *agama*, (2) *hukum*, and (3) *adat-istiadat*—which are often respectively glossed as "religion," "law," and "traditional

custom." Quite apart from the circularity and deferral engendered in such "definition," he noted that this equation of *agama* and *adat* is at odds with state bureaucratic efforts to distinguish the universality and legitimacy of religion (*agama*) from the particularity and backwardness of local custom (*adat-istiadat*).

10. See, e.g., H. Geertz 2000; Picard 2011c, 3.

11. See, e.g., appendices to H. Geertz and C. Geertz 1975; and Hobart 1979.

12. By *polity* I mean to suggest a form of complex agency (Hobart 1991b; Inden 1990) articulated, and rearticulated, through ongoing and variously mediated public argument over the nature and pursuit of shared goods. Developing out of the critique of practice (see chapters 4 and 5), I use this term specifically in contrast to *society*, which tends to figure as an objective fait accompli ready and waiting for analysis (cf. Strathern 2005; Inden n.d.).

13. To be clear, this is not to suggest that "the common good" is understood in identical terms by all involved. Its articulation and pursuit is an open-ended matter, continually up for debate. Consequently, the ward community may itself be seen as constituted by the ongoing argument over shared goods and the means best suited to realizing them.

14. It must be emphasized that neither the ward (B. *banjar*) nor the village (B. *désa*) was ever the discrete village republic (D. *dorpsrepubliek*) of Dutch colonial imagination. The ward was simply one—admittedly crucial—form of collectivity among several (e.g., irrigation society, temple congregation, descent group) that have historically made up the social life of Balinese.

15. Picard (2011a) has attributed the formulation of the *Panca-sraddha* to Narendra Dev Pandit's 1955 publication of a booklet entitled *Intisari Hindu Dharma*. However, as he noted, although they were promoted as early as 1964, it was not until 1967 that that these five "pillars of belief" were adopted as a formal doctrine for *Agama Hindu* (see PHD 1967).

16. Although Balinese tend to use this form (viz. *atma*) in conversation, the form found in official documents and public speeches commonly includes the final *-n* from the Sanskrit stem, *ātman* (e.g., as it appears in philologically ordered dictionaries). The latter seems to be a relatively novel form for Balinese, perhaps reflecting a desire to be "Sanskritically correct," with all that implies. On the treatment of *-n* stems more generally in Sanskrit loanwords, see Gonda [1973] 1998, 420.

17. See contributions to Picard and Madinier 2011.

18. See Becker 1995c; cf. Leavitt 2014; McDowell 2000.

19. "To put it crudely: because the languages of Third World societies—including, of course, the societies that social anthropologists have traditionally studied—are 'weaker' in relation to Western languages (and today, especially to English), they are more likely to submit to forcible transformation in the translation process than the other way around" (Asad 1986a, 157–58).

20. Vološinov's phrasing raises the interesting question of what must be presupposed in translating an utterance, as opposed to translating the idealized form of "the sentence" or "statement."

21. It is also evident in the improvisational dramas that have long figured as a privileged arena for social and political commentary (Fox 2013b).

22. See, e.g., Bateson and Mead 1942, 251; Hinzler 1986, 496; Vickers 2012, 81.

23. With the term *anthropologies* I mean to suggest something like *projects* or *processes of becoming human*—a notion for which Balinese have a most useful phrase, *dadi manusa*.

24. Her prior boyfriend was an only child, and his family was both local and reasonably affluent—and so potentially able to prevent a wedding to which they objected. By contrast, Gdé was from a distant village, and his family was relatively impoverished—and so would have little recourse should they wish to complain.

25. The situation was complicated by the fact that her elder sister had an acrimonious relationship with their father. As I understand it, a long-standing and relatively muted antagonism had broken out into open conflict a couple of years beforehand, when the elder sister discovered that their father was having an extramarital affair. The wider family was all too aware that this, too, may have played a part in the push for Dani to remain in the houseyard. The elder sister was by all accounts looking forward to leaving.

26. It is also commonly linked to *purus*, a word for "penis" in the honorific register (Warna 1990, 558; see Hobart 1979, 313–14).

27. In other words, the idea of *human being* constituted by such Indically inflected notions as *atma* and *purusa* seems to have been out of step with this particular set of events.

28. See note 23.

29. This is not to say that Balinese are engaging in "translation" per se. My point is rather that the indeterminacy of these terms has allowed for a certain degree of slippage, which Balinese have often played to various kinds of advantage. When it comes to the linguistic operations we conceive as "translation," Balinese do not have a ready term for what is called *terjemah* (commonly glossed as "translate") in Indonesian. Yet there is a rich language about language, including terms for "glossing" (B. *ngartiang/ngartos*; see Hobart 2000, 191) and "imitating" (B. *ngojah*) the speech of others, which becomes particularly important in dramatic performances making use of multiple linguistic registers.

30. See, e.g., Duff-Cooper 1985, 153; Howe 2005, 71; Stuart-Fox 2015, 91; cf. concluding section of chapter 3.

31. The link between purity and efficacy has been noted by others (see, e.g., Hobart 1979, 461–73; Connor 1982b, 295–96. And the relationship between *suci* and *sakti* may at times be a case of Balinese holding together what Europeans and Americans are wont to separate. Yet my conversations in Batan Nangka would suggest there is more to the play on *suci* than a simple association of ideals.

32. On the relationship between translation and more general hermeneutics, see Nida 1964; Gadamer 1993, 384–89; Palmer 1969, 26–31.

8. Wagging the Dog

1. See chapter 5, note 1. I have borrowed the phrase *prologue to action* from MacIntyre's (1988, 16–23) discussion of the various ways in which translators have dealt with the Homeric notion of *thumos*.

2. See chapter 7, "Religious Differences" section.

3. Although my characterization of the problem differs in several respects, this is very roughly analogous to what Bourdieu recognized in the gap between "logical logic" and the "logic of practice." For reasons addressed in chapter 5, the analogy ends there.

4. Pollock asked rhetorically, "And when will we begin to see that among the facts that are important in these texts is their textuality itself; that the creation of the fame and virtue of the king through a celebration of his virtue and fame is what this textuality is meant to do; that the metaphors of the texts are metaphors people lived by, and the education and cultural virtuosity they evince is a whole way of being?" (1996, 243).

Works Cited

Manuscripts

K   Gedong Kirtya Manuscript Collection, Gedong Kirtya, Singaraja, Bali, Indonesia.

HKS   Hooykaas-Ketut Sangka Collection, Balinese Manuscript Project, University of Leiden, Netherlands (see Hinzler 1983; some 1,500 of the more recent additions to the Collection are not yet available at the University; access to pertinent materials was generously provided by Dr. Hinzler).

LOr.   Leiden Oriental Manuscript Collection, University of Leiden, Netherlands.

Anak oeboeh, Singaraja (K 1759).
Babacakan caru, Jrowan, Abang, Karangasem (HKS 7045).
Bhamakretih, Puri Madhura, Amlapura, Karangasem (HKS 7769).
Caru pambalik sumpah mwang resigana, Griya Bêng, Gianyar (HKS 7377).
Dharma ning astakosali, Jasri, Karangasem (HKS 6958).
Tatulak agung, Griya Bungaya, Karangasem (HKS 6826).
Tatulak Mpu Siwagandu, Br. Tegalsari, Singaraja, Buleleng (HKS 1111, LOr. 13.569).
Tatulak Sang Hyang Panca Bayu, Br. Liligundi, Singaraja, Buleleng (HKS 3394, LOr. 16.538).
Tatulak Sang Hyang Resigana, Banyuning, Buleleng (HKS 6464).

Tatwa bhama kretih, Sibang Kaja, Badung (HKS 7480).
Tutur lebur gangsa, Sidan, Gianyar (HKS 2491, K 3660, LOr. 15.635).

Printed Works

Abu-Lughod, Lila. 2013. *Do Muslim Women Need Saving?* Cambridge, MA: Harvard University Press.

Acri, Andrea. 2006. "The Sanskrit-Old Javanese *Tutur* Literature from Bali: The Textual Basis of *Śaivism* in Ancient Indonesia." *Rivista di studi sudasiatici* 1:107–37.

———. 2010. "On Birds, Ascetics, and Kings in Central Java: *Rāmāyana* Kakawin, 24.95-126 and 25." *Bijdragen tot de taal-, land- en volkenkunde* 166 (4): 475–506.

———. 2011. "A New Perspective for 'Balinese Hinduism' in the Light of the Premodern Religious Discourse: A Textual-Historical Approach." In *The Politics of Religion in Indonesia*, edited by Michel Picard and Rémy Madinier, 142–66. London: Routledge.

———. 2013. "Modern Hindu Intellectuals and Ancient Texts: Reforming Śaiva Yoga in Bali." *Bijdragen tot de taal-, land- en volkenkunde* 169 (1): 68–103.

———. 2016. "Imposition of the Syllabary (*svaravyañjana-nyāsa*) in the Old Javano-Balinese Tradition in the Light of South Asian Tantric Sources." In *The Materiality and Efficacy of Balinese Letters: Situating Scriptural Practice*, edited by Richard Fox and Annette Hornbacher, 123–65. Leiden: Brill.

Acri, Andrea, and Arlo Griffiths. 2014. "The Romanization of Indic Script Used in Ancient Indonesia." *Bijdragen tot de taal-, land- en volkenkunde* 170 (2/3): 365–78.

Addams, Charles. 1964. *The Addams Family*. Beverly Hills: MGM Television and American Broadcasting Company.

Aditjondro, George. 1995. "Bali, Jakarta's Colony: Social and Ecological Impacts of Jakarta-Based Conglomerates in Bali's Tourism Industry." Working Paper No. 58. Asia Research Centre, Murdoch University, Perth.

Ahearn, Laura M. 2001. *Invitations to Love: Literacy, Love Letters, and Social Change in Nepal*. Ann Arbor: University of Michigan Press.

Althusser, Louis. 1971. "Ideology and Ideological State Apparatuses (Notes toward an Investigation)." In *Lenin and Philosophy and Other Essays*, translated by Ben Brewster, 127–86. New York: Monthly Review Press.

Apte, Vaman Shivram. (1890) 2014. *The Practical Sanskrit-English Dictionary*. Poona, India: Shiralkar. http://www.sanskrit-lexicon.uni-koeln.de/scans/AP90Scan/2014/web/webtc/indexcaller.php.

Arcana, Putu Fajar. 2006. "Misi Kebudayaan: Kartu Pos dari Bali." *Kompas*, December 12, 2006. http://www.kompas.com/kompas-cetak/0612/12/humaniora/3156619.htm.

Århem, K., and G. Sprenger, eds. 2016. *Animism in Southeast Asia*. London: Routledge.

Arwati, Ni Made Sri. 2003. *Bhyakala, tebasan durmanggala dan prayascita*. Denpasar, Bali: s.n.

———. 2008. *Berbagai jenis caru*. Denpasar, Bali: s.n.

Asad, Talal. 1986a. "The Concept of Cultural Translation in British Social Anthropology." In *Writing Culture: The Poetics and Politics of Ethnography*, edited by James Clifford and George Marcus, 141–64. Berkeley: University of California Press.

———. 1986b. "The Idea of an Anthropology of Islam." Occasional Papers Series, Center for Contemporary Arab Studies, Georgetown University, Washington, DC.

Austin, Peter K., and Julia Sallabank, eds. 2011. *The Cambridge Handbook of Endangered Languages*. Cambridge: Cambridge University Press.

Bagus, I Gusti Ngurah. 1980. *Aksara dalam kebudayaan Bali: Suatu kajian antropologi. Pidato pengukuhan jabatan guru besar dalam ilmu antropologi budaya pada Fakultas Sastra Universitas Udayana yang diucapkan pada tanggal 20 Desember 1980*. Denpasar, Bali: Universitas Udayana.

Bali Post, Bali Orti. 2013a. "Cakepan lontar, sinunggil koléksi dokuméntasi budaya Bali." April 21, 2013, 7.

———. 2013b. "Nénten mesti setata katengetang." April 21, 2013, 7.

———. 2013c. "Ngiring lestariang tetamian budaya druéné." April 21, 2013, 7.

Barber, C. Clyde. 1979. *Dictionary of Balinese-English*. 2 vols. Aberdeen University Library Occasional Publications 2. Aberdeen: University of Aberdeen.

Barth, Fredrik. 1993. *Balinese Worlds*. Chicago: University of Chicago Press.

Barthes, Roland. 1972. *Mythologies*. New York: Hill and Wang.

———. 1974. *S/Z*. Oxford: Blackwell.

Barton, David. 2007. *Literacy: An Introduction to the Ecology of Written Language*. Oxford: Blackwell.

Barton, David, and Uta Papen, eds. 2010. *The Anthropology of Writing: Understanding Textually-Mediated Worlds*. London: Continuum.

Bateson, Gregory. 1972. *Steps to an Ecology of Mind: Collected Essays in Anthropology, Psychiatry, Evolution, and Epistemology*. London: Jason Aronson.

Bateson, Gregory, and Margaret Mead. 1942. *Balinese Character: A Photographic Analysis*. New York: New York Academy of Sciences.

Becker, Alton L. 1979. "Text-Building, Epistemology, and Aesthetics in Javanese Shadow Theater." In *The Imagination of Reality: Essays in Southeast Asian Coherence Systems*, edited by Alton L. Becker and Aram A. Yengoyan, 211–43. New Jersey: Ablex.

———. 1995a. "Aridharma: Framing an Old Javanese Tale." In *Beyond Translation: Essays toward a Modern Philology*, 137–81. Ann Arbor: The University of Michigan Press.

———. 1995b. "Biography of a Sentence: A Burmese Proverb." In *Beyond Translation: Essays toward a Modern Philology*, 185–210. Ann Arbor: University of Michigan Press.

———. 1995c. "Silence across Languages." In *Beyond Translation: Essays toward a Modern Philology*, 283–94. Ann Arbor: University of Michigan Press.

Bellos, David. 2012. *Is That a Fish in Your Ear? The Amazing Adventure of Translation*. New York: Penguin Books.

Belo, Jane. 1953. *Bali: Temple Festival*. Locust Valley, NY: J. J. Augustin.

Bentor, Yael. 1996. *Consecration of Images and Stūpas in Indo-Tibetan Tantric Buddhism*. Leiden: E. J. Brill.

Besnier, Nico. 1995. *Literacy, Emotion, and Authority: Reading and Writing on a Polynesian Atoll*. Cambridge: Cambridge University Press.

Bhadra, I Wayan. 1937. "Het 'mabasan' of de beoefening van het oud-Javaansch op Bali." *Mededeelingen van de Kirtya Liefrinck-van der Tuuk* 5, supplement. Surabaya, Java: Bijlage.

Bird-David, Nurit. 1999. "'Animism' Revisited: Personhood, Environment, and Relational Epistemology." *Current Anthropology* 40 (S1): S67–91.

Bizot, François. 1981. "Notes sur les yantra bouddhiques d'indochine." In *Tantric and Taoist Studies in Honour of R. A. Stein*, edited by Michel Strickmann, 156–91. Brussels: Institut Belge des Hautes Études Chinoises.

Bloch, Maurice. 1998. *How We Think They Think: Anthropological Approaches to Cognition, Memory and Literacy*. Boulder, CO: Westview.

Blommaert, Jan. 2008. *Grassroots Literacy: Writing, Identity and Voice in Central Africa*. New York: Routledge.

Boeles, Jan Jetso. 1947. "The Migration of the Magical Syllable Oṃ." In *India Antiqua: A Volume of Oriental Studies Presented by His Friends and Pupils to Jean Philippe Vogel, C.I.E. on the Occasion of the Fiftieth Anniversary of His Doctorate*, edited by Frederik David Kan Bosch, Theodoor van Erp, August Johan Bernet Kempers, Rudolf Aernoud Kern, Franciscus Bernardus Jacobus Kuiper and Pieter Hendrik Pott, 40–56. Leiden: E. J. Brill.

Boon, James A. 1977. *The Anthropological Romance of Bali, 1597–1972*. Cambridge: Cambridge University Press.

Bourdieu, Pierre. 1977. *Outline of a Theory of Practice*. Cambridge: Cambridge University Press.

——. 1984. *Distinction: A Social Critique of the Judgement of Taste*. Cambridge, MA: Harvard University Press.

——. 1990. *The Logic of Practice*. Stanford, CA: Stanford University Press.

——. 1993. *The Field of Cultural Production: Essays on Art and Literature*. New York: Columbia University Press.

Bourdieu, Pierre, and Loïc Wacquant. 1992. *An Invitation to Reflexive Sociology*. Chicago: University of Chicago Press.

Burke, Kenneth. 1973. "Semantic and Poetic Meaning." In *The Philosophy of Literary Form*, 138–67. Berkeley: University of California Press.

Burns, Kathryn. 2010. *Into the Archive: Writing and Power in Colonial Peru*. Durham, NC: Duke University Press.

Butler, Judith. 1999. *Gender Trouble: Feminism and the Subversion of Identity*. 10th anniversary ed. New York: Routledge.

——. 2004. "Betrayal's Felicity." *Diacritics* 34 (1): 82–87.

——. 2009. "The Sensibility of Critique: A Response to Asad and Mahmood." In *Is Critique Secular? Blasphemy, Injury and Free Speech*, 101–36. Townsend Papers in the Humanities No 2. Berkeley: Townsend Center for the Humanities.

Carbine, Jason A. 2011. *Sons of the Buddha: Continuities and Ruptures in a Burmese Monastic Tradition*. Berlin: de Gruyter.

Cole, Michael, and Jennifer Cole. 2006. "Rethinking the Goody Myth." In *Technology, Literacy and the Evolution of Society*, edited by David R. Olson and Michael Cole, 305–24. Mahwah, NJ: Lawrence Erlbaum.

Collingwood, Robin George. (1946) 1993. *The Idea of History*. Rev. ed. Oxford: Oxford University Press.

———. 2005. *An Essay on Philosophical Method*. Rev. ed. Oxford: Clarendon.

Collins, James. 1995. "Literacy and Literacies." *Annual Review of Anthropology* 24:75–93.

Collins, James, and Richard K. Blot. 2003. *Literacy and Literacies: Texts, Power, and Identity*. Cambridge: Cambridge University Press.

Connor, Linda. 1982a. "The Unbounded Self: Balinese Therapy in Theory and Practice." In *Cultural Conceptions of Mental Health and Therapy*, edited by Anthony J. Marsella and Geoffrey M. White, 251–67. Dordrecht: D. Reidel.

———. 1982b. In *Darkness and Light: A Study of Peasant Intellectuals in Bali*. PhD Diss., University of Sydney.

———. 1986. "Ethnographic Notes on *The Medium Is the Masseuse*." In *Jero Tapakan: Balinese Healer: An Ethnographic Film Monograph*, edited by Linda Connor, Patsy Asch, and Timothy Asch, 177–210. London: Cambridge University Press.

———. 1995. "Acquiring Invisible Strength: A Balinese Discourse of Harm and Well-Being." *Indonesia Circle* 66:124–53.

Cooper, Marilyn M. 1986. "The Ecology of Writing." *College English* 48 (4): 364–75.

Couldry, Nick. 2010. "Theorising Media as Practice." In *Theorising Media and Practice*, edited by Birgit Bräuchler and John Postill, 35–54. New York: Berghahn Books.

Couldry, Nick, and Mark Hobart. 2010. "Media as Practice: A Brief Exchange." In *Theorising Media and Practice*, edited by Birgit Bräuchler and John Postill, 77–84. New York: Berghahn Books.

Crapanzano, Vincent. 2000. "Transfiguring Translation." *Semiotica* 128 (1/2): 113–36.

Creese, Helen. 2004. *Women of the Kakawin World: Marriage and Sexuality in the Indic Courts of Java and Bali*. London: Routledge.

———. 2009. "Singing the Text: On-Air Textual Interpretation in Bali." In *Lost Times and Untold Tales of the Malay World*, edited by Jan van der Putten and Mary Kilcline Cody, 210–26. Singapore: National University of Singapore Press.

———. 2014. "The *Utsawa Dharma Gita* Competition: The Contemporary Evolution of Hindu Textual Singing in Indonesia." *Journal of Hindu Studies* 7:296–322.

———. 2016. "Im-Materiality: Where Have All the Aksara Gone?" In *The Materiality and Efficacy of Balinese Letters: Situating Scriptural Practices*, edited by Richard Fox and Annette Hornbacher, 166–90. Leiden: Brill.

Darma Putra, I Nyoman, and Helen Creese. 2012. "More than Just 'Numpang Nampang.'" *Indonesia and the Malay World* 40 (118): 272–97.

Derrida, Jacques. 1974. *Of Grammatology*. Baltimore: Johns Hopkins University Press.

———. 1981. *Dissemination*. Chicago: University of Chicago Press.

Descola, Philippe. 2013. *Beyond Nature and Culture*. Chicago: University of Chicago Press.

Descombes, Vincent. 1987. "Je m'en Foucault." *London Review of Books*, March 3, 1987, 20–21.

Douglas, Mary. 1972. "Self-Evidence: The Henry Myers Lecture 1972." *Proceedings of the Royal Anthropological Institute of Great Britain and Ireland* 1972:27–43.

DPPD (Dinas Pengajaran Propinsi Daerah Tk. I Bali). 1978. *Ejaan bahasa daerah Bali yang disempurnakan (huruf latin)*. Denpasar, Bali: s.n.

Duchêne, Alexandre, and Monica Heller, eds. 2007. *Discourses of Endangerment: Ideology and Interest in the Defense of Languages*. London: Continuum.

Duff-Cooper, Andrew. 1985. "Hierarchy, Purity, and Equality among a Community of Balinese on Lombok." In *Contexts and Levels: Anthropological Essays on Hierarchy, Oxford*, edited by R. H. Barnes, Daniel de Coppet, and R. J. Parkin, 153–66. JASO Occasional Papers No. 4.

Duncan, Christopher R. 2009. "Reconciliation and Revitalization: The Resurgence of Tradition in Postconflict Tobelo, North Maluku, Eastern Indonesia." *Journal of Asian Studies* 68 (4): 1077–1104.

———. 2013. *Violence and Vengeance: Religious Conflict and Its Aftermath in Eastern Indonesia*. Ithaca, NY: Cornell University Press.

Dwyer, Leslie, and Degung Santikarma. 2003. "'When the World Turned to Chaos': 1965 and Its Aftermath in Bali, Indonesia." In *The Specter of Genocide: Mass Murder in Historical Perspective*, edited by Robert Gellately and Ben Kiernan, 289–305. Cambridge: Cambridge University Press.

Enfield, Nick J. 2005. "Areal Linguistics and Mainland Southeast Asia." *Annual Review of Anthropology* 34:181–206.

Engler, Steven, and Gregory P. Grieve, eds. 2005. *Historicizing "Tradition" in the Study of Religion*. Berlin: de Gruyter.

Errington, Shelley. 1979. "Some Comments on Style in the Meanings of the Past." *Journal of Asian Studies* 38 (2): 231–44.

———. 1983. "Embodied Sumange' in Luwu." *Journal of Asian Studies* 42 (3): 545–70.

Evans-Pritchard, Edward E. 1934. "Lévy-Bruhl's Theory of Primitive Mentality." *Bulletin of the Faculty of Arts* (Egyptian University, Cairo) 2 (1): 1–26.

Evens, T. M. S. 1983. "Mind, Logic, and the Efficacy of the Nuer Incest Prohibition." *Man* 18:111–33.

Feyerabend, Paul. 1975. *Against Method*. London: New Left Books.

Finnegan, Ruth H. 1973. "Literacy versus Non-literacy: The Great Divide?" In *Modes of Thought: Essays on Thinking in Western and Non-Western Societies*, edited by Ruth H. Finnegan and Robin W. G. Horton, 112–44. London: Faber.

Florida, Nancy. 1995. *Writing the Past, Inscribing the Future: History as Prophecy in Colonial Java*. Durham, NC: Duke University Press.

Foucault, Michel. (1976) 1990. *The History of Sexuality; Volume 1: An Introduction*. New York, Vintage Books.

———. (1966) 2002. *The Order of Things: An Archaeology of the Human Sciences*. London: Routledge.

Fox, Richard. 2003. "Substantial Transmissions: A Presuppositional Analysis of 'the Old Javanese Text' as an Object of Knowledge, and Its Implications for the Study of Religion in Bali." *Bijdragen tot de taal-, land- en volkenkunde* 159 (1): 65–107.

———. 2005. "Plus ça change . . . Recent Developments in Old Javanese Studies and Their Implications for the Study of Religion in Contemporary Bali." *Bijdragen tot de taal-, land- en volkenkunde* 161 (1): 63–97.

———. 2010. "Why Media Matter: Religion and the Recent History of 'the Balinese.'" *History of Religions* 41 (4): 354–92.

———. 2011. *Critical Reflections on Religion and Media in Contemporary Bali*. Numen Series in the History of Religions 130. Leiden: Brill.

——. 2012. "*Ngelidin sétra, nepukin sema?* Thoughts on Language and Writing in Contemporary Bali." *Jurnal kajian Bali* 2 (2): 21–48.

——. 2013a. "Indonesian Hinduism." In *Brill's Encyclopedia of Hinduism*, edited by Knut Jacobsen, 5:252–56. Leiden: Brill.

——. 2013b. "*Om Swasty-Alaikum* . . . Interpreting Religio-Ethnic Humor on the Balinese Stage." *Archipel: Études interdisciplinarires sur le monde insulindien* 86 (2): 43–72.

——. 2015. "Why Do Balinese Make Offerings? On Religion, Teleology and Complexity." *Bijdragen tot de taal-, land- en volkenkunde* 171 (1): 29–55.

——. 2016a. "The Meaning of Life, or How to Do Things with Letters." In *The Materiality and Efficacy of Balinese Letters: Situating Scriptural Practices*, edited by Richard Fox and Annette Hornbacher, 23–50. Leiden: Brill.

——. 2016b. "Postscript." In *The Materiality and Efficacy of Balinese Letters: Situating Scriptural Practices*, edited by Richard Fox and Annette Hornbacher, 208–16. Leiden: Brill.

——. 2017. "Of Family, Futures and Fear in a Balinese Ward: Some Preliminary Thoughts toward a New Project." *Jurnal kajian Bali* 7 (1): 213–48.

Fox, Richard, and Annette Hornbacher, eds. 2016. *The Materiality and Efficacy of Balinese Letters: Situating Scriptural Practices*. Leiden: Brill.

Frake, Charles O. 1983. "Did Literacy Cause the Great Cognitive Divide?" *American Ethnologist* 10:368–71.

Gadamer, Hans-Georg. 1993. *Truth and Method*. 2nd ed. London: Sheed and Ward.

Geertz, Clifford. 1960. *The Religion of Java*. Chicago: University of Chicago Press.

——. 1968. *Islam Observed: Religious Development in Morocco and Indonesia*. Chicago: University of Chicago Press.

——. 1973. "Deep Play: Notes on the Balinese Cockfight." In *The Interpretation of Cultures: Selected Essays*, 412–53. New York: Basic Books.

——. 1980. *Negara: The Theater State in Nineteenth-Century Bali*. Princeton, NJ: Princeton University Press.

Geertz, Hildred. 1994. *Images of Power: Balinese Paintings Made for Gregory Bateson and Margaret Mead*. Honolulu: University of Hawai'i Press.

——. 1998. "The Scholarly Achievements of Dr. I Gusti Ngurah Bagus." In *Proses and protes budaya, persembahan untuk Ngurah Bagus*, edited by A. M. Mbete et al., 305–10. Denpasar, Bali: Penerbit Bali Post.

——. 2000. "How Can We Speak about Balinese Religion?" Paper presented at the seminar "Bali in Reformation: Religious Change and Socio-political Transformation," July 11–13. Denpasar, Bali.

——. 2004. *Life of a Balinese Temple: Artistry, Imagination, and History in a Peasant Village*. Honolulu: University of Hawai'i Press.

——. 2005. *Tales from a Charmed Life: A Balinese Painter Reminisces*. Honolulu: University of Hawai'i Press.

——. 2016. *Storytelling in Bali*. Leiden: Brill.

Geertz, Hildred, and Clifford Geertz. 1975. *Kinship in Bali*. Chicago: University of Chicago Press.

Gibson, James J. 1979. *The Ecological Approach to Visual Perception*. Boston: Houghton Mifflin.

Gibson, Thomas. 1994. "Childhood, Colonialism and Fieldwork among the Buid of the Philippines and the Konjo of Indonesia." In *Enfants et sociétés d'Asie du Sud-Est*, edited by Jeannine Koubi and Josiane Massard-Vincent, 183–205. Paris: L'Harmattan.

Gonda, Jan. (1973) 1998. *Sanskrit in Indonesia*. 2nd ed. New Delhi: International Academy of Indian Culture and Aditya Prakashan.

———. 1987. *Rice and Barley Offerings in the Veda*. Leiden: E. J. Brill.

Goody, Jack, ed. 1968. *Literacy in Traditional Societies*. Cambridge: Cambridge University Press.

———. 1986. *The Logic of Writing and the Organization of Society*. Cambridge: Cambridge University Press.

Goris, Roelf. 1926. *Bijdrage tot de kennis der oud-Javaansche en Balineesche theologie*. Leiden: Vros.

Goudriaan, Teun, and Christiaan Hooykaas. 1971. *Stuti and Stava (Bauddha, Śaiva and Vaiṣṇava) of Balinese Brahman Priests*. Verhandelingen der Koninklijke Nederlandse Akademie van Wetenschappen, Afdeling Letterkunde, Nieuwe Reeks 76. Amsterdam: North-Holland.

Gramsci, Antonio. 1971. *Selections from the Prison Notebooks*. Edited and translated by Quintin Hoare and Geoffrey Nowell Smith. London: Lawrence and Wishart.

Granoka, Ida Wayan Oka. 2007. *Reinkarnasi budaya: Manifestasi dari dorongan kuat untuk bereinkarnasi di dalam tubuh kebudayaan yang berbhinneka tunggal ika*. Denpasar, Bali: Yuganadakalpa, Yoga Musik Maha Bajra Sandhi.

Grenoble, Lenore A. 2011. "Language Ecology and Endangerment." In *The Cambridge Handbook of Endangered Languages*, edited by Peter K. Austin and Julia Sallabank, 27–44. Cambridge: Cambridge University Press.

Hale, Ken, Michael Krauss, Lucille J. Watahomigie, Akira Y. Yamamoto, Colette Craig, LaVerne Masayesva Jeanne, and Nora C. England. 1992. "Endangered Languages." *Language* 68 (1): 1–42.

Halperin, David. 2002. *How to Do the History of Homosexuality*. Chicago: University of Chicago Press.

Halverson, John. 1991. "Olson on Literacy." *Language in Society* 20 (4): 619–40.

———. 1992a. "Goody and the Implosion of the Literacy Thesis." *Man*, n.s., 27 (2): 301–17.

———. 1992b. "Havelock on Greek Orality and Literacy." *Journal of the History of Ideas* 53 (1): 148–63.

Hanks, William F. 2014. "The Space of Translation." In "Translating Worlds: The Epistemological Space of Translation," special issue, *Hau: Journal of Ethnographic Theory* 4 (2): 17–39.

Hanks, William F., and Carlo Severi. 2014. "Translating Worlds: The Epistemological Space of Translation." In "Translating Worlds: The Epistemological Space of Translation," special issue, *Hau: Journal of Ethnographic Theory* 4 (2): 1–16.

Harman, Graham. 2009. *Prince of Networks: Bruno Latour and Metaphysics*. Melbourne: re.press.

Hauser-Schäublin, Brigitta. 2012. "The Diversion of the Village Gods: A Criminal Turn in the Biography of Balinese Copperplate Inscriptions." *Bijdragen tot de taal-, land- en volkenkunde* 168 (1): 74–99.

———, ed. 2013. *Adat and Indigeneity in Indonesia Culture and Entitlements between Heteronomy and Self-Ascription*. Göttingen, Germany: Universitätsverlag Göttingen.

Havelock, Eric A. 1963. *Preface to Plato*. Cambridge, MA: Harvard University Press.

———. 1986. *The Muse Learns to Write: Reflections on Orality and Literacy from Antiquity to the Present*. New Haven, CT: Yale University Press.

Hayashi, Yukio. 2003. *Practical Buddhism among the Thai-Lao: Religion in the Making of a Region*. Kyoto: Kyoto University Press.

Hefner, Robert H. 2011. "Where Have All the *Abangan* Gone? Religionization and the Decline of Non-standard Islam in Indonesia." In *The Politics of Religion in Indonesia*, edited by Michel Picard and Rémy Madinier, 71–91. London: Routledge.

Herzfeld, Michael. 2003. "The Unspeakable in Pursuit of the Ineffable: Representations of Untranslatability in Ethnographic Discourse." In *Translating Cultures: Perspectives on Translation and Anthropology*, edited by Paula G. Rubel and Abraham Rosman, 109–34. Oxford: Berg.

Hill, Jane H. 2002. "'Expert Rhetorics' in Advocacy for Endangered Languages: Who Is Listening, and What Do They Hear?" *Journal of Linguistic Anthropology* 12 (2): 119–33.

Himmelmann, Nikolaus P. 2008. "Reproduction and Preservation of Linguistic Knowledge: Linguistics' Response to Language Endangerment." *Annual Review of Anthropology* 37 (1): 337–50.

Hinzler, H. I. R. 1983. "The Balinese Manuscript Project." *Southeast Asia Library Group Newsletter* 25:7.

———. 1986. *Catalogue of Balinese Manuscripts in the Library of the University of Leiden and Other Collections in the Netherlands*. Vol. 2, *Descriptions of the Balinese Drawings from the van der Tuuk Collection*. Codices Manuscripti 23. Leiden: E. J. Brill/Leiden University Press.

———. 1988. "On Balinese Name-Giving Rituals." In *Papers from the IIIrd European colloquium on Malay and Indonesian Studies, Naples, 2–4 June 1981*, edited by Luigi Santa Maria, Faizah Soenoto Rivai, and A. Sorrentino, 121–46. Italy: Napoli.

———. 1993. "Balinese palmleaf manuscripts." *Bijdragen tot de taal-, land- en volkenkunde* 149 (3): 438–74.

Hirschkind, Charles. 2006. *The Ethical Soundscape: Cassette Sermons and Islamic Counterpublics*. New York: Columbia University Press.

Hobart, Mark. 1975. "Orators and Patrons: Two Types of Political Leader in Balinese Village Society." In *Political Language and Oratory in Traditional Society*, edited by Maurice Bloch, 65–92. London: Academic Press.

———. 1979. "A Balinese Village and Its Field of Social Relations." PhD diss., University of London.

———. 1991a. "The Art of Measuring Mirages, or Is There Kinship in Bali?" In *Cognation and Social Organization in Southeast Asia*, edited by Frans Hüsken and Jeremy Kemp, 33–53. Verhandelingen van het Koninklijk Instituut voor Taal, Land- en Volkenkunde 145. Leiden: KITLV.

———. 1991b. "The Patience of Plants: A Note on Agency in Bali." *Review of Indonesian and Malaysian Affairs* 24(2): 90–135.

———. 1992. *Beyond Reason? A Human Comedy.* Sociaal-antropologische cahiers, no. 25. Nijmegen, Netherlands: Instituut voor Culturele en Sociale Antropologie.

———. 2000. *After Culture: Anthropology as Radical Metaphysical Critique.* Yogyakarta, Indonesia: Duta Wacana University Press.

———. 2007. "Rethinking Balinese Dance." *Indonesia and the Malay World* 35(101): 107–28.

———. 2010. "What Do We Mean by 'Media Practices'?" In *Theorising Media and Practice*, edited by Birgit Bräuchler and John Postill, 55–76. New York: Berghahn Books.

———. 2015. "Beyond the Whorfs of Dover: A Study of Balinese Interpretive Practices." *Heidelberg Ethnology*, Occasional Paper No. 1. http://journals.ub.uni-heidelberg.de/index.php/hdethn/article/view/18998.

Hobsbawm, Eric, and Terence Ranger, eds. 1983. *The Invention of Tradition.* Cambridge: Cambridge University Press.

Hodgson, Dorothy L., ed. 2011. *Gender and Culture at the Limit of Rights.* Philadelphia: University of Pennsylvania Press.

Hollis, Martin, and Steven Lukes, eds. 1982. *Rationality and Relativism.* Oxford: Blackwell.

Hooykaas, Christiaan. 1963. "Books Made in Bali." *Bijdragen tot de taal-, land- en volkenkunde* 119 (4): 371–86.

———. 1964. *Āgama Tīrtha: Five Studies in Hindu-Balinese Religion.* Verhandelingen der Koninklijke Nederlandse Akademie van Wetenschappen, Afdeling Letterkunde, Nieuwe Reeks 70, no. 4. Amsterdam: Noord-Hollandsche Uitgevers Maatschappij.

———. 1975. "*Pañca-Yajña*-s in India and Bali." *Adyar Library Bulletin* 39:240–59.

———. 1977. *A Balinese Temple Festival.* The Hague: Martinus Nijhoff.

———. 1978. *The Balinese Poem Basur: An Introduction to Magic.* The Hague: Martinus Nijhoff.

———. 1980. *Drawings of Balinese Sorcery.* Leiden: Brill.

Hooykaas, Jacoba. 1959. "A Yantra of Speech Magic in Balinese Folklore and Religion." *Bijdragen tot de taal-, land- en volkenkunde* 115 (2): 176–91.

Hooykaas-van Leeuwen Boomkamp, Jacoba. 1961. *Ritual Purification of a Balinese Temple.* Verhandelingen der Koninklijke Nederlandse Akademie van Wetenschappen, Afd. Letterkunde, Nieuwe Reeks 68, no. 4. Amsterdam: N. V. Noord-Hollandsche Uitgevers Maatschappij.

———. 1963. *Märchen aus Bali.* Zurich: Verlag die Waage.

Hornbacher, Annette. 2014. "Machtvolle Zeichen: Schrift als Medium esoterischer Spekulation, ritueller Wirkung und religiöser Kanonisierung in Bali." In *Erscheinungsformen und Handhabungen Heiliger Schriften*, edited by Joachim Friedrich Quack and Daniela Christina Luft, 311–36. Materiale Textkulturen 5. Berlin: De Gruyter.

———. 2016a. "The Body of Letters: Balinese Aksara as an Intersection between Script, Power and Knowledge." In *The Materiality and Efficacy of Balinese Letters: Situating Scriptural Practices*, edited by Richard Fox and Annette Hornbacher, 70–99. Leiden: Brill.

———. 2016b. "Introduction—Balinese Practices of Script and Western Paradigms of Text: An Anthropological Approach to a Philological Topic." In *The Materiality and Efficacy of Balinese Letters: Situating Scriptural Practices*, edited by Richard Fox and Annette Hornbacher, 1–22. Leiden: Brill.

Howe, Leopold E. A. 1983. "An Introduction to the Cultural Study of Traditional Balinese Architecture." *Archipel: Études interdisciplinarires sur le monde insulindien* 25 (1): 137–58.

———. 2005. *The Changing World of Bali: Religion, Society and Tourism.* London: Routledge.

Hunter, Thomas M. 1988. "Balinese Language: Historical Background and Contemporary State." PhD diss., University of Michigan.

———. 2007. "The Poetics of Grammar in the Javano-Balinese Tradition." In *The Poetics of Grammar and the Metaphysics of Sound and Sign*, edited by Sergio La Porta and David Shulman, 271–303. Leiden: Brill.

———. 2016. "The Medium Is the Message: Chirographic Figures in Two Traditions." In *The Materiality and Efficacy of Balinese Letters: Situating Scriptural Practices*, edited by Richard Fox and Annette Hornbacher, 100–122. Leiden: Brill.

Illich, Ivan, and Barry Sanders. 1988. *ABC: The Alphabetization of the Popular Mind.* San Francisco: North Point.

Inden, Ronald. 1990. *Imagining India.* Oxford: Blackwell.

———. n.d. "Human Agency in the Social Sciences." Unpublished manuscript.

Ingold, Tim. 2000. *The Perception of the Environment: Essays in Livelihood, Dwelling and Skill.* London: Routledge.

Jendra, I Wayan. 1996. "Kedwibahasaan bahasa Bali dan bahasa Indonesia dalam aktivitas seni mabebasan di Bali." PhD diss., Universitas Gajah Mada.

Johnson, William A., and Holt N. Parker, eds. 2009. *Ancient Literacies: The Culture of Reading in Greece and Rome.* Oxford: Oxford University Press.

Kennedy, George A. 1999. *Classical Rhetoric and Its Christian and Secular Tradition, from Ancient to Modern Times.* 2nd ed. Chapel Hill: University of North Carolina Press.

Kersten, J. 1984. *Bahasa Bali.* Ende, Flores: Nusa Indah.

Kitiarsa, Pattana. 2012. *Mediums, Monks, and Amulets: Thai Popular Buddhism Today.* Chiang Mai: Silkworm Books in association with University of Washington Press.

Knight, Kelvin. 1998. Introduction to *The MacIntyre Reader*, edited by Kelvin Knight, 1–27. Notre Dame, IN: Notre Dame University Press.

———. 2007. *Aristotelian Philosophy: Ethics and Politics from Aristotle to MacIntyre.* Cambridge, UK: Polity.

———. 2008. "Practices: The Aristotelian Concept." *Analyse und Kritik* 30:317–29.

Koentjaraningrat. 1985. *Javanese Culture.* Singapore: Oxford University Press.

Korn, V. E. 1932. *Het adatrecht van Bali.* 2nd ed. The Hague: Naeff.

———. 1960. "The Village Republic of Tenganan Pegĕringsingan." In *Bali: Studies in Life, Thought, and Ritual*, edited by W. F. Wertheim et al., 77–100. The Hague: W. van Hoeve.

Kridalaksana, Harimurti. 1978. "Spelling Reform 1972: A Stage in the Process of Standardization of Bahasa Indonesia." In *Papers from the Conference on the Standardisation of Asian Languages, Manila, Philippines, December 16–21*, edited by Alejandrino Q. Perez, A. O. Santiago, and Nguyen Dang Liem, 305–17. Canberra: Pacific Linguistics.

Kuhn, Thomas S. (1962) 1996. *The Structure of Scientific Revolutions.* 3rd ed. Chicago: University of Chicago Press.

Laclau, Ernesto. 2005. *On Populist Reason.* London: Verso.

Laclau, Ernesto, and Chantal Mouffe. (1985) 2001. *Hegemony and Socialist Strategy: Towards a Radical Democratic Politics.* London: Verso.

Laidlaw, James. 2014. *The Subject of Virtue: An Anthropology of Ethics and Freedom.* Cambridge: Cambridge University Press.

Lakatos, Imre. 1970. "History of Science and its Rational Reconstructions." In *PSA 1970: Boston Studies in the Philosophy of Science,* edited by R. C. Buck and R. S. Cohen, 8:91–136. Dordrecht: Reidel.

Lakoff, George, and Mark Johnson. 1980. *Metaphors We Live By.* Chicago: University of Chicago Press.

Lanus, Sugi. 2014. "Puja Tri Sandhyā: Indian Mantras Recomposed and Standardised in Bali." *Journal of Hindu Studies* 7:243–72.

Larson, Joanne. 1996. "Challenging Autonomous Models of Literacy: Street's Call to Action." *Linguistics and Education* 8:439–45.

Latour, Bruno. 2005. *Reassembling the Social: An Introduction to Actor-Network Theory.* Oxford: Oxford University Press.

Lausberg, Heinrich. 1963. *Elemente der literarischen Rhetorik: Eine Einführung für Studierende der klassischen, romanischen, englischen und deutschen Philologie.* Munich: Max Hueber Verlag.

Leach, Edmund. 1973. "Ourselves and Others." *Times Literary Supplement,* July 6, 1973, 771–72.

Leavitt, John. 2014. "Words and Worlds: Ethnography and Theories of Translation." In "Translating Worlds: The Epistemological Space of Translation," special issue, *Hau: Journal of Ethnographic Theory* 4 (2): 193–220.

Lévy-Bruhl, Lucien. 1926. *How Natives Think.* Translated by L. A. Clare. London: Allen and Unwin.

Lloyd, Geoffrey Ernest Richard. 2014. "On the Very Possibility of Mutual Intelligibility." Hau: *Journal of Ethnographic Theory* 4(2): 221–35.

Lord, Albert B. (1960) 1971. *The Singer of Tales.* New York: Atheneum.

Lovric, Barbara J. A. 1987. "Rhetoric and Reality: The Hidden Nightmare: Myth and Magic as Representations and Reverberations of Morbid Realities." PhD diss., University of Sydney.

Lutz, Christopher S. 2004. *Tradition in the Ethics of Alasdair MacIntyre: Relativism, Thomism, and Philosophy.* Lanham, MD: Lexington Books.

——. 2012. *Reading Alasdair MacIntyre's "After Virtue."* New York: Continuum International.

MacIntyre, Alasdair. (1979) 1998. "Social Science Methodology as the Ideology of Bureaucratic Authority." In *The MacIntyre Reader,* edited by Kelvin Knight, 53–68. Notre Dame, IN: University of Notre Dame Press.

——. (1981) 2010. *After Virtue: A Study in Moral Theory.* 3rd ed. Notre Dame, IN: University of Notre Dame Press.

——. 1988. *Whose Justice? Which Rationality?* Notre Dame, IN: University of Notre Dame Press.

——. 1990. *Three Rival Versions of Moral Enquiry: Encyclopaedia, Genealogy, and Tradition.* Gifford Lectures. Notre Dame, IN: University of Notre Dame Press.

——. 1991. "Précis of *Whose Justice? Which Rationality?*" *Philosophy and Phenomenological Research* 51 (1): 149–52.

——. 2006. "Epistemological Crises, Dramatic Narrative, and the Philosophy of Science." In *The Tasks of Philosophy: Selected Essays*, 1:3–23. Cambridge: Cambridge University Press.

MacRae, Graham, and Samuel Parker. 2002. "Would the Real Undagi Please Stand Up? On the Social Location of Balinese Architectural Knowledge." *Bijdragen tot De Taalen Volkenkunde* 158 (2): 253–81.

Mahmood, Saba. 2005. *Politics of Piety: The Islamic Revival and the Feminist Subject*. Princeton, NJ: Princeton University Press.

Malinowski, Bronislaw. 1948. *Magic, Science and Religion and Other Essays*. Glencoe, IL: Free Press.

McDaniel, Justin Thomas. 2011. *The Lovelorn Ghost and the Magic Monk: Practicing Buddhism in Modern Thailand*. New York: Columbia University Press.

McDowell, John H. 2000. "Collaborative Ethnopoetics: A View from the Sibundoy Valley." In *Translating Native Latin American Verbal Art*, edited by Kay Sammons and Joel Sherzer, 211–32. Washington, DC: Smithsonian Institution Press.

Meillassoux, Quentin. 2008. *After Finitude: An Essay on the Necessity of Contingency*. London: Continuum.

Messick, Brinkley. 1993. *The Calligraphic State: Textual Domination and History in a Muslim Society*. Berkeley: University of California Press.

Monier-Williams, Monier. 1899. *A Sanskrit-English Dictionary: Etymologically and Philologically Arranged with Special Reference to Cognate Indo-European Languages*. Oxford: Clarendon.

Morgan, David, ed. 1969. *Biological Science: The Web of Life*. Canberra: Australian Academy of Science.

Mouffe, Chantal. 2000. *The Democratic Paradox*. London: Verso.

Mühlhäusler, Paul. 1992. "Preserving Languages or Language Ecologies? A Top-Down Approach to Language Survival." *Oceanic Linguistics* 31 (2): 163–80.

Nagel, Thomas. 1995. "MacIntyre versus the Enlightenment." In *Other Minds: Critical Essays, 1969–1994*, 203–9. New York: Oxford University Press.

Nala, Ngurah. 2006. *Aksara Bali dalam usada*. Surabaya, Java: Penerbit Pāramita.

Newland, Lynda. 2001. "The Deployment of the Prosperous Family: Family Planning in West Java." *Feminist Formations* 13 (3): 22–48.

Nida, Eugene A. 1964. *Toward a Science of Translating: With Special Reference to Principles and Procedures Involved in Bible Translating*. Leiden: Brill.

Niehof, Anke, and Firman Lubis, eds. 2003. *Two Is Enough: Family Planning in Indonesia under the New Order, 1968–1998*. Leiden: KITLV.

Noszlopy, Laura. 2002. *The Bali Arts Festival—Pesta Kesenian Bali: Culture, Politics and the Arts in Contemporary Indonesia*. PhD Diss., University of East Anglia.

Nussbaum, Martha C. 1989. "Recoiling from Reason." Review of *Whose Justice? Which Rationality?*, by Alasdair MacIntyre. *New York Review of Books*, December 7, 1989, 36–41.

Olson, David R. 1994. *The World on Paper: The Conceptual and Cognitive Implications of Writing and Reading*. Cambridge: Cambridge University Press.

——. 1996. "Language and Literacy: What Writing Does to Language and Mind." *Annual Review of Applied Linguistics* 16:3–13.

——. 2009. "Language, Literacy and Mind: The Literacy Hypothesis." *Psykhe* 18 (1): 3–9.

Ong, Walter J. 1958a. *Ramus, Method, and the Decay of Dialogue: From the Art of Discourse to the Art of Reason.* Chicago: University of Chicago Press.

——. 1958b. *Ramus and Talon Inventory: A Short-Title Inventory of the Published Works of Peter Ramus (1515–1572) and Omer Talon (Ca. 1510–1562) in Their Original and in Their Variously Altered Forms.* Cambridge, MA: Harvard University Press.

——. 1967. *The Presence of the Word: Some Prolegomena for Cultural and Religious History.* New Haven, CT: Yale University Press.

——. 1982. *Orality and Literacy: The Technologizing of the Word.* London: Routledge.

——. 1986. "Writing Is a Technology That Restructures Thought." In *The Written Word: Literacy in Transition; Wolfson College Lectures 1985,* edited by Gerd Baumann, 23–50. Oxford: Clarendon.

Ortner, Sherry B. 1984. "Theory in Anthropology since the Sixties." *Comparative Studies in Society and History* 26 (1): 126–66.

——. 1990. "Patterns of History: Cultural Schemas in the Foundings of Sherpa Religious Institutions." In *Culture through Time: Anthropological Approaches,* edited by Emiko Ohnuki-Tierney, 57–93. Stanford, CA: Stanford University Press.

Ottino, Arlette. 2000. *The Universe Within: A Balinese Village through Its Ritual Practices.* Paris: Éditions Karthala.

Overing, Joanna, ed. 1985. *Reason and Morality.* ASA Monographs 24. London: Tavistock.

Palmer, Richard E. 1969. *Hermeneutics: Interpretation Theory in Schleiermacher, Dilthey, Heidegger, and Gadamer.* Northwestern University Studies in Phenomenology and Existential Philosophy. Evanston, IL: Northwestern University Press.

Patton, Thomas N. 2012. "In Pursuit of the Sorcerer's Power: Sacred Diagrams as Technologies of Potency." *Contemporary Buddhism: An Interdisciplinary Journal* 13 (2): 213–31.

Pemberton, John. 1994. "Recollections from 'Beautiful Indonesia' (Somewhere beyond the Postmodern)." *Public Culture* 6:241–62.

Perda 3/1992. 1992. *Peraturan daerah propinsi daerah tingkat I Bali, nomor 3, tahun 1992, tentang bahasa, aksara dan sastra Bali.* Lembaran Daerah Propinsi Daerah Tingkat I Bali. Nomor 385, Tahun 1992, Seri D No. 379.

PHD (Parisada Hindu Dharma). 1967. *Upadeça tentang adjaran-adjaran Agama Hindu.* Denpasar, Bali: s.n.

PHDKT (Parisada Hindu Dharma Kabupaten Tabanan). 1979. *Kumpulan keputusan seminar kesatuan tafsir terhadap aspek-aspek Agama Hindu, 1976 s/d 1978.* Tabanan, Bali: Departemen Agama Kabupaten Tabanan.

Picard, Michel. 1990. "'Cultural Tourism' in Bali: Cultural Performances as Tourist Attraction." *Indonesia* 49:37–74.

——. 1996. *Bali: Cultural Tourism and Touristic Culture.* Singapore: Archipelago.

——. 1999. "The Discourse of *Kebalian*: Transcultural Constructions of Balinese Identity." In *Staying Local in the Global Village: Bali in the Twentieth Century,* edited by Rachelle Rubinstein and Linda H. Connor, 15–49. Honolulu: University of Hawai'i Press.

——. 2004. "What's in a Name? *Agama Hindu Bali* in the Making." In *Hinduism in Modern Indonesia: A Minority Religion between Local, National, and Global Interests*, edited by Martin Ramstedt, 56–75. London: RoutledgeCurzon.

——. 2008. "From *Kebalian* to *Ajeg Bali*: Tourism and Balinese Identity in the Aftermath of the Kuta Bombing." In *Tourism in Southeast Asia: Challenges and New Directions*, edited by Michael Hitchcock, Victor T. King, and Michael Parnwell, 99–131. Copenhagen: NIAS Press.

——. 2011a. "Balinese Religion in Search of Recognition: From *Agama Hindu Bali* to *Agama Hindu* (1945–1965)." *Bijdragen tot de taal-, land- en volkenkunde* 167 (4): 482–510.

——. 2011b. "From Agama Hindu Bali to Agama Hindu and Back: Toward a Relocalization of the Balinese Religion?" In *The Politics of Religion in Indonesia*, edited by Michel Picard and Rémy Madinier, 117–41. London: Routledge.

——. 2011c. "Introduction: 'Agama,' 'Adat,' and Pancasila." In *The Politics of Religion in Indonesia*, edited by Michel Picard and Rémy Madinier, 1–20. London: Routledge.

Picard, Michel, and Rémy Madinier, eds. 2011. *The Politics of Religion in Indonesia: Syncretism, Orthodoxy, and Religious Contention in Java and Bali*. London: Routledge.

Pitana, I Gdé. 1999. "Status Struggles and the Priesthood in Contemporary Bali." In *Staying Local in the Global Village*, edited by Rachelle Rubinstein and Linda H. Connor, 181–201. Honolulu: University of Hawai'i Press.

Poerbatjaraka, R. Ng. 1926. "*Arjuna-Wiwāha*, tekst en vertaling." *Bijdragen tot de taal-, land- en volkenkunde* 82:181–305.

Pollock, Sheldon. 1996. "The Sanskrit Cosmopolis, 300–1300: Transculturation, Vernacularization, and the Question of Ideology." In *Ideology and the Status of Sanskrit: Contributions to the History of Sanskrit Language*, edited by Jan E. M. Houben, 197–247. Leiden: Brill.

——. 2006. *The Language of the Gods in the World of Men: Sanskrit, Culture and Power in Premodern India*. Berkeley: University of California Press.

——. 2009. "Future Philology? The Fate of a Soft Science in a Hard World." *Critical Inquiry* 35:931–61.

——. 2014. "Philology in Three Dimensions." *Postmedieval: A Journal of Medieval Cultural Studies* 5: 398–413.

——. 2015. "Philologia Rediviva?" *Bulletin of the American Academy of Arts and Sciences* 68 (4): 34–36.

Postill, John. 2003. "Knowledge, Literacy and Media among the Sarawak: A Reply to Maurice Bloch." *Social Anthropology* 11 (1): 79–100.

——. 2010. "Introduction: Theorising Media and Practice." In *Theorising Media and Practice*, edited by Birgit Bräuchler and John Postill, 1–32. New York: Berghahn Books.

Postman, Neil. 2000. "The Humanism of Media Ecology." Keynote address delivered at the Inaugural Media Ecology Association Convention, Fordham University, New York, June 16–17. In *Proceedings of the Media Ecology Association*, vol. 1. http://www.media-ecology.org/publications/MEA_proceedings/v1/humanism_of_media_ecology.html.

Quine, Willard van Orman. (1951) 1994. "Two Dogmas of Empiricism." In *From a Logical Point of View*, 20–46. Cambridge, MA: Harvard University Press.

——. 1960. *Word and Object*. Cambridge, MA: MIT Press.

Rama, Angel. 1996. *The Lettered City*. Edited and translated by J. C. Chasteen. Durham, NC: Duke University Press.

Ramstedt, Martin, ed. 2004. *Hinduism in Modern Indonesia: A Minority Religion between Local, National, and Global Interests*. London: RoutledgeCurzon.

Raphael, Vicente L. 1988. *Contradicting Colonialism: Translation and Christian Conversion in Tagalog Society under Early Spanish Rule*. Ithaca, NY: Cornell University Press.

Rappaport, Joanne, and Tom Cummins. 2012. *Beyond the Lettered City: Indigenous Literacies in the Andes*. Durham, NC: Duke University Press.

Reddy, Michael J. 1979. "The Conduit Metaphor: A Case of Frame Conflict in Our Language about Language." In *Metaphor and Thought*, 2nd ed., edited by Andrew Ortony, 164–201. Cambridge: Cambridge University Press.

Retsikas, Konstantinos. 2010. "Unconscious Culture and Conscious Nature: Exploring East Javanese Conceptions of the Person through Bourdieu's Lens." *Journal of the Royal Anthropological Institute* 16 (S1): S140–57.

Rhoads, Elizabeth. 2007. "Bali Standing Strong." *Inside Indonesia*, April–June 2007. http://www.insideindonesia.org/index.php/edition-89/19-bali-standing-strong-ed-89.

Ricci, Ronit. 2011. *Islam Translated: Literature, Conversion, and the Arabic Cosmopolis of South and Southeast Asia South Asia across the Disciplines*. Chicago: University of Chicago Press.

Ricklefs, Merle C. 2006. *Mystic Synthesis in Java: A History of Islamization from the 14th to the Early 19th Centuries*. Norwalk, CT: EastBridge Books.

Robinson, Geoffrey. 1995. *The Dark Side of Paradise: Political Violence in Bali*. Ithaca, NY: Cornell University Press.

Robson, Stuart O. 1972. "The Kawi Classics in Bali." *Bijdragen tot de taal-, land- en volkenkunde* 128:308–29.

Romain, J. 2011. "Indian Architecture in the 'Sanskrit Cosmopolis': The Temples of the Dieng Plateau." In *Early Interactions between South and Southeast Asia: Reflections on Cross-Cultural Exchange*, edited by Pierre-Yves Manguin, A. Mani, and Geoff Wade, 299–316. Singapore: Institute of Southeast Asian Studies.

Rubinger, Richard. 2007. *Popular Literacy in Early Modern Japan*. Honolulu: University of Hawai'i Press.

Rubinstein, Rachelle. 1993. *"Pepaosan*: Challenges and Change." In *Balinese Music in Context: A Sixty-Fifth Birthday Tribute to Hans Oesch*, edited by Danker Schaareman, 85–113. Forum Ethnomusicologicum 4. Winterthur, Switzerland: Amadeus.

——. 2000. *Beyond the Realm of the Senses: The Balinese Ritual of Kekawin Composition*. Verhandelingen van het KITLV 181. Leiden: KITLV Press.

Salmond, Amiria J. M. 2013. "Transforming Translations (Part I): 'The Owner of These Bones.'" *Hau: Journal of Ethnographic Theory* 3 (3): 1–32.

——. 2014. "Transforming Translations (Part 2): Addressing Ontological Alterity." *Hau: Journal of Ethnographic Theory* 4 (1): 155–87.

Salmond, Anne. 1989. "Tribal Words, Tribal Worlds: The Translatability of Tapu and Mana." In *Culture, Kin and Cognition in Oceania: Essays in Honor of Ward Goodenough*, edited by Mac Marshall and John L. Caughey, 55–78. American Anthropological Association Monographs No. 25.

Salomon, Frank, and Mercedes Niño-Murcia. 2011. *The Lettered Mountain: A Peruvian Village's Way with Writing*. Durham, NC: Duke University Press.

Santikarma, Degung. 2003. "Bali Erect." *Latitudes* 43:13–17.

Santoso, Soewito. 1975. *Sutasoma: A Study in Javanese Wajrayana*. Sata-Pitaka Series 213. New Delhi: International Academy of Indian Culture.

Schatzki, Theodore R. 1996. *Social Practices: A Wittgensteinian Approach to Human Activity and the Social*. Cambridge: Cambridge University Press.

Schulte Nordholt, Henk. 1986. *Bali: Colonial Conceptions and Political Change, 1700–1940: From Shifting Hierarchies to "Fixed Order."* Comparative Asian Studies Programme. Rotterdam: Erasmus University.

———. 1991. *State, Village, and Ritual in Bali: A Historical Perspective*. Amsterdam: Vrije University Press.

———. 1996. *The Spell of Power: A History of Balinese Politics, 1650–1940*. Verhandelingen van het Koninklijk Instituut voor Taal-, Land- en Volkenkunde. Leiden: KITLV Press.

———. 1999. "The Making of Traditional Bali: Colonial Ethnography and Bureaucratic Reproduction." In *Colonial Subjects: Essays in the Practical History of Anthropology*, edited by Peter Pels and Oscar Salemink, 241–81. Ann Arbor: University of Michigan Press.

———. 2007. *Bali: An Open Fortress, 1995–2005: Regional Autonomy, Electoral Democracy and Entrenched Identities*. Singapore: National University of Singapore Press.

Scott, James C. 2009. *The Art of Not Being Governed: An Anarchist History of Upland Southeast Asia*. New Haven, CT: Yale University Press.

Sedgwick, Eve Kosofsky. 1990. *Epistemology of the Closet*. Berkeley: University of California Press.

Severi, Carlo. 2014. "Transmutating Beings: A Proposal for an Anthropology of Thought." *Hau: Journal of Ethnographic Theory* 4 (2): 41–71.

Shastri, Narendra Dev Pandit. 1955. *Intisari Hindu Dharma*. Denpasar, Bali: s.n.

Silverstein, Michael. 1979. "Language Structure and Linguistic Ideology." In *The Elements: A Parasession on Linguistic Units and Levels*, edited by Paul R. Clyne, William F. Hanks, and Carol L. Hofbauer, 193–247. Chicago: Chicago Linguistic Society.

Simpen, I Wayan. (1973) 1995. *Pasang aksara Bali*. Denpasar, Bali: Upada Sastra.

Skeat, Walter William. 1900. *Malay Magic: Being an Introduction to the Folklore and Popular Religion of the Malay Peninsula*. London: Macmillan.

Soebadio, Harayati. 1971. *Jñānasiddhânta; Secret Lore of the Balinese Śaiva Priest*. Bibliotheca Indonesica 7. The Hague: Nijhoff.

Stephen, Michele. 2005. *Desire, Divine and Demonic: Balinese Mysticism in the Paintings of I Ketut Budiana and I Gusti Nyoman Mirdiana*. Honolulu: University of Hawai'i Press.

Strathern, Marilyn. 2005. "For the Motion: The Concept of Society Is Theoretically Obsolete." In *Key Debates in Anthropology*, edited by Tim Ingold, 50–55. London: Routledge.

Street, Brian. 1984. *Literacy in Theory and Practice*. New York: Cambridge University Press.

———. 2003. "What's 'New' in New Literacy Studies? Critical Approaches to Literacy in Theory and Practice." *Current Issues in Comparative Education* 5 (2): 77–91.

Stuart-Fox, David J. 1974. *The Art of the Balinese Offering*. Yogyakarta, Java: Penerbitan Yayasan Kanisius.

———. 2002. *Pura Besakih: Temple, Religion and Society in Bali*. Leiden: KITLV Press.

———. 2015. *Pray, Magic, Heal: The Story of Ketut Liyer—Bali's Famous "Eat, Pray, Love" Folk Healer*. With Mangku Ketut Liyer. New York: New Saraswati.

Suhardana, K. M. 2009. *Bhama kretih; Penyucian pekarangan panes, berbagai caru dan sarananya*. Surabaya, Java: Penerbit Paramita.

Sumarta, I Ketut. 2001. "Between Globalisation and Illiteracy." In *Bali: Living in Two Worlds*, edited by Urs Ramseyer and I Gusti Raka Panji Tisna, 51–62. Basel, Switzerland: Museum der Kulturen.

Supomo, S. 2000. "Kama in the Old Javanese Kakawin." In *Society and Culture of Southeast Asia: Continuities and Changes*, edited by Lokesh Chandra, 263–81. New Delhi: International Academy of Indian Culture/Aditya Prakashan.

Swastika, I Ketut Pasek. 2008. *Bhuta yajña: Saiban, caru, tawur dan nangluk mrana*. Denpasar, Bali: Pustaka Bali Post.

Swearer, Donald. 2004. *Becoming the Buddha: The Ritual of Image Consecration in Thailand*. Princeton, NJ: Princeton University Press.

Sweeney, Amin. 1987. *A Full Hearing: Orality and Literacy in the Malay World*. Berkeley: University of California Press.

Tannenbaum, Nicola. 1987. "Tattoos: Invulnerability and Power in Shan Cosmology." *American Anthropologist* 14 (4): 693–711.

Terwiel, Barend Jan. 2012. *Monks and Magic: An Analysis of Religious Ceremonies in Central Thailand*. Copenhagen: NIAS Press.

Thacker, Eugene. 2010. *After Life*. Chicago: University of Chicago Press.

Tschacher, Torsten. 2009. "Circulating Islam: Understanding Convergence and Divergence in the Islamic Traditions of Ma'bar and Nusantara." In *Islamic Connections: Muslim Societies in South and Southeast Asia*, edited by R. Michael Feener and Terenjit Sevea, 48–67. Singapore: Institute of Southeast Asian Studies.

Tsumura, Fumihiko. 2009. "Magical Use of Traditional Scripts in Northeastern Thai Villages." In *Written Cultures in Mainland Southeast Asia*, edited by Masao Kashinaga, 63–77. Senri Ethnological Studies 74. Osaka: National Museum of Ethnology.

Turner, Stephen. 1994. *The Social Theory of Practices: Tradition, Tacit Knowledge and Presuppositions*. Chicago: University of Chicago Press.

Undang-Undang Dasar Negara Republik Indonesia Tahun 1945 [1945 Constitution of the Republic of Indonesia].

Undang-Undang Republic Indonesia Nomor 24, Tahun 2009, tentang bendera, bahasa, dan lambang negara, serta lagu kebangsaan [Law of the Indonesian Republic Number 24, year 2009, regarding the state flag, language, and symbols, and the national anthem].

van der Tuuk, Herman Neubronner. 1897–1912. *Kawi-Balineesch-Nederlandsch woordenboek*. 4 vols. Batavia [Jakarta]: Landsdruk-kerij.

Vickers, Adrian. 1984. "When Is a Text Not a Text? The Malat and Philology." *Review of Indonesian and Malaysian Affairs* 18:73–86.

———. 1989. *Bali: A Paradise Created*. Berkeley: Periplus Editions.

———. 1991. "Ritual Written: The Song of the Ligya, or The Killing of the Rhinoceros." In *State and Society in Bali: Historical, Textual and Anthropological Approaches*, edited by Hildred Geertz, 85–136. Leiden: KITLV Press.

———. 2011. "Bali Rebuilds Its Tourist Industry." *Bijdragen tot de Taal-, Land en Volken-kunde* 167 (4): 459–81.

———. 2012. *Balinese Art: Paintings and Drawings of Bali, 1800–2010.* Singapore: Tuttle.

Viveiros de Castro, Eduardo. 2004. "Perspectival Anthropology and the Method of Controlled Equivocation." *Tipití: Journal of the Society for the Anthropology of Lowland South America* 2 (1): 3–22.

———. 2015. *The Relative Native: Essays on Indigenous Conceptual Worlds.* Chicago: Hau Books.

Vološinov, Valentin Nikolaevich. 1973. *Marxism and the Philosophy of Language,* translated by Ladislav Matejka and I. R. Titunik. Cambridge, MA: Harvard University Press.

Wacquant, Loïc. 2014. "Putting Habitus in Its Place: Rejoinder to the Symposium." *Body and Society* 20 (2): 118–39.

Warna, I Wayan et al. 1990. *Kamus Bali-Indonesia.* Denpasar, Bali: Dinas Pendidikan Dasar Propinsi Dati I Bali.

Warren, Carol. 1993. *Adat and Dinas: Balinese Communities in the Indonesian State.* Oxford: Oxford University Press.

Waterson, Roxana. 2009. *The Living House: An Anthropology of Architecture in South-East Asia.* Tokyo: Tuttle.

Weck, Wolfgang. 1937. *Heilkunde und Volkstum auf Bali.* Stuttgart, Germany: Ferdinand Enke.

White, Hayden. 1973. *Metahistory: The Historical Imagination in Nineteenth-Century Europe.* Baltimore, MD: Johns Hopkins University Press.

Wiener, Margaret J. 1995. *Visible and Invisible Realms: Power, Magic, and Colonial Conquest in Bali.* Chicago: University of Chicago Press.

———. 2007. "The Magical Life of Things." In *Colonial Collections Revisited,* edited by Pieter ter Keurs, 45–70. Leiden: CNWS Publications.

———. 2016. "'The World Is Full of Letters': Graphic Ideologies, Graphic Technologies, and Transformative Practice in Bali." In *The Materiality and Efficacy of Balinese Letters: Situating Scriptural Practice,* edited by Richard Fox and Annette Hornbacher, 51–69. Leiden: Brill.

Wijaya, Nyoman. 2012. *Menerbos badai: Biografi intelektual Prof. Dr. I Gusti Ngurah Bagus.* Denpasar, Bali: Pustaka Larasan.

Wikarman, I Nyoman Singgin. 2006. *Caru pelemahan dan sasih.* Surabaya, Java: Penerbit Paramita.

Willerslev, Rane. 2007. *Soul Hunters: Hunting, Animism, and Personhood among the Siberian Yukaghirs.* Berkeley: University of California Press.

Wilson, Brian, ed. 1970. *Rationality.* Oxford: Blackwell.

Winch, Peter. 1964. "Understanding a Primitive Society." *American Philosophical Quarterly* 1 (4): 307–24.

Wirz, Paul. 1928. *Der Totenkult auf Bali.* Stuttgart, Germany: Strecker und Schröder.

Wittgenstein, Ludwig. (1953) 2009. *Philosophical Investigations. The German Text with an English Translation by G.E.M. Anscombe, P.M.S. Hacker and Joachim Schulte.* Rev. 4th ed. by P. M. S. Hacker and Joachim Schulte. Oxford: Blackwell.

Wolters, Oliver William. 1999. *History, Culture, and Region in Southeast Asian Perspectives.* Ithaca, NY: Cornell University Southeast Asia Program Publications.

Woodbury, Anthony C. 1993. "A Defense of the Proposition, 'When a Language Dies, a Culture Dies.'" *Texas Linguistic Forum* 33:101–129.

Woods, Teresa. 2007. "Magic, Morality and Medicine: Madness and Medical Pluralism in Java." PhD diss., University of Washington.

Worsley, Peter J. 1972. *Babad Bulèlèng: A Balinese Dynastic Chronicle.* The Hague: Nijhoff.

Yahya, Farouk. 2015. *Magic and Divination in Malay Illustrated Manuscripts.* Leiden: Brill.

Zoetmulder, P. J. 1982. *Old Javanese-English Dictionary.* With Stuart O. Robson. 2 vols. The Hague: Nijhoff.

——. 2007. "The Significance of the Study of Culture and Religion for Indonesian Historiography." In *An Introduction to Indonesian Historiography,* edited by Soedjatmoko, 326–43. Jakarta: Equinox.

Zurbuchen, Mary S. 1981. "The Shadow Theater of Bali: Explorations in Language and Text." PhD diss., University of Michigan, Ann Arbor.

——. 1984. "Contexts and Choices: Spoken Indonesian in Bali." In *Aesthetic Tradition and Cultural Transition in Java and Bali,* edited by Stephanie Morgan and Laurie Jo Sears, 247–66. Madison: Center for Southeast Asian Studies, University of Wisconsin.

——. 1987. *The Language of the Balinese Shadow Theater.* Princeton, NJ: Princeton University Press.

——. 1989. "Internal Translation in Balinese Poetry." In *Writing on the Tongue,* edited by Alton L. Becker, 215–79. Michigan Papers on South and Southeast Asia 33. Ann Arbor: Center for South and Southeast Asian Studies.

INDEX

Page numbers in italics refer to figures (f) and photos (p).

Acri, Andrea, 7

adat (as tradition), as an Arabic loanword in Indonesian, 122, 124, 154; legal distinction from *dinas* (as administrative membership), 161

adat-istiadat (as traditional custom), 209–10n9

Addams, Charles, 64

Aditjondro, George, 188n6

Agama, in Balinese, as constitutive of both its subject and its community, 162, 164–65; in Indonesian, dictionary glossing of, 157, 183–84n4; and the pursuit of the common good, 160, 164; in Soekarno's Nasakom, 149

Agama Hindu (state-bureaucratic Hinduism), local rites and activities in relation to, xiii; and *maagama* Hindu, 159–62; *Panca-sraddha* (five "pillars of belief") of, 162–63,

168, 198n11, 210n15; psychologization of destructive forces, 117–18, 203n19; recognition by the Indonesian Ministry of Religion, 47–48; and *rumah sehat* ("healthy home"), 117; ward regulations associated with, 159, 162

Ajeg Bali, Granoka's criticism of, 143; and the hegemonic aspirations of Balinese urban elite, 188n13, 204–5n12

Aksara, and competing articulations of agency, matter, and what it means to be "alive," 174–75; dangerously ambivalent power of, 69–71, 178; *dasabayu* ("ten forces") configuration of, *44f2.4a–b*, 45, 67, 191n38; as a form of *sadana*, 141; nine uses and acts of, 57; purity associated with, 61; traditional healers as manipulators of, 36, 70, 191n42. *See also* Grebeg Aksara; script-bearing objects

JML

CPSIA information can be obtained
at www.ICGtesting.com
Printed in the USA
BVHW07s0741040818
523345BV00004B/128/P